W9-CGZ-532

Once Upon a Time in a Different World

a Different World

Issues and Ideas in African American Children's Literature

Neal A. Lester

Routledge
Taylor & Francis Group
New York   London

Routledge is an imprint of the
Taylor & Francis Group, an informa business

Routledge
Taylor & Francis Group
270 Madison Avenue
New York, NY 10016

Routledge
Taylor & Francis Group
2 Park Square
Milton Park, Abingdon
Oxon OX14 4RN

Printed in the United States of America on acid-free paper
10 9 8 7 6 5 4 3 2 1

International Standard Book Number-10: 0-415-98019-4 (Hardcover)
International Standard Book Number-13: 978-0-415-98019-7 (Hardcover)

Library of Congress Cataloging-in-Publication Data

Lester, Neal A.
   Once upon a time in a different world : issues and ideas in African American children's literature / Neal Lester.
      p. cm. -- (Children's literature and culture ; v. 42)
     ISBN 0-415-98019-4 (alk. paper)
     1. American literature--African American authors--History and criticism.
   2. Children's literature, American--History and criticism. 3. African American children--Books and reading. 4. African American children in literature. 5. African Americans in literature. I. Title.

PS153.N5L45 2006
809'.89282'08996--dc22
                                                    2006020261

Visit the Taylor & Francis Web site at
http://www.taylorandfrancis.com

and the Routledge Web site at
http://www.routledge-ny.com

PERMISSION ACKNOWLEDGMENTS

"(Un)Happily Ever After: Fairy Tale Moral, Moralities and Heterosexism in Children's Texts" originally appeared in *Journal of Gay and Lesbian Issues in Education: An International Quarterly Devoted to Research, Policy, and Practice* 4.2 (Winter 2006): 55–74.

"'Life for me ain't been no crystal stair': Readin', Writin', and Parental (Il)Literacy in African American Children's Books" originally appeared in *Children's Folklore Review* (Issue 25: 2002–2003, pp. 75–100).

"'Sticks and Stones may break my bones…': Airbrushing the Ugliest of Ugly in African American Children's Books" originally appeared in *Obsidian III: Literature in the African Diaspora 3* (Fall/Winter 2001–2002): 10–34.

"Nappy Edges and Goldy Locks: African American Daughters and the Politics of Hair" originally appeared in *The Lion and the Unicorn: A Critical Journal of Children's Literature* 24.2 (2000): 201–224. Reprinted courtesy of The Johns Hopkins University Press.

"Beyond Big Hair and a Bad Hair Day: Carolivia Herron's *Nappy Hair* Pieces" originally appeared in *Children's Literature in Education: An International Quarterly* (Issue 30, September 1999: 171–183). Reprinted with kind permission of Springer Science and Business Media.

"Don't Condemn White Teacher over *Nappy Hair*" originally appeared in *The Arizona Republic* (30 December 1998): B6.

"Angels of Color: Divinely Inspired or Socially Constructed?" Originally appeared in *Diversity: A Journal of Multicultural Issues* 2 (Spring 1994): 65–79.

"'Alabama Angels' Descending into the Past" originally appeared in *Journal of American Culture* 17 (Summer 1994): 97–98.

"Review of Kelly McWilliams's *Doormat*," "Review of *Teacher's Guide to the Bluford Book Series*," "Review of Angela Johnson's *The First Part Last*," "Review of Anne Schraff's *Until We Meet Again*," "Review of Anne Schraff's *Lost and Found*," and "Review of Anne Schraff's *A Matter of Trust*" all originally appeared in *Journal of Adolescent and Adult Literacy*.

"If You're Happy to be Nappy, Clap Your hands!": A Review of bell hooks's *Happy to Be Nappy*" originally appeared in *Children's Folklore Review* 22 (1999): 45–55.

"Review of Joyce Carol Thomas's *Crowning Glory: Poems*" originally appeared in *QBR: The Black Book Review* 9 (November / December 2002): 9–10.

"A Potpourri of Children's Activities that Entertain and Teach: A Review of *Juba This & Juba That: 100 African American Games for Children*" originally appeared in *Birmingham Times* (28 March 1996): 11.

To Jasmine and Jared, whose lives continue to transform my own more profoundly than they may ever realize—and to Adelina, whose patience, support, and understanding are boundless.

CONTENTS

PART II: DIALOGUING REVIEWS

PART III: EXTENDING DISCOURSES

SERIES EDITOR'S FOREWORD

Dedicated to furthering original research in children's literature and culture, the Children's Literature and Culture series includes monographs on individual authors and illustrators, historical examinations of different periods, literary analyses of genres, and comparative studies of literature and the mass media. The series is international in scope and is intended to encourage innovative research in children's literature with a focus on interdisciplinary methodology.

Children's literature and culture are understood in the broadest sense of the term "children" to encompass the period of childhood up through adolescence. Owing to the fact that the notion of childhood has changed so much since the origination of children's literature, this Routledge series is particularly concerned with transformations in children's culture and how they have affected the representation and socialization of children. While the emphasis of the series is on children's literature, all types of studies that deal with children's radio, film, television, and art are included in an endeavor to grasp the aesthetics and values of children's culture. Not only have there been momentous changes in children's culture in the past fifty years, but there have also been radical shifts in the scholarship that deals with these changes. In this regard, the goal of the Children's Literature and Culture series is to enhance research in this field and, at the same time, point to new directions that bring together the best scholarly work throughout the world.

Jack Zipes

FOREWORD

Neal Lester's writings first came to my attention several years ago. The journal I edit, *Children's Folklore Review*, published his review article, "Nappy Happy: A Review of bell hooks's *Happy to Be Nappy*," in the 1999 issue and his article, "'Life for Me Ain't Been No Crystal Stair': Readin', Writin', and Parental (Il)literacy in African American Children's Books," in the 2003 issue. *The Lion and the Unicorn*, for which I served as guest editor of a special issue on "Folklore in/and Children's Literature," published his article, "Nappy Edges and Goldy Locks: African American Daughters and the Politics of Hair," in the 2000 issue. I am delighted to see these and other essays included in *Once Upon a Time in a Different World: Issues and Ideas in African American Children's Literature*.

As a folklorist, I can attest that most of my colleagues are much more comfortable examining cultures other than their own, the culture of the Trobriand Islanders, for example, as opposed to the culture of the college campuses, regions, or families in which they live. Neal Lester, however, has not shrunk from the challenge and has shown himself willing to look within his own culture, at his family and their traditions, and at himself as a tradition bearer. At times, he has contrasted his own African American folklore with the folklore and expectations of European Americans.

But, there is more. Lester has been able to look at these materials—such as African American hair, hairstyles, and practices in comparison with or contrast to European American hair, hairstyles, and practices—in a way that is free from bias, a difficult thing to do when one is examining one's own traditions. In fact, I would like to focus for a moment on "Nappy Edges and Goldy Locks: African American Daughters and the Politics of Hair" as that article illustrates the multiple perspectives from which Lester is able to approach a topic.

In the first section of the article, Lester begins with personal anecdotes, explaining that he had not thought much about hair and culture until the birth of his daughter, and he then reflects on his son's hair and his mother's hair before telling a couple of stories about himself, ways in which he has worn his hair, and various reactions to his hair. Lester begins the second section with a historical note about Madame C. J. Walker, "the first self-made woman millionaire [who] made her fortune with . . . black hair care products," and then discusses the history of African Americans' hair and hair care from slavery times to the present, concluding the section with interwoven comments on professional academic scholarship dealing with African Americans' hair and on African Americans' hair in popular culture.

Sections III and IV of the article deal primarily with children's literature. Lester opens Section III with the statement that, "Black folks' hair . . . has not been dealt with so prolifically and to the same extent in children's literature . . . [as in] African American adult literature." He then discusses some of that literature in which brown children struggle with their "kinky" hair and contrasts those books to such popular culture icons as the flowing hair of Rapunzel, Goldilocks, and Barbie before discussing the few children's picture books that do deal with hair. In Section IV, Lester deals with longer texts, both fiction and nonfiction, beginning and ending the section, as one might expect, with Carolivia Herron's *Nappy Hair*. He concludes the article with an unpublished poem by student Isis Jones, "Nappy Hair," which is "a message of cultural celebration and self-acceptance [that] rings loudly and proudly." There are also five pages of notes with supportive details and further information appended to the article.

Lester's rhetorical strategy is very effective. By beginning with personal anecdotes, especially the ones about himself but also the ones about his children, his mother, and his grandmother, which he then connects to an historical and cultural context, Lester removes his essay on African American hair from the world of abstract academic topics and gives it a sympathetic, human face; moreover, he does this without suggesting that anyone is at fault or that there is anyone to blame—for creating the stereotype of culturally approved straight hair, for creating a cosmetic industry to appeal to those who wish to have such culturally approved straight hair, or for using very painful chemical (and other) treatments or buying any number of wigs to attain that straight hair. Instead, he regards the situation as one of "competing mythologies . . . [that] signify for me continuing racial and gender biases about head hair both within and outside black cultural perceptions." He tells one particularly interesting story about his own dreadlocks:

> As I was sitting browsing through books at a multicultural children's book festival recently, a little white boy, probably about three or four years old, came over to me and started lifting my dreadlocks with his hands and playing with them. While I was amused at his curious boldness, his mother was mortified and unnecessarily apologetic.

It is Lester's amused tolerance that puts the human face on the topic of African Americans' hair, and it is also the amused tolerance (along with his multifaceted approach to his topic) that is, I think, one of the keys to this article and this book.

Once Upon a Time in a Different World has an obvious three-part structure within which the reader is provided a multivalent conversation about a number of topics and ideas in addition to the above-referenced material on hair. Part I contains eight essays by Lester, each of which is followed by a short response by eight other people: educators, scholars, students, parents, and/or critics. Part II is a father–daughter dialogue in which Lester and his teenaged daughter, Jasmine, separately review the same novels, something they have done in *The Journal of Adolescent and Adult Literacy*. Part III contains Lester's reviews of books and related teaching resource materials. Both Parts II and III conclude with responses from other experts in the field.

Once Upon a Time in a Different World presents the reader with essays on, among other things, prescribed heterosexism in children's texts, the assumptions about the cultural idolatry of alphabet literacy, the use or non-use of the word "nigger" in children's texts, and the representations of angels in literature—in addition to the pieces about hair. The broad range of topics and the responses to those topics (and to the reviews in Parts II and III) make this book one that is sure to spark discussion and debate among its readers in the classroom and elsewhere.

Neal Lester has succeeded in providing a book that is both scholarly and accessible, and an important resource for parents, students, educators, and anyone interested in an informed, interesting, and multitextured study of children's literature.

C. W. Sullivan III

ACKNOWLEDGMENTS

If this volume means anything to anyone, it is because it is the collaborative efforts of others who also care about and are committed to creating a safer and more diverse environment for our children, for their complete intellectual and spiritual growth. I thank especially my colleague Alleen Nilsen for opening up to me the wondrous possibility of sustained teaching and research in this already vibrant field of children's and young adult literature. I thank as well my respondents—Stacey Augustine, Jim Blasingame, ben clark, Kim Curry-Evans, Olga Davis, Joe Graves, Clotte Hammon, Vincenza Mangiolino, Khafilah McCurdy, Elizabeth McNeil, Chip Sullivan, and Nathan Winesett—to acknowledge the value of their participation in this project. I am grateful to my research assistants, Stephanie Maroney and Karin Simelaro, for their steadfast punctuality, their keen attention to detail, and their patience. Finally, I am deeply indebted to Jack Zipes, who saw the value of this dialogue and conversation about a world that ultimately may not be so different after all.

INTRODUCTION
Moistening the Desert Landscapes

I can see them standing politely on the wide
pages that I was still learning to turn,
Jane in a blue jumper, Dick with
his crayon-brown hair;
Playing with a ball or exploring the
cosmos of the backyard,
Unaware that they are the first characters,
the boy and girl who begin fiction.

—Billy Collins, "First Reader" (1999)

I.

As an African American parent of two teenagers, I am always looking for texts—books, stories, greeting cards, toys, dolls, and other forms of representation—that legitimize the presence and experiences of families and children who look like us. Long before talk show host Oprah Winfrey announced her somewhat futile efforts to find brown angel figurines and ornaments and then was flooded with brown angel gifts from millions of her fans, my foray into the different world of African American children's literature came in the late 1980s with my personal search for a brown angel tree topper for my family's Christmas tree. That search for a tree topper, which led me to short stories, children's books, and even to the special Christmas issue of *Newsweek*, then morphed into one of my first critical pieces on the peculiar absence of angels of color in popular culture and literature. Mary Hoffman's delightfully refreshing children's picture book *An Angel Just Like Me* (1997)—the story of Tyler, a young African American boy who is critically perceptive enough to question the fact that "none of the angels on the Christmas cards or wrapping paper looked like him" and that none of the Santas looked like his own brown dad—underscores the painful reality of African American absence and invisibility historically in mainstream representations. Tyler's surprise Christmas gift is "the most beautifully carved wooden angel [that] looked just like [him]." The narrative concludes that, once Tyler's friends of color see the brilliance of his angel, they too want "angels just like them."

As a teacher of African American literature and cultural studies, I have for these past sixteen years recognized the value and vitality of integrating children's texts in all of my college instruction. To explore the nuances and to tease out the timeliness of gender and racial identity issues in Toni Morrison's first novel *The Bluest Eye* (1970) invites the opportunity to discuss the range of 1950s Fisher-Price toys, Barbie dolls, Mary Jane peanut butter candy wrappers, Raggedy Ann and Andy tea sets, Mickey and Minnie Mouse Learn-to-Zip-Button-and-Tie dolls, and samples of 1940s *Fun with Dick and Jane* early readers that evidence black absence or invisibility. Indeed, as readers witness the pain of black Pecola Breedlove's fervent and futile prayer to have the bluest eyes, Morrison reminds readers that who and what we are as adults is definitively connected with how and what the adult world created for and presented to us as children:

> Adults, older girls, shops, magazines, newspapers, window signs—all the world had agreed that a blue-eyed, yellow-haired, pink-skinned doll was what every girl child treasured. "Here," they said, "this is beautiful, and if you are 'worthy' you may have it." (20) … Each night, without fail, she prayed for the blue eyes. Fervently, for a year she had prayed. Although somewhat discouraged, she was not without hope. To have something as wonderful as that happen would take a long, long time. (40)

My personal and professional dedication comes in showing my own brown children and my rainbow of college students that, as performance artist Anna Deavere Smith contends, "the mirrors of society do not mirror society" (1993). Indeed, my extensive research, teaching, and public lectures over these past sixteen years have meant to challenge assumptions about the alleged insignificance of children's literature categorically and of African American children's literature more specifically.

II.

In the early and mid-1990s as the lone and first tenured African American professor teaching African American literature in the English Department at the University of Alabama—yes, the 1963-George Wallace-door-blocking university—I described my teaching and countless public-speaking engagements across the state as my efforts to "bring water to those thirsting in the desert." Although the state of Alabama had a considerably larger black population than does Arizona, my new home since the fall of 1997, very little about African American culture had become part of public school or university curriculum. I left that university largely because its then-seven-year-old minor in African American studies was wilting from administrative and curricular neglect.

Never had I imagined my Alabama water-to-the-desert metaphor coming to pass as in my nine years in the Department of English at Arizona State University. Against others' skepticism about uprooting my young family and moving to yet another politically conservative, not-many-black-folks-in-that-state state—rejecting attractive offers from schools in Iowa, Oklahoma, Indiana, Michigan, and Pennsylvania—I journeyed to a place where my interracial family and I might see and be with more people who look like us and are not perceived as "transgressors." I was welcomed into a department where at least four others, two of them African American, were teaching African American literature and to an institution with an African American studies program fast becoming an autonomous unit.

Before becoming department chair some three years ago, I had reminded each of my three white department chairs and colleagues in my annual performance reviews—to contextualize my student evaluation scores and summaries—that teaching African American literature in the Southwest is considerably more challenging than teaching this same subject in the Southeast. In Georgia, Tennessee, and Alabama—my homes at various junctures of my academic career—the black–white color line is clear both geographically and psychologically, despite the reality of African American influence on southern white culture—speech, food, and music, for example. In major public Deep South spaces, blacks are here, whites there. To talk about black–white race relations is easier in many respects because all are painfully aware of racial difference and separation historically, politically, educationally, economically, and socially. The reality of tense race relations, by no means unique to the South, is as palpably drenching as the humidity that made us all so physically uncomfortable during long, sweltering southern summers.

In the dry, dusty Sonoran Desert, I continue to find a disturbing number of my white students greeting me with unsolicited apologies for having had no prior contact with African Americans before my class. Never in the nine years of teaching in Alabama did anyone make that particular public confession to me. Students here soon learned that there are no racial experience prerequisites determining their success in my ethnic courses. The full experience of taking my African American literature courses does, however, invite all students to open their minds to difference and to value and recognize racial difference as global enhancement rather than as individual or communal threat. This possibility of a different way of thinking about the world and forming different perspectives met with individual and occasionally collective resistance when I challenged my always predominantly white students' basic assumptions about black people and about blacks' experiences through the lens of literary and cultural expression. I realized quickly from many white students born and raised in Arizona or transplanted from New Hampshire or Utah that such resistance derives from African American absence or a basic unawareness prior to their experiences with me. Unfortunately, there are still so few African American professors and students at Arizona State University, a particularly large metropolitan university, that it is easy for them to imagine that racism, even its most subtle forms, does not affect them.

When a white, middle-class, fifty-something female in my first African American literature survey course at Arizona State University stated almost as self-congratulations that she is "unaware that racism exists because it doesn't affect [her]," it was the first time that my publishing, teaching, and public-speaking mission had been articulated so earnestly and rawly by another. Based on that comment alone, I, as a responsible university educator, had to show her and others who felt similarly "by any means necessary" that racism and racial bigotry affect her and all of us on some fundamental level. Having a black "professional" next-door neighbor with whom she had never had a meaningful conversation or who had never been invited into her home or she into his suggested to me that her environment was not as racially "integrated" as she imagined. When I meet white neighbors and other white professionals here who, on hearing that I work at Arizona State University, assume that I am a coach or who, on hearing that I am a professor, assume that I teach only first-year composition (and there is nothing "lowly" about teaching first-year composition), I realize that moisture needs to settle this blinding dust. When my kidney stone doctor is, in his words, "astounded" that I have both a master's and doctorate, I have to replenish my pots, pans, bowls, and buckets for thirsty desert dwellers. When a white colleague from another department on campus assumes that all the students in my African American literature courses are black, I reach for my nearest water source.

Still, my stay in the desert has thus far been satisfying overall. Apart from being tenured at Arizona State University, I know that I will always have a job somewhere in this country because people are thirsty, even those who do not realize or acknowledge their thirst. I like to think that, as a public scholar and a researcher, I continue to bring cups of water to soothe parched tongues, providing moisture to settle the dust in the scorched landscapes of many people's minds. When my students and neighbors in Arizona are Asian, Hispanic, Native American, Latino, African American, multiracial, and Euro-American, I know that my decision to light out for this southwestern territory both challenges and rewards. I also know that my droppers, spoonfuls, cups, and buckets of water can only enhance the beauty of the desert's moisture-deprived landscape.

Indeed, this metaphor extends to my research and teaching in African American children's literature. Since coming to the desert, I have found a wellspring of research possibilities and celebrations in children's literature among colleagues, one of whom enticed and supported me in putting together my first course in African American children's literature. That course has been taught a number of times to very enthusiastic students. In fact, when it was last taught, it carried with it University Service Learning credit, whereby about half of the class interned at a predominantly African American and Hispanic elementary school. Here, interns tested the theories and engaged in the practices we had explored. Even with that class, however, I had to struggle with the College of Education to legitimize the course for their education majors. The question raised was, "Does it have sufficient multicultural content?" How can a course in African American children's literature that touches on young adult literature and even American Indian children's literature *not* be sufficiently multicultural? I add that even the announcement of the new course as a feature piece with the title "New Class to Focus on Kids' Books that Aren't Anglo-centric" in the university student newspaper (*State Press*, 4 November 1998) met with public resistance from a white student contending that a class that "explored the ways in which African Americans have been portrayed in dolls, in literature and [popular culture]" allegedly widened the cultural and racial divide. This senior business major, in his letter to the editor of November 16 1998, protests:

> I would ask why we need another course in the African American
> Studies Department whose aim is to prepare the next 200 years

by studying the past 200 years? Is it impossible for this institution to create a course that actually helps to unite people instead of divide them?

In the hope that we can progress as a nation, as a society, together, we should concentrate on uniting with one another. Desire, determination and ability should do this, not the color of our skin.

Aside from the multiple faulty assumptions and wrong facts this respondent articulates—for instance, as an English professor, my course was an English Department course, not an African American Studies Department course, and the article for which I was interviewed made this clear—the larger issue is that this naïve and greatly uninformed perspective argues that to talk about difference leads to or widens an existing divide. It surely does not. My efforts to legitimize African American children's literature as a viable research and teaching area continues, and I proffer this collection as yet another means of culturally and spiritually moistening many desert landscapes, both immediate and afar.

III.

As a teacher and scholar of African American children's literature, I continue to be disappointed at the scarcity of critical pieces that explore in meaningful and more complicated ways issues in contemporary African American children's literature. I hope that this collection contributes to the intellectual and ideological discourse on this body of literature, not necessarily as a guide in how to teach or select the discussed texts. Furthermore, as a single-authored collection, it avoids the often repetitive and overlapping details and perspectives in other single-focused or themed collections with multiple contributors. It also seeks to tease out more complicated issues in the genre than are usually touched on when an editor conceives of a collection primarily to introduce others to the genre. My collection offers a convenient and multitextured perspective of children's literature, asserting the importance of this genre and exploring both overt and implied critical issues as well as their probable effects on young readers.

This collection proposes to cover a range of issues relevant to any discussion of race and gender identity politics. It fills a gap left by the absence of so few critical single texts that address a range of issues particular to African American children, and by extension to all children, and to adults responsible for those children. The ideas presented in this collection will surely spawn new and important conversations about representation in children's texts by and about other ethnic groups. These conversations about children and what they are exposed to become conversations also about adults who create and present these texts to children.

My hope is that this collection will serve as an important resource for parents, high school and college students, educators, and librarians; particularly those with some formal or lay involvement in areas of ethnic studies, American studies, American literature, African American literature, women's studies, and children's literature, because its format provides materials that are accessible to each of these readership levels. The essays will serve both pedagogical and practical purposes by introducing readers to nuanced issues in African American children's literature and expanding complex discussions of identity politics and constructions. The range and complexity of essay topics will underscore the extent to which this body of literature is a viable means of making the invisible visible, responding directly to author Ralph Ellison's profoundly relevant assertion about African American identity in a world that refuses to legitimize that existence:

> I am invisible; understand, simply because people refuse to see me. Like the bodiless heads you see sometimes in the circus sideshows, it is as though I have been surrounded by mirrors of hard, distorting glass. When they approach me they see only my surroundings, themselves, or figments of their imagination—indeed, everything and anything except me. (Prologue to *Invisible Man*, Vantage, 1947)

The collection has a three-part structure: Part I: A "Call-and-Response" Conversation; Part II: Dialoguing Reviews; and Part III: Extending Discourses. The first part consists of focus essays, at this point published in leading journals in the field of children's literature, each of which I have authored. Because these essays were published in different venues and with different readerships, there is some repetition unexcised to maintain the integrity of the initial pieces. A unique and useful feature in this first part is its call-and-response format as a critical and political "conversation" about issues and ideas in African American children's literature. Specifically, the essays cover the following topics that will contribute to larger discussions of identity, gender, sexuality and race relations: heterosexism in children's texts, treatments of parental (il)literacy, the absence of "nigger" in children's texts, the race and gender politics of African American hair, the controversial children's book *Nappy Hair*, the absence of angels of color in literature and popular culture, and Toni Morrison's first two children's books as primers on better parenting and better adulting. Offering broad and informed responses to each of my essays are carefully selected educators, scholars, students, parents, and/or critics. I have selected each respondent based on a number of diversity factors, such as gender balance, perspectives and backgrounds, and experiences with children's literature and ethnic studies. Such a format inherently provides readers with multiple perspectives along with a larger threaded conversation about this literature. Each essay and response is followed by a section called *Talking Out Loud: Ideas for Discussion* with leading inquiries provided by the respondent and me to generate ideas for written and/or discussion purposes. These questions following each pairing consider larger critical issues that emerge from the calls and responses in this section.

Part II of this collection is a father–daughter dialoguing that blurs the line between African American children's literature and young adult literature. It includes my reviews of adolescent novels and my seventeen-year-old daughter's reviews of those same novels—reviews written independently but published as companion pieces. Not only do I routinely include young adult authors in my African American children's literature course—Christopher Paul Curtis, Nikki Grimes, Jacqueline Woodson, and Mildred Taylor, for instance—but also as my own children have grown, I have remained invested in knowing what and how they read and what holds their interest. Toward that end, my teen daughter, Jasmine Z. Lester, and I have engaged in a father–daughter book review exercise in *The Journal of Adolescent and Adult Literacy.* We have looked at the same texts—typically new books coming out—and offered separate critical responses. The basis of this exercise is my awareness that what adults think is important about texts is not necessarily what target audiences of teens and preteens see as important. This exercise has given my daughter and me another shared opportunity to celebrate literacy and parent–child and adult–child dialoguing. That my daughter and I have reviewed these books shows the extent to which my profession as an educator, as a literature teacher, as a scholar of ethnic literature, and my role as a parent may or may not influence my daughter's responses to these texts, to these ideas. Very interesting and provocative discussions about movies and books have grown out of these dialoguing moments.

Part III is a section of reviews I have written on specific African American children's books. These reviews have always contextualized a specific book within the larger contexts of children's literature or African American literature. Indeed, as I have written them, these reviews are not just about individual books under review but rather are about larger issues of identity and culture within and beyond these reviewed books.

I

A "Call-and-Response" Conversation

1

(UN)HAPPILY EVER AFTER

*Fairy Tale Morals, Moralities, and
Heterosexism in Children's Texts*

I'd heard my calling by age 6. We had a word for boys like me.
(Punk). … At age 11 we moved to Georgia. I graduated to new
knowledge. (Homo)

—Marlon Riggs, "Tongues Untied" (1991)

I had known [that I was gay] since I was a little boy but never felt
I could share my secret with anyone. I'd been taught that being
homosexual was wrong, a sin against God, so all my life I'd tried
to run from the way I felt.

—R. Robotham, "Still Friends" (1997)

As a white, middle-class male, I learned through my family, my
school, and my church how to dress, what to think, and when to
repent. I learned to write within the broad lines of my ruled paper
as I sat beneath an American flag and a scantily clothed, crucified
Christ. I learned that God punished sinners but loved the repen-
tant. I learned that homosexuality was sinful; that *I* was a sinner.

—James T. Sears, "Teaching Queerly" (1999)

3

INTRODUCTION

In Randall Kenan's short story "Run, Mourner, Run" (1992), Dean Williams is a young adult, white, gay male paralyzed by an unresolved identity crisis. As the story focuses on the intricacies of Dean's economic, social, and emotional life in the present, Kenan underscores Dean's negative self-perception as a gay male as rooted in early childhood experiences that taught him connections between sexual identity and morality. At school, for instance, Dean's education is that of any child continually subjected to heterosexist social prescriptions even when sexual orientation is not the subject of the formal lesson plan:

> Once upon a time—what now seems decades ago rather than ten or fifteen years—Dean had real dreams. In first grade, he wanted to be a doctor; in second, a lawyer; third, an Indian chief. He read fairy stories and nursery rhymes, those slick shiny oversized books, over and over, and Mother Goose became a Bible of sorts. If pigs could fly and foxes could talk and dragons were for real, then surely he could be anything he wanted to be. Not many years after that he dropped out and learned to dream more mundane dreams. Yet those nuggets from grade school stayed with him. (164)

To be a doctor, a lawyer, an Indian chief, and even Mother Goose characters, according to Dean's multiple sources of authorial teachings, was presumably to be heterosexual; there were no other options for physical safety and security, for social legitimacy and success. Kenan's story—even with this "once upon a time" (164) fairy-tale trope—is not a children's text. It nonetheless offers as its premise the extent to which the range of childhood texts from fairy tales to nursery rhymes and ditties inherently carries social expectations, prescriptions, and dictates that can negatively impact any youngster's emotional and psychological growth. It is a reality of limitations and dangers based not necessarily on what an individual does, but rather on what an individual is: "Surely he could be anything he wanted to be" (164). Although Dean does not choose his same-sex attraction, he has nevertheless absorbed lessons about the "wrongness" of that attraction. He feels then that he will never be the "good boy" that Little Jack Horner is—"sitting in a corner and eating his Christmas pie"—not because of anything he has done but because he is not heterosexual. Indeed, such normalization of heterosexuality is common in early childhood formal education and is the centerpiece of a popular learning strategy in a Phoenix, Arizona, elementary school. With all the pomp and circumstance of traditional wedding ceremonies, members of a kindergarten class learn their alphabets by performing a mock wedding:

> This is the sixth year [that] teacher Pat Jackson has coordinated the wedding of Mr. Q and Miss U in her kindergarten class at Kyrene Monte Vista Elementary School. She thought the event would be a fun way to introduce a spelling lesson to her students, as one girl would play the bride and hold a stuffed letter U and a boy would be the Q-holding groom, with the rest of the class in bridal party roles. Everyone is dressed up and equipped with flowers and boutonnieres. (Yara, 2002, A1)

Similarly, in my own Southern hometown church in Jefferson, Georgia, youngsters participate in a Tom Thumb wedding with wee ones as all the players, another early lesson on the social and moral "rightness" of marriage and heterosexuality. Kathy Bickmore (1999) contends in her essay that heterosexuality, intricately woven into the fabric of our early education system, must be challenged:

> Moral precepts are indeed taught in elementary schools, but (by virtue of being implicit and avoiding controversy) they tend to reinforce dominant viewpoints and narrow notions of normalcy, thereby minimizing the possibility of democratic social change. … Gender identity and sexuality are to some degree inescapable in literature and social studies lessons, because the characters in human dramas virtually all have gender identities and intimate relationships. … The vast number of [those lessons] … quietly include sexuality in the form of normalized nuclear family characters and heterosexual relationships. (18–19)

This chapter then considers the extent to which children's texts perpetuate a limiting heteronormalcy that negatively impacts identity development for those who do not fit this model of behavior and desire. It challenges educators and parents to acknowledge that children's sexual identities are impacted in subtle and overt lessons that affect any child's overall social, spiritual, and psychological adult well-being. Betsy J. Cahill and Rachel Theilheimer (1999) claim that "children who develop into gay or lesbian young people with negative perceptions about being gay are at 'high risk for physical and psychological dysfunction'" (41). This chapter further challenges all adults, educators in particular, to take responsibility in creating for all children the safest, most nurturing, and most open environments both inside and outside the classroom.

INCLUSION THAT EXCLUDES

In the foreword to his multicultural revision of Mother Goose rhymes, Douglas W. Larche (1985) acknowledges that childhood nursery rhymes and fairy tales can have an impact on adults and children in more ways than we might realize: "Nursery rhymes can be a powerful socializing force in children. In the innocence of early childhood, it is vital that nursery rhymes in their subtle but simple way implant the ideals *we* espouse" (emphasis added, 7). Assuming that "we" understand and acknowledge our own social and political biases, there continues to be a need to revise the "classics" to include every child. Sara Ward reiterates the importance of these stories to our adult development:

> Because [fairy tales] were often explicitly didactic, teaching values and other important life lessons, children were (and still are) especially receptive to those messages communicated. ... They might not have the critical skills necessary to challenge the way things are, even if they can recognize that these tales establish strong lines of dissension between what is to be male and what is to be female. Subtleties are conveyed that reveal to young children what their specific role in life should be. (n.d., 2)

Certainly, today's climate of presumed sensitivity to and awareness of multiple layers of political correctness dictates that age-old fairy tales and nursery rhymes be revised to challenge race, class, and gender biases. Feminists liberate Cinderella and Rapunzel from their cages of female passivity, as female characters in these new tellings need not rely on a prince to rescue them from fairyland entrapment. Larche's (1985) is clearly an equal opportunity revision with images of physically challenged and multiethnic individuals, and with a Jill who has Jack's agility: "Jack be nimble, Jack be quick, Jack jump over the candlestick! Jill be nimble, jump it too, If Jack can do it, so can you!" (8). The feminist cause has achieved such legitimacy that it is coopted in marketing schemes, as in this Honda car advertisement: "Jack, be nimble. Jack, be quick. Jill's already at the finish line. (The Honda Awards for 26 years, honoring the best collegiate women athletes)." Here, American Honda Motor Company referees a mock race between males and females buying Honda automobiles at the same time it promotes women's accomplishments in sports. This same feminist revision characterizes Ms. Foundation's tenth anniversary "Take Your Daughters to Work Day" campaign that includes these public service announcements: "Mary had a little lamb at a corporate luncheon honoring her promotion," and "Little Miss Muffet sat on the board of directors of a Fortune 500 company" (Galley,

2002). Such revisions challenge the status quo gender roles of traditional fairy tales and nursery rhymes, granting agency to females personally, socially, and politically in the present, agency that eluded many a childhood representation of females in the antiquated past.

African Americanists and other ethnic studies scholars also value "colorizing" whitewashed fairy tales. Junior high school and middle school teacher Fred H. Crump, Jr., Afrocentrized familiar tales by imaging African Americans, assigning characters more Afrocentric names, and including African costumes and geographic settings: "Jamako and the Beanstalk"; "Afrotina and the Three Bears"; "The Ebony Duckling"; and "Hakim and Grenita." Crump (1991) comments on his motivation for his revisionist work:

> My specific reason for undertaking this project was an attempt to bring the "mainstream" fairy tales into more black kids' lives in a format they could relate to *and* enjoy. I first got the idea at a Book Fair at school in 1981 when I overheard two of my black students say there were no books there for them. There was an Ezra Jack Keats and maybe Michael Jackson. ...
>
> As I worked, I took Xerox copies to show my black students, and received very positive responses, lots of smiles, many good suggestions. I began to see it as a possible "self-esteem" boost for them. I feel we underestimate the impact of "lack of self-esteem." (letter to the author, 5 December 1990)

Notions of (in)visibility and inclusivity are equally central to Alile Sharon Larkin (1991), whose children's video replaces the typical white and blond straight-haired female with a "cinnamon brown child [named Nimi] with lots of pretty African curls on her pretty little cinnamon brown head." And, writing for an adult audience, Eve Merriam (1996) challenges class assumptions of traditional rhymes. In her introduction to the biting satire, poet Nikki Giovanni (1998) elucidates Merriam's objectives in taking on this revisionist project:

> Eve Merriam took the spirit of "Mother Goose" to the inner city to give voice to those who were being silenced. She did not have the luxury of code. She had the moral indignation of a just cause. ... Agony should not be ignored. ... Merriam gave voice to the inner city to let them know there are some who hear. (2)

Conjoining familiar germs of *Mother Goose* (2002) with sharp social critique, Merriam (1996) disrupts the romanticized and seemingly safe world of "happily ever after": "Now I lay me down to sleep, I pray the double lock will keep; May no brick through the window break, And no one rob me till I wake" (17). These lines remind us that the middle class ritual of putting children to bed is a privilege and safety not every child experiences.

Similarly, Toni Cade Bambara (1995) challenges the heroic ideals of Western fairy tales. Offering that such standards and classics are potentially "con" texts, Bambara's revision signifies on "Goldilocks and the Three Bears," boldly questioning the ethics of Goldilocks's unorthodox and socially irresponsible actions inside the home of the three bears: She's invasive, careless, destructive, irresponsible, and deliberately misrepresents truth. Bambara challenges critical thinkers to question how we arrive at and accept truth:

> I heard that this little yellow-haired gal was a childhood hero of yours. … Well, then do you think it is hip, healthy, or wise to inflict little children with the *official* version of the golden bandit [Goldilocks] before we have assumed the necessary task of encouraging and equipping the young in a critical habit? … A critical habit is crucial, wouldn't you say, afflicted as we are every day with … authorized versions. Lies. Cover-ups. Dis-information. (210)

Bambara reminds that all texts are political and insists that all readers approach any and all texts with a critically literate eye.

Indeed, there are many ways such revisions are accomplished, from colorizing illustrations as in E. M. Oliver's (1981) book, to revising narratives to mirror a specific cultural landscape as in Kroll's (1995) writings, to utilizing the vehicles of language and music as in singer Patti Austin's 1992 hip-hop versions. Such contemporary rhythms, Afrocentric costumes, and African American vernacular demystify the fairy tale world, offering an immediacy and relevance to modern-day storytelling rituals. To make visible those typically absent from conventional representations underscores the focus of the highly acclaimed Home Box Office series "Happily Ever After: Fairy Tales for Every Child" project with African Americanist versions of "The Frog Prince," "Jack and the Beanstalk," "The Valiant Young Tailor," and "Beauty and the Beast." "Sleeping Beauty," "Hansel and Gretel," and "Cinderella" celebrate Hispanic culture. Asians are featured in "Little Red Riding Hood," "The Emperor's New Clothes," "The Little Mermaid," and "The Princess and the Pea." Those participating in this revisionist project fully recognized the importance of making every child see himself or herself in these cartoon images. Producer Donna Brown-Guillaume and actor husband Robert Guillaume "wanted their [African American] adolescent daughter, Rachel, to be able to identify with fairy tale characters the way white children did, and wondered if other black parents felt the same" (R. Miller, 1995, E1, E6). They found a bevy of actors, writers, animators, composers, and musicians of color eager to lend their voices and talents to this important work. The need for such a project underscores Latina actor Liz Torres's sentiments precisely: "I spent my childhood imagining myself as Goldilocks, Cinderella, and the rest until 'the pie of reality' hit me in the face" (E6). Although the series strives to include cultural representations of children from diverse ethnic backgrounds, in its first seasons the series failed to challenge traditional gender role social prescriptions.

While feminist and multicultural efforts to revise "traditional" children's texts continue to be socially and politically necessary, they too fall short of being as inclusive as they could be. They fail to critique prevalent heterosexual hegemony and coercion. As author Raymond Hitchcock contends, "It's a shame there aren't any gay fairy tales. It would be nice to see the girl kiss the frog, it turns into a princess, and they live happily forever after. There's got to be innumerable lessons from that one" (Carvin, 2001, 7). Gay and lesbian revisionist fairy tales exist but clearly only for adult audiences: Peter Cashorali's (1997) book and William Hunter's XXX-rated *Goldie Locks and the Bi Bears* (1997), which features bisexual African American males as the three bears and a white blond female as Goldilocks. Michael Ford's (1996a, 1996b) edited collections also revise and challenge heterocentric lessons of deeply entrenched master narratives. Ford admits his early desires to rewrite the gender role scripts of his childhood fairy tales:

> Perhaps more than anything else, fairy tales represent the wide-eyed innocence of childhood, a time when our minds were open to any and all possibilities. ... As a budding queer, I suppose I gave some passing thought to the princes they [female characters] were usually searching for; but deep down, I always imagined myself as the one doing the searching. ... Often, I would dress up and act out my favorite tales, blind to gender stereotypes or what my "expected" role was. ... As I grew older, the fairy world grew a little dimmer as childhood dreams were replaced by different desires. (1996b, 1–2)

Ford (1996a) acknowledges the tensions between his public and private identities. Even in his childhood, he was able to see the privileged position of heterosexuality as social and political power. He adds:

> Often the stories we were told as children are meant to teach us something about what will happen to us when we leave the

nursery and start venturing forth on our own. ... The greatest
lesson-teachers of all were fairy tales. Often read to us merely as
precursors to bedtime by harried loved ones who simply wanted
to put us to sleep so they could enjoy some quiet time, these simple
stories were treasure chests of information that taught us, knowingly or not, about love, life, and what was expected of us. ...

   Ironically, we pass these stories and ideas down through generations, in what many consider one of the dearest traditions of
childhood. What more beautiful image is there than of a father
reading to his son the same stories his father read to him as a boy.
Little does he know that inside the sleepy-eyed head, his little man is
dreaming of the prince who will take him in his arms. (1996a, 1–2)

Such an account underscores that even as a child grows up in a heterocentric environment, the values, goals, and rules of behavior in that
environment can run counter to the child's own private attractions,
desires, and curiosities.

ADULT PERSPECTIVES THROUGH CHILDREN'S EYES

Traditional fairy tales, nursery rhymes, and childhood ditties inherently conjoin morality and sexual identity. Heterosexuality is good
and right, alternatives bad and sinful. In his essay, Jonathan Ned Katz
(2000) details the historical evolution of labels that allegedly helped to
order, define, and inadvertently limit erotic desire and behavior. Trac-
ing connections between a "production-oriented procreative" and a
purely "consumerist pleasure principle," Katz comments on the political and social normalizing of heterosexuality that was led by the medical profession in the late nineteenth and early twentieth centuries:

   The idea of heterosexuality as the master sex from which all others deviated was (like the idea of the master race) deeply author-
   itarian. The doctors' normalization of a sex that was hetero
   proclaimed a new heterosexual separatism—an erotic apartheid
   that forcefully segregated the sex normals from the sex perverts.
   ... Strict boundaries made the emerging erotic world less poly-
   morphous—safer for sex normals. (142)

While such constructions sought to create public order among the
masses, the same constructions inevitably created chaos for and
silenced those who early on knew they were outside the boundaries
of "normalcy." Indeed, it is not uncommon for gay, lesbian, and bisexual individuals awakening to their sexual orientations at surprisingly
young ages to know the wrongness of their being at ages when they

are scarcely able to understand the complex ramifications of what their private desires might mean for their lives and to others. Caitlin Ryan, director of Policy Studies at the Institute on Sexuality, Inequality, and Health at San Francisco State University, explains:

> Adults who came out in the 1970s and early 80s first became aware of same-sex attraction around age 13, while adolescents who came out in the late 1980s and early 1990s experienced this as early as age 9; self-identification as lesbian or gay occurred between ages 19 and 23 for the adults and between 14 and 16 for the adolescents. (Shenitz, 2002, 103)

A thirty-something African American gay male friend speaks to this simultaneous awakening and silencing, also at an early age:

> I knew I was gay as early as 8 or 9. My best friend [male] and I started playing around then and it lasted well into my teens. I was never attracted to the opposite sex and never had any encounter with the opposite sex. [At that early age,] I knew that something was NOT quite right, and I certainly kept the feelings hidden. (e-mail message to author, 6 February 2002)

Even when this individual had no language to articulate his responses and attractions, he was nevertheless keenly aware of the wrongness of having such attractions. An editorial (1983) posits that, despite the myriad public messages that encourage, reward, and even dictate the rightness of heterosexuality, homosexual orientation is realized early in one's life whether or not it is publicly acted on:

> Though the direction of one's sexual activity *is* a matter of choice for a small percentage of adults, the majority of lesbians and gay men become aware that they are somehow "different" from the heterosexual "norm" when they are quite young. This awareness generally occurs in profoundly anti-gay social settings and in spite of a heterosexist society that "proselytizes" superiority of hetero-sexuality and the inferiority of homosexuality. Given the perva-siveness of heterosexual influences (the media, the educational system, countless role models, etc.), the fact that lesbians and gay men succeed in discovering their identities at all provides a strong argument that sexual orientation is not influenced by "proselytiz-ing." ("Why CIBC is dealing with homophobia," 9)

Thus, youngsters awakening to their heterosexuality find socially condoned childhood outlets for and expressions of their budding heterosexual identity through "playing house" and "playing mommy and daddy" and through such popular childhood rhymes as "John and Suzie, sittin' in a tree K-I-S-S-I-N-G. First comes love; then comes marriage. Here comes Suzie with a baby carriage." The appropriateness of physical attraction between boys and girls who subsequently marry and procreate reinforces alternatives to heterosexuality as deviant, socially irresponsible, and hence morally wrong. And, these lessons abound. Of 295 rhymes in *The Real Mother Goose* (B. Wright, 1944), more than fifty highlight heterosexuality with direct references to marriage of husbands and wives; references to romantic intimacies such as kissing or courting between boys and girls, men and women; having children; marriage proposals; fathers and mothers; and weddings. While parenting and marriage are not exclusive to heterosexuals, heterosexuality is the prescribed norm. Even the illustrations and visual pairings of children characters reiterate this heterosexual norm. Only seven rhymes suggest any possibility of fluid or nonheterosexual identities: "Why May I Not Love Johnny?" (45); "Two Pigeons" (55); "Robin and Richard" (although two males are in bed, the verse clarifies that the men are "brothers") (20); "Curly-Locks" (39); "Bessy Bell and Mary Gray" (90); "Bobby Snooks" (72); and "A Week of Birthdays" (87).

Inclusivity, acceptance, and equity in public policy become even more important in the face of current events in which the president of the United States supports a constitutional ban on gay marriage (2004). While the U.S. Supreme Court rules to strike down laws that infringe on the right to privacy for gays and lesbians (2003), Canada opens its door to gay marriage and Vermont to gay civil unions, conservatives protest such developments on the basis of morality, not on the basis of the alleged "equality and justice for all." Such is the response of a female Virginian to an editorial, "God is Watching" (Letters, 2003):

> The Supreme Court may have struck down the Texas law against sodomy declaring that the government has no place in peoples' bedrooms, but they can't keep out God. ... Deciding a certain behavior is no longer illegal doesn't change the fact that it is still a sin according to God, who is the ultimate judge. May he have mercy on this nation. (A11)

Amanda Udis-Kessler and Cooper Thompson (1995) question the following misconceptions in their brochure:

> In the United States, some of the most broadly held standards [of sexual conduct] include the following: being married to the "opposite sex" is the most appropriate expression of an adult sex-

ual relationship; having a relationship with someone of your own gender is somewhere on a continuum from abnormal to immoral; and expressing one's sexuality is synonymous with wanting or having genital contact. (1)

Clearly, no such socially acceptable outlets exist for children with nonheterosexual identities and curiosities. Only in recent years have a few high schools across the country begun to sponsor gay and lesbian proms. Furthermore, children may know that acting on heterosexual impulses through such early experimentation as "playing doctor" is frowned on, but they do not experience that what and who they are is wrong, just their precocious behavior. In fact, for heterosexist parents, this young experimentation through heterosexual performance may confirm for them that their children are heading in the "right" direction toward sexual normalcy.

MORALITIES AND SEXUAL IDENTITIES

Acknowledging Cheryl Clarke's (1983) assertion that "a tremendous amount of pressure is brought to bear on men, women, and children to be heterosexual to the exclusion of every other erotic impulse" (200), revisionist children's texts across the board must participate in critiquing social inscriptions that connect sexual identity with morality. They must challenge the Bible-thumping public pronouncements that "homosexuality is an abomination to God," and that "if God condoned homosexuality, he would have created Adam and Steve, not Adam and Eve." Few question the extent to which society continues to fail youngsters moving toward sexual identities that are not socially rewarded or morally sanctioned. Explaining the inner emotional turmoil of publicly masking his own gayness, an African American adult male in an *Essence* interview underscores the wrongness of his homosexual difference:

> Ever since I can remember, I've been attracted to men. Every part of society told me *it was wrong*, so I tried everything not to be. I dated women. I tried to completely block it out of my mind, I tried therapy. But my heart has a voice that speaks to me: Because it is part of who I am, I couldn't make it go away. … I tried so hard to get rid of it, but I couldn't. The only thing [I could] do is choose not to act on it. (Villarosa, 1993, 64)

Interconnecting race and homosexuality as "deviance," Molefi Kete Asante (1988), insists that "an Afrocentric perspective recognizes its existence but homosexuality cannot be condoned or accepted as good for the national development of a strong people. It can be and must be tolerated until such time as our families and schools are engaged in Afrocentric instructions for males" (57). Asante's limited perspective does not even acknowledge the possibility of women's attraction to other women or bisexuality as it condemns male homosexuality. Youngsters absorb adult perspectives about acceptable and unacceptable public behavior and feelings even when the youngsters do not fully understand the complexities, manifestations, and ramifications of these perspectives:

> If our society celebrated sexuality in all its variations, we could imagine children and adults expressing their sexuality in many ways, and we could imagine that these feelings, thoughts, and behaviors might change over a lifetime. Actually, young children do explore their sexuality with some degree of freedom. But our society and the sub-cultures in which we live impose standards for sexual conduct that influence how we think and feel about our sexuality, and, especially, how we behave. (Udis-Kessler and Thompson, 1995, 1)

A twenty-something gay white male acknowledges multileveled wrongness in his early (homo)sexual curiosities and explorations:

> In third grade, the boy that sat next to me one day put his penis in my hand. I really liked it. So I asked him to do it again. I gave him pencils so that I could touch it. This happened three or four times over the course of a week or two and then it never happened again.
>
> I believe [these encounters were] more than curiosity. What prompted him [in third grade] in the first place? And why me—the child who ended up being gay? Could he sense this? There were other boys in the class, but I remember that we were doing something "wrong" and we needed not to get caught. This was during school. (e-mail message to author, 13 December 2001)

To pretend that youngsters are not experiencing and consciously responding to sexual urges and sensations is to reveal adult naïveté and unawareness. King and Schneider (1999) acknowledge: "Elementary children do consider sexualities—theirs and others'—talk about it, and some practice with it. When we refuse to talk about it, the value of sexual talk of all kinds increases on the black market of linguistic transactions" (131). Access to honest, age-appropriate information that includes multiple and diverse personal, cultural, and political perspectives is the cornerstone of a democratic society of individuals free and at peace within themselves. Equally problematic then is the assumption that public performances of heterosexuality mirror innermost desires.

Deeds do not define doers, especially when those desires have been determined socially dangerous and morally wrong.

WHEN ENOUGH IS NOT ENOUGH

While there is a growing body of fiction and nonfiction dealing with nonheterosexual identities, as evidenced by various bibliographies of children's books with gay and lesbian characters (*Annotated Bibliography of Children's Books with Gay and Lesbian Characters* by Sandra Chapman and *Gay and Lesbian Characters and Themes in Children's Books*), the issue of the (homo)sexuality of children themselves thrusts us into more socially sensitive and skeptical terrain. Unsurprisingly, most children's books that deal with the issue of homosexuality—at the expense of public outrage and controversy, as in "Court Battle Looms for Children's Books on Homosexuality" (2002)—focus exclusively on gay/lesbian adults and adult relationships, usually gay parents of presumably straight children, such as Michael Wilhoite's *Daddy's Roommate* (1991) and *Daddy's Wedding* (1996); Lois Abramchik's *Is Your Family Like Mine?* (1996); and Lesléa Newman's *Heather Has Two Mommies* (1989), to name a few. Anthologies detailing experiences of growing up gay/lesbian are also available. However, these are for adolescent and young adult audiences: Bennett Singer's *Growing up Gay/Lesbian: A Literary Anthology* (1994), Amy Sonnie's *Revolutionary Voices: A Multicultural Queer Youth Anthology* (2000), and Kevin Jennings's *Becoming Visible: A Reader in Gay and Lesbian History for High School and College Students* (1994).

The very presence of this literature responds to important personal, social, and political needs. However, such books—many of them currently out of print—do not address a child's developing gay, lesbian, or bisexual orientation, which obviously precedes and largely defines gay adult identity, attitudes, and behaviors. As gay and lesbian youngsters publicly acknowledge their sexual orientations at earlier ages—as young as nine and perhaps earlier—it becomes necessary to consider the impact of heterosexual hegemony and coercion in the earliest texts to which we expose all children. And although "there are children in almost every elementary/middle school classroom who are gay or lesbian ... few gay children have any support or guidance, the way children of color and with disabilities have public and private support systems in place" ("Why CIBC Is Dealing with Homophobia," 1983, 3). Articulating this urgent need to have books for gay, lesbian, and bisexual adults and children, Barbie's House Books Publishing issues the following public service announcement with details about Barbara Lynn Edmonds's *Mama Eat Ant, Yuck!* (2000):

> All parents of newborns have this in common: none know their baby will be heterosexual, homosexual, or bisexual. The more we can do now to erase homophobia, the safer all our children will be in the future. Gay-friendly preschool literature is a long overdue resource for parents and educators, both gay and straight. (n.d., 2)

Can heterosexual parents, teachers, and young classmates imagine that Jack might prefer a romantically innocent hike up the hill with John instead of Jill, that Georgy Porgy may be "passing" when he kisses girls publicly but really wants to kiss boys, or that Cinderella would happily accept a princess as the bearer of her lost glass slipper? Some exploration into the common Jack-and-Jill rhyme reveals that an early Scandinavian version narrated the scenario of two boys, Jack and Gill:

> Now hang on to your hats for this one! The earliest illustrations of the [Jack and Jill] rhyme showed not a boy and girl, but two boys climbing a hill—Jack and Gill! The rhyme comes from an ancient Scandinavian myth about the markings on the moon. The moon god Mani captured two Norse children, Hjuki and Bill, while they were drawing water from a well. When the moon was full, the children could be seen with a bucket on a pole between them. This story, with the names changed to Jack and Jill, has evolved into our tale of heads over tails. (*Mother Goose Rhymes,* n.d.)

Sexualization of this rhyme and its accompanying morality explain this adult commentator's implicit and explicit unease at naming the same-sex encounter, even as it is not uncommon for children to engage in same-sex play well into their teen years and beyond. A popular street revision that includes boys kissing boys and girls in a presumed public intimacy, however innocent, is again mocked as social wrongness: "Georgy Porgy, pudding and pie. Kissed the girls and made them cry. When the boys came out to play, He kissed them too, coz he was gay" (*Nursery Rhymes for Grown Ups,* n.d., 1). Tonally, that Georgy Porgy also kisses boys is not a cause for celebration but rather for moral and social disapproval, as is true in this street revision of "Little Boy Blue" called "Little Boy Blew," from the same source: "Little Boy blew. Hey! He needed the money" (*Nursery Rhymes for Grown Ups,* n.d., 1). Here, a presumably public homosexual act of intimacy is allegedly deviant and born of economic desperation rather than of individual celebration and social acceptance.

If we can colorize and inversely engender these childhood classics, how then do we make the classics sensitive to multiple sexual identities?

Can we imagine a text that both colorizes and provides viable and visible alternatives to heterocentrism? Can adults accept that the fictions of boys and girls and sexual identity are inherently connected?

> I can see them standing politely on the wide pages
> that I was still learning to turn,
> Jane in a blue jumper, Dick with his crayon-brown hair,
> playing with a ball or exploring the cosmos
> of the backyard, unaware they are the first characters,
> the boy and girl who begin fiction. (B. Collins, 1999)

Here, Father and Mother and Jane and Dick join Adam and Eve as they weave complex social constructions regarding gender, race, class, and sexual identity. Both the Dick-and-Jane and brother–sister relationships take on heterosexual, albeit incestual, normalcy, in the provocative t-shirt featuring the familiar image of Dick standing before a kneeling Jane with the caption: "Jane loves Dick." Indeed, as Sears (1999) admits, "Elementary teachers unmindfully enforce 'compulsory heterosexuality' through stories of nuclear animal families and questions about mommies and daddies" (11).

Current revisionist rhymes such as this one, which was popular among my daughter's middle school classmates, implies another heterosexist connection between Jack and Jill: "Jack and Jill went up the hill to smoke some marijuana. Jack got high and unzipped his fly, and Jill said, 'I don't wanna.'" Is it possible that Jill has no interest in romantic/sexual contact with Jack or any other male? Revisionist limericks and rhymes that continue this heterosexist bent are commonplace in contemporary Internet folklore, thus mirroring the social mainstream: "Jack and Jill went up the hill to have some hanky panky. Silly Jill forgot her pill, and now there's little Franky" (*Nursery Rhymes for Grown Ups*, n.d., 1).

Exposing all children to texts with age-appropriate intimacies and interactions between same-sex characters would not only validate the experiences of gays or bisexuals, but might also counter early rampant and aggressive homophobia that often goes without social consequence (Schenden, 1999, 2). It is surely no difficult task to find public examples of aggressive and even self-righteous homophobia. Consider, for example, the sentiments of one-time Detroit mayoral candidate Kwame Kilpatrick: "There are things my impressionable children don't need to see at this age—a man kissing a man, a woman kissing a woman. That's not hatred. It's just that I want to raise strong, proud men that love women" ("Rants and Raves," 2003, 12). Kilpatrick's own homophobia is one matter; that his own "impressionable children" might well be gay is an arena into which he could easily step. Similarly, a family friend unashamedly confessed that she and her self-proclaimed, ultra-masculinist husband were really worried when their ten-year-old son expressed too intense an interest in figure skating and playing with dolls. They breathed a sigh of relief when they successfully steered him away from such "girly" activities to "all-boy" sports like football and basketball. They may never know the extent to which their working against his interests might have impacted him negatively. Further, their exercise in persuasion merely highlights their ignorance about sexual identity rather than their power to mold such an identity in their likeness. While gay-friendly/gender stereotype–busting children's books such as Harvey Fierstein's *The Sissy Duckling* (2002) and Lesléa Newman's *The Boy Who Cried Fabulous* (2004) are not likely to change such parents' attitudes, should these books fall into a child's hands at a public library or school, they could work toward counteracting the potential damaging effect of such parental behavior.

Within this context, Tomie dePaola's (1979) children's book is an example of efforts to challenge prevailing gender stereotyping that early on affects youngsters' behaviors and thoughts about themselves. Although the story is not about Oliver's attraction to girls or boys, it considers social and parental biases that prescribe and ascribe certain behaviors and ideals for boys, certain others for girls. While girls can be tomboys without much social and personal consequence, boys are more restricted in their public performances. The character Oliver Button, having no interest in sports or other allegedly "boy things," endures hurtful teasing from his classmates because he enjoys dancing, acting, singing, drawing, dressing up in costumes, playing with paper dolls, jumping rope, and reading—allegedly "girl activities": he "didn't like to do things that boys are supposed to do" (dePaola, 1979). Only after an undaunted Oliver proves his skills as a tap dancer at the school talent show is he miraculously accepted for his decision to take the path less traveled. Still, even if we accept dancing as a boy-appropriate activity, tap dancing, like break dancing, one might add, rates higher on the heterosexual male scale of social acceptability than would ballet, for instance. Unsurprisingly, Oliver's father tries to straighten him up: "Don't be such a sissy! Go out and play basketball or football or baseball. Any kind of ball!" Here exists the prevalent, though faulty, correlation between sports acumen and heterosexuality.

While there is a need for more books such as dePaola's (1979) that explode gender stereotypes, such books are much more accepted into mainstream society in ways that books exploring children's homosexuality are not. Children's texts might address the young Oliver Button's purely innocent attraction to John, or Jane's attraction to Susie and John, in the same way that Sam and Amy Lou share an unspoken but obvious elementary school flirtation in Joan M. Lexau's (1985) children's book. Just as the crush between Sam and Amy Lou is not sexualized, the same kind of presentation might serve to present same-sex romantic pairings without social threat or moral judgment. Or, there might be same-sex innocent crushes that go beyond routine homosocial childhood behavior and performance. Such instances would not be encouraging or persuading but rather validating and responsive to the potential needs of all young ones.

Gender stereotypes and homophobia can surely lead to uncertainty and emotional turmoil among heterosexual children as well. Journalist and author Robert Lipsyte's (2003) editorial response to the award-winning 2003 Broadway play *Take Me Out*—about gays in sports—sees the play as a lesson for adults and youngsters in dispelling the myth that sports is a heterosexuals-only arena. Lipsyte acknowledges his heterosexual privilege in an unapologetically homophobic high school environment:

> Being heterosexual is no protection against homophobia. I didn't suffer the pain some [gay] professional athletes have described so vividly recently [in their coming out stories]. ... Nor have I been one of the thousands of gay youngsters persecuted and driven out of sports. ... But I remember how gay slurs could stir my own adolescent fear and confusion. I can still hear the junior high gym teacher ordering me to stand up to a fast pitch ("Don't hit like a girl!") and the high school gym teacher urging me up the rope ("Climb, don't be a sissy!"). In college boxing class, the coach yelled at me to "Stop hitting like a faggot!" Panicky, I slugged a friend after the bell to prove I was a man. (A13)

To counteract homophobia in the classroom, gay and nongay children are entitled to honest information about sexuality or any other topic relevant to their lives.[1] Verbal mockery such as "sissy" and "fag" can escalate to physical threats and attacks for no particular reason other than acting out disapproval of another's perceived or lived homosexual identity, thereby publicly laying claim to the perpetrator's own privileged heterosexuality. A young preteen boy in my son's boys choir was on indefinite leave of absence because other boys teased him unmercifully about being "gay"—derived primarily from his "unboyish" self-discipline, respect for authority, attentiveness, and conformity. To my probing response to his mass e-mail about disciplining a female student who called a male classmate a "faggot motherfucker," a young beginning white teacher friend reminds me that his south side Chicago class of African American (75%) and Hispanic (25%) eighth-graders—ages 13 to 15—routinely engages in anti-gay performances with abandon:

> One of the most common insults or put downs that I find kids in my community using is to call someone (or something) "gay" or a "faggot." Last year I had a student who really didn't like me, and practically every other word out of his mouth was "faggot." I think there may be a few reasons for this kind of homophobia: 1. Most of the kids in the community I teach in have extremely little time outside of it. Nearly all of them don't know any gay people (or think they don't) and base their conceptions of homosexuality on what they see in movies and TV; 2. They know that the Bible and their church communities say *homosexuality is wrong*, and this message is usually reinforced by their parents and families; 3. This is just a conjecture, but I suspect that the kids either consciously or subconsciously associate homosexuality with whiteness or white people (as in, most homosexuals are white), which is yet another reason why it is anathema. (e-mail message to author, 25 September 2004)

It is thus not uncommon to connect verbal assaults with physical violence, as Bruce Shenitz (2002) recounts in his story about a gay teen's suffering:

> At the beginning of his sophomore year in Reno's Galena High School, it didn't look like life could get any worse for a 14-year-old out gay student Derek Henkle: He was jeered at on the school bus, pushed into lockers in the hallway, and spat on in the cafeteria. But the worst was still to come: In September 1995, while Derek was walking back to school at the end of a break, he recalls, a group of male students surrounded him in the parking lot and "took out a lasso and said, 'Let's lasso a fag and tie him to the back of the truck and drag him down the highway.'" In fear for his life, "a survival instinct took over," he says. He dodged in and out of the parked cars as the gang pursued him. "They got the lasso around my neck three times, and I was able to get it off each time," he says. "But had they been any better at lassoing, I probably wouldn't be here." (99)

Derek transferred to three different schools, and the verbal and physical harassments followed whenever there was any public acknowledgment of his homosexuality. He eventually dropped out of school. Derek's story is not an uncommon one; Shenitz announces this crisis in public education and by extension in society at large: "As gay people have become more visible and kids arrive at self-knowledge about their sexuality earlier, it has become harder for gay kids to slip under the radar of intolerant peers. Verbal and physical harassment at school sometimes escalates to [physically] dangerous levels" (100).

Worse still, physical aggression toward homosexuals is often ignored or condoned. A 1988 Dallas, Texas, case, for instance, illustrates such tolerance toward violence in our legal system. Two homosexuals were killed, and a judge offered the following comments about the wrongness of the slain victims' sexual orientation:

> A judge says he sentenced an 18-year-old killer to 30 years in prison instead of the maximum life term partly because the two men he shot to death were homosexuals.
>
> "The two guys that got killed wouldn't have been killed if they hadn't been cruising the streets picking up teenage boys," District Judge Jack Hampton told the *Dallas Times Herald* in an interview.
> ...
> "I don't much care for homosexuals cruising the streets picking up teenage boys. ... I've a teenage boy." ("Judge: Light Sentence Given," 1988)

The legal, social, and political endorsement of violence against individuals because of their perceived "deviant" sexual identities is evidence of the degree to which homophobia is woven into our society's fabric. Children's books that normalize alternatives to heterosexism can help dissipate homophobia by addressing it at its roots—in childhood. King and Schneider (1999) offer sound pedagogical strategies for "infusing" age-appropriate gay and lesbian themes and lessons into the elementary education curriculum in their essay. They insist that all responsible educators who are critically and culturally literate "must look for occasions to convene conversations on homosexuality as a social fact" (128).

CONCLUSION

My position makes no grand claim that nonheterosexual adults are psychologically or otherwise permanently scarred by the absence of gay, lesbian, or bisexual childhood texts that legitimize their earliest (homo)sexual desires and feelings. The emphasis here is rather to challenge, in the same way feminists and multiculturalists challenge "conventional" representations, another limitation that affects a young person's physical, social, psychological, and spiritual development. Just as we accept that childhood toys, cartoons, songs, books, and greeting cards (Murphy, 2004, 25) affect children's perceptions of themselves and their world, adults must see fairy tales and nursery rhymes as cultural markers and master narratives that have an impact on children's developing sexual identities and self-worth. Maria Tatar (1999) reiterates the importance of these children's texts as cultural artifacts:

> Although fairy tales are still arguably the most powerful formative tales of childhood and permeate mass media for children and adults, it is not unusual to find them deemed of marginal cultural importance and dismissed as unworthy of critical attention. Yet the staying power of these stories, their widespread and enduring popularity, suggests that they must be addressing issues that have significant social function—whether critical, conservative, compensatory, or therapeutic. ... Fairy tales register an effort on the part of both men and women to develop maps for coping with personal anxieties, family conflicts, social frictions, and the myriad frustrations of everyday life. (xi)

In the case of nonheterosexual individuals, fairy tales may conversely be a major source of their "personal anxieties, family conflicts, social frictions, and the myriad frustrations of everyday life" (Tatar, 1999, xi). Children, like adults, read their environments and the lessons variously manifested, either molding their behavior to reap the rewards of conformity or challenging consciously or unconsciously the boundaries, sometimes at great risk. Jonathan Ned Katz (2000) explains public behavioral performances as constructions relative to sexual identity:

> Women and men make their own sexual histories. But they do not produce their own sexual lives just as they please. They make their sexualities within a particular mode of organization given by the past and altered by their changing desire, their present power and activity, and their vision of a better world. (147)

Ward's (n.d.) comments about gender roles and sexuality further underscore fundamental realities about right and wrong sexual identities:

> By so supplanting stories targeting towards children, fairy tale authors have ultimately fashioned their fantasies into the reality of children. ... Boys and girls learn what it means to be classified as a boy or girl and what they must do to properly maintain that distinction. Boys must be valiant and regal; girls must be beautiful and pure and must also look to the boy for a sense of self-realization. (3)

To live the proverbial "happily ever after," boys and girls must perform the heterosexual's script. As every man, woman, boy, and girl is not included in that celebrated paradigm of privilege, King and Schneider (1999) insist that as responsible adults who are parents, educators, guardians, family members, and neighbors, "we can no longer afford this heterosexist elitism" (131).

Because there are individuals whose experiences are deliberately absent from childhood texts, no socially and morally responsible adult has the luxury of ignoring the need to continue creating revisionist, age-appropriate texts that are as all-inclusive as possible. That the complexities of sexual identities can be effectively discussed with youngsters and preadolescents is evidenced in Debra Chasnoff and Helene Cohen's (1999) award-winning educational video. The film offers snapshots of some six American public schools from first to eighth grades, from California to New York, engaging in classroom discussions about gay and lesbian social and political tolerance. While the film tries to do more than suggest that mainstream nongay Americans—both adults and children—revise their misconceptions and misinformation about those who do not practice heterosexuality, it is a carefully choreographed sampling of progay politics. The film remains focused on adult sexual identity and does not directly address children with alternative sexual attractions, desires, and curiosities. Still, the film is a valuable teaching and learning tool, validating that such age-appropriate, curricularly sound discussions are important and necessary if we are to move to the level of respecting difference on all levels. Cahill and Theilheimer (1999) contend that "gay and lesbian issues belong in the classrooms":

> Although some people believe young children lack the developmental readiness to deal with gay and lesbian issues, our assumption ... is that children are capable of understanding "difference." Research on children's early concepts of race, gender, and physical difference indicates that by age four most children are aware of color, racial, and gender differences, and that awareness is affectively laden. We believe that children have the cognitive capacity also to understand "difference" in family configurations and affectional preferences. (40)

Unsurprisingly, the Chasnoff and Cohen film and its inclusion in schools met with moral and political opposition in claims that the film was "an attempt to 'recruit' children into a 'homosexual lifestyle'" (Schenden, 1999, 2).

Resources and pedagogical strategies for "infusing" sexual identities into elementary classroom discussions are outlined in the comprehensive and groundbreaking collection of twenty-two essays edited by William J. Letts IV and James T. Sears (1999). In his introduction to that collection, Kevin Jennings, executive director of the Gay, Lesbian, and Straight Education Network, contends that "schools are the place where children spend more of their time than anywhere else between the ages of five and eighteen, and thus play a seminal role in either confirming prejudice or combating it" (Letts and Sears, 1999, x). The collection's succinct chapters, excellent annotated reference bibliography, and its sensitivity to multicultural perspectives make it an invaluable resource for educators. In addition, Kevin Jennings's (2003) book is a readable resource for parents of nonheterosexual children. While the book deals with parents of nonheterosexual teens, Jennings's autobiographical introduction clarifies for nervous and resistant parents and educators that sexuality is not a teen-specific reality:

> From an early age, I realized that something was amiss. I knew I was gay long before I had heard the word or knew what it meant. I remember at age six or seven being more fascinated by my brother's bodybuilding magazines than by his *Playboy*'s [sic], but somehow knowing that this was information I should keep quiet. As I grew up and came to understand what these feelings meant, I recoiled in horror from myself. (1)

It is then incumbent on all responsible for the well-being of youngsters to attend to all dimensions of their growth and development.

Andrea Dworkin (as cited in Tatar, 1999) articulates the dangers of exposing children only to conventional fairy tales—and by extension nursery rhymes and other childhood ditties—and questions the extent to which we can ever fully dismantle the racism, classism, sexism, heterosexism, and homophobia prevalent in these cultural texts:

> We have not formed that ancient world [of fairy tales]—it has formed us. We ingested it as children whole, had its values and consciousness imprinted on our minds as cultural absolutes long before we were in fact men and women. We have taken the fairy tales of childhood with us into maturity, chewed but still lying in the stomach, as real identity. Between Snow-white and her heroic prince, our two great fictions, we never did have much of a chance. At some point the Great Divide took place: they (the boys) dreamed of mounting the Great Steed and buying Snow-white from the dwarfs; we (the girls) aspired to become that object of every necrophiliac's lust—the innocent, *victimized* Sleeping Beauty, beauteous lump of ultimate, sleeping good. (xiii)

The impact of imagining early childhood affirmation of alternative sexual desires can be profound for those searching to locate themselves even in a fantasy world that renders them invisible. A thirty-something-year-old African American gay male admits such:

> It would have been nice to have some form of "positive" reinforcement [about my sexual attraction to boys when I was younger]. I think it would be good for children's books to acknowledge some form of intimacy (emotional or otherwise) with same-sex "characters"—be they animal or whatever—just so that children will have their feelings confirmed and validated. (e-mail message to author, 6 March 2002)

Regarding whether it would have made a big difference if the gay characters were black or white, he adds:

> It didn't matter to me then because I didn't know any better. There weren't that many books with black characters, and I didn't feel any particular way about that either. But in hindsight, I think it would have been great to have characters more like me, racially and sexually. (e-mail message to author, 6 March 2002)

The value of such specific revisionist children's texts is further recognized when an adult African American gay male admits:

> Although I think that people become aware of [their] sexuality at very different ages, I recall distinctly being attracted to boys in my mid-teens, but culturally and religiously, that attraction was totally unacknowledgeable. I had been targeted for being gay even earlier though I had no knowledge of sexuality. Guess I was a late bloomer. ... I remember being 13 and in 9th grade and having kids put signs on my clothes that said things like "Kick Me. I'm Gay!" I also remember kids making up songs about me on the bus. I specifically remember them singing—almost in unison—"Jeff, Jeff Smith, whoop, your freaky butt." Now, I have no idea where this was coming from. I'm sure I was effeminate. I now accept being a queen, but I don't think I was attracted to anyone at that time in a sexual manner. And I definitely had crushes on girls.
>
> I think having those types of [early childhood] images would be invaluable. It legitimizes the emotions. It says it's OK. Of course, there still would be family pressures and religious pressures, but at least there would be something, ... especially as kids are coming out earlier and earlier, ... largely due to the greater visibility of lesbian, gay, bisexual and transgendered [adults]. (e-mail message to author, 11 September 2001)

Every adult and educator must recognize additional limitations of traditional master narratives such as childhood tales and rhymes and accept responsibility in "demystify[ing] these sacred texts ... [by] break[ing] their magical spells; [understanding that] social change is possible once we become aware of the [limitations of] the stories that have guided our social, moral, and personal development" (Tatar, 1999, xvii). Every adult and educator must first imagine then create and maintain "classrooms [and homes] that challenge categorical thinking, promote interpersonal intelligence, and foster critical consciousness. ... Childhood innocence is a veneer that we as adults impress onto children, enabling us to deny desire comfortably and to silence sexuality" (Sears, 1999, 5, 9).

MAYBE THE PRINCE SHOULD KISS THE FROG

BY STACY AUGUSTINE

I ponder the question of how to introduce the idea of homosexuality and gays and lesbians to my twin daughters, now nine years old. Believe it or not, my little girls are quite innocent of this concept, probably because we watch no commercial television and see very few movies. When we do watch movies, it is often at home—an old musical checked out from the library, say, *Oklahoma*.

I cannot stand the way gays and lesbians are depicted in popular culture. As out of it as I am, I still see the stereotypes everywhere: the gay guy as great decorator and snappy dresser, the woman as dyke. *Queer Eye* jumps right to mind. I also continue frequently to see the relationship between gay bigotry and misogyny. My daughters' physical education teacher still insults the boys when they lose in competition to the girls; they are "wimps" and "sissies." He calls all the girls and even a particularly unathletic boy "hon." When giving sexual harassment training, these are the kinds of examples I would have made up. Who would have thought that twenty-five-year-olds would be talking like this—and worse, thinking like this—in this day and age? At my children's small private school, there is (as yet) no insult of "fag" or the trendy "that's so gay." My honors college niece, however, reports that use of these expressions is commonplace among her peers.

The gays and lesbians I know are boring—indistinguishable from the rest of their class. In considering this chapter and what I really believe about the idea of same-sex partners in fairy tales and nursery rhymes, my mind continually turned to Bill. Like me, Bill is a lawyer. Since I'm a stay-at-home mom, I don't run into him much these days. However, I used to run into him fairly often. Back in my dating days, Bill and I would often go to the same places—theater, restaurants, work-related parties—the same places I would see my heterosexual peers. After I married a pediatrician, I continued to run into Bill at historic home tours, at benefits—again and still, the usual. He was often with his life partner. Like many lawyers, including my (heterosexual) father, his significant other was a teacher. Bill's partner died a couple years ago, of a hereditary kidney disease that has killed several other members of his family. Grieving, Bill has thrown himself into charitable work; I noticed he has just received an award from the governor. Bill is a good guy and a good lawyer, but he's *boring*. He's ordinary. Like other gays and lesbians and like his hetero peers, he is trying to live his life and get through it, to make sense of it all, and is consumed with the normal and typical problems of his age and stage of life.

Is there a bathhouse culture out there, with rampant promiscuity? Sure. And, there is an equivalent in the hook-up, sexed-up, aggressive popular heterosexual culture. This is a culture that forces sex on people. This is a culture in which physical involvement is way out in front of emotional engagement, where people are "hotties," and 10-year-olds wear shorts with "Juicy" splayed across their bottoms. This is the "That's hot!" culture of Paris Hilton. And I hate it.

I believe in the power of literature and of fairy tales. When my girls were little, I was one of those who snuck in references to an identity I wanted them to have. The girls in the stories were engineers, mathematicians, scientists. They celebrated Chanukah, Rosh Hashanah, and Passover. As I embellished traditional fairy tales, I likewise frequently read from books like *Not One Damsel in Distress*.

I'm not worried about influencing my children to become homosexual or otherwise confusing their identity. When I was in my early twenties, I was in a "fag drag show," held in a theater instead of a bar. How I got there was pretty much accidental. A man I knew slightly, from work, was organizing the show, and I was going to work the box office. He then told me someone was sick, so they needed another dancer and asked if I would step in. As a game gal with many years of dance training, I did it. At the last minute, I ended up reading a "dark and stormy night" comedy piece. The day of the show, I passed a man at a phone—we still used pay phones, back then—he was so excited, saying, "We've got everything in this show! We've got gays, lesbians, transsexuals—we've even got a straight woman." Ahem. That would be me. In that world, I was a freak. They were glad to have me, though I could really dance back then, and it was a great opportunity for social anthropology.

I spent a fair amount of time hanging around with the guys, talking. I would ask them when they came out, who knew, and when they knew they were gay. They had stories of hiding, shame, and suffering. Without exception, they told me, they knew as early as elementary school. Similarly, I've known my girls were heterosexual for years, since they walked in to see "Viva Las Vegas" on the television screen. We were going to see the Manhattan Transfer at the local theater, and I'd randomly tuned in as I got ready. When my girls walked in and saw Elvis Presley, their jaws simultaneously dropped. They became very still and sat down, riveted. It was comedic—they stared as if their eyes had been replaced with cartoon swirls. One said, "Mommy, who's that?" My normally compliant children refused to go to the theater until I promised that I would buy them a DVD of that movie the very next day.

In the 1980s, just as AIDS was becoming understood and known, I remember going to a showcase house that benefited an AIDS charity. There was as yet no effective treatment; people were dying by the score, it seemed, with the arts world losing an entire generation. All the workers at the showcase were gay. It was a beautiful day and a lovely house with gorgeous gardens. Everyone there was so nice. Areas of the garden were set apart as "outdoor rooms," one of which had a memorial listing of names—friends of these guys, friends who had died of AIDS. I'm not sure why it hit me so hard—maybe it was the ephemeral beauty of the day, maybe it was that the men there were being so nice to me and I liked them so much, maybe it was the simple recognition that each of these names had been a real person that had loved and lived and cared and died too early. In any event, I recognized not a single name. I read them all, and I wept.

I would like homosexuality to be normalized. I do not want people to live in terror of being "outed." I do not want them to be ashamed because of their sexual orientation. Just as I wanted my twin daughters to see themselves as "normal" in the stories I read them, I would like homosexual children, too, to see someone ordinary, not freakish, who is like them in important ways. Speaking personally, it would also be helpful to me, as a mother, in helping my children understand that, first and foremost, gays and lesbians are people.

POSTSCRIPT

While we were visiting extended family in New Jersey over Thanksgiving, my girls went over to play with Sadie, who has two mothers, Susan and Gloria. We were planning to go down to the Brandywine River Valley about noon that day, so could only work in a short visit. My daughters, Helene and Marcella, are almost ten, and Sadie is nine. The girls have seen each other once a year or so since they were very small.

They are not actually related but have family in common: Susan is my husband's nephew's sister-in-law, to be exact.

As arranged with Susan the night before, we arrived around ten Sunday morning. The house is charming, made of logs and originally a vacation home, right across the street from the small lake that Sadie swims in during the summer. Sadie was waiting at the door, and as it opened, we could smell the brownies Gloria was baking. We left the girls, who began playing together immediately, and went about our business for the next two hours.

When we returned, all the girls—big and little—were playing a board game in the sunny family room at the back of the house. Susan gave us a house tour while Gloria helped the girls collect their shoes, socks, gloves, and hats. As we left, I could not help but think how lovely it all was and how completely unremarkable otherwise.

Later that night, we visited Longwood Gardens, near Wilmington. The gardens had on their holiday finery—lights and decorations—and Helene and I walked hand-in-hand on the grounds and through the conservatories. As we stood on a terrace and looked down on a tree covered in ice-blue lights, Helene commented, "Mommy, I don't understand how Sadie can have two mothers."

"Well," I said, "you know how our neighbors, Bruce and Sherry, decided they wanted to spend their lives together, then decided they wanted children? They adopted their children, so that they could have a family together. It's not just like that with Susan and Gloria, but it's kind of like that—Gloria is Susan's special friend, that she wants to spend her life with, and they wanted to have a child together, and Sadie is that child." The truth is actually more complicated, involving donor sperm, but I thought it best to reduce it to the simplest common denominator. As it was, I could see Helene really working to make sense of this.

We walked the promenade, flanked by the enormous trees with lights in an alternating pattern of green and red. Helene said, "But I don't understand. How can that be?" I repeated that the two were each other's "special friends," who wanted to be a family together. Suddenly, Helene dropped my hand and jumped back, peering into my face. She said,

> "Do you mean as if she were a husband?"
> "Yes," I replied.
> "That's disgusting!"
> "Why is it disgusting?"
> "Is Sadie adopted, then?"
> "Actually, one of them gave birth to Sadie. I think it was Susan."
> "Susan, yes, it was Susan."

> "I don't think it's disgusting to care about someone and
> want to spend your life with them. I think this way is
> hard, and it is not something I would want for you."

And here, my friends, is the crowning remark. She tells me, "Don't worry about it! It won't happen!" Then she was finished with that topic. For now.

This exchange, of course, gave me food for thought. Why did she react so strongly? Some might say that this is evidence that homosexuality is inherently repulsive to heterosexuals, but I do not think so. Could I have done a better job of laying groundwork, so that Helene would have been less taken by surprise? I have been quite aggressive in making sure my children know there is an entire world of people with varying physical characteristics. I have been sure to make them aware of the differing socioeconomic situations to be found. We have begun to ensure that they have an understanding of social justice issues and how these involve culture, color, and class. In contrast, until now, I have given little consideration to the potential consequences of heterosexist perspective. I want my children to appreciate relationships built on love and respect, regardless of the gender of those involved. In laying the necessary groundwork, would it have been helpful to have read some stories including same-sex parents? I think it would have been. I hope this discussion does, in some small way, contribute to the creation and use of nonheterosexist children's literature.

TALKING OUT LOUD: IDEAS FOR DISCUSSION

1. What is homosexuality?
2. What is heterosexuality?
3. How does society normalize homosexuality?
4. What fears arise from the normalization of homosexuality? Is an acknowledgment of homosexual legitimacy a threat to the legitimacy of heterosexuality?
5. To what extent is sexual identity performative?
6. What factors contribute to an individual's sexual identity?
7. To what extent does children's literature affect identity formation, or is its impact dwarfed by parents and other social and direct life experiences?
8. How might the larger, presumably heterosexual, society benefit through early awareness of the existence of healthy and positive homosexual relationships?

9. To what extent do children's texts—toys, songs, books, cartoons—have an impact on other aspects of our self-identity constructions?
10. Discuss the potential fluidity of sexual identities.

2

"LIFE FOR ME AIN'T BEEN NO CRYSTAL STAIR"[1]

Readin', Writin', and Parental (Il)Literacy in African American Children's Books

Learning would *spoil* the best nigger in the world. Now ... if you teach that nigger ... how to read, there would be no keeping him. It would forever unfit him to be a slave.

—Frederick Douglass, *Narrative* (1845)

Mass literacy is a relatively new social goal. A hundred years ago people didn't need to be good readers in order to earn a living. But in the Information Age, no one can get by without knowing how to read well and understand increasingly complex material.

—*Newsweek* (22 November 1999)

This project makes no claims to being an exhaustive exploration of parental illiteracy in African American children's books. It nevertheless recognizes the grave misinformation and incomplete information available to children with nonreading parents.[2] Failure to address parental illiteracy in children's texts in many ways furthers the marginalization of those unable to read and write. Treatments cited here are sadly rudimentary and grossly inadequate. To equate illiteracy with hopelessness, immorality, lack of self-love, limited quality family relations, latchkey childhood, parental dishonesty, and limited social participation—as do Vashanti Rahaman's *Read for Me, Mama* (1997) and Dolores Johnson's *Papa's Stories* (1994)—is to accept the cultural bias associated with literacy and to remain ignorant to complicated personal, social, political, and historical realities. As a professor of education clarifies, "The great divide in literacy is not between those who can read and write and those who have not yet learned to. It is between those who have discovered what kinds of literacy society values and how to demonstrate their competencies in ways that earn recognition" ("Quotations about Literacy," 1991, 1). Sojourner Truth, an illiterate former slave and one of the first black feminist abolitionists, "protested against discriminatory laws that denied the ballot to women, ... blacks, and illiterate citizens. After she was once turned away from a voting booth, she said, 'I can't read a book, but I can read the people.'" (Krass, 1988, 97). Indeed, her comment speaks to a dimension of (il)literacy that must be considered in order to eradicate myths and stereotypes used to determine individual self- and social worth. Such an exploration here reveals that children's books' authors can be totally unaware of the complexities of (il)literacy and the multitude of literate practices at the core of social, cultural, and individual identity formations. Among African Americans, the issue of (il)literacy must be further contextualized not as a way of condoning not learning to read and write, but as a way of understanding more fully that nonreading and writing is seldom if ever a simple matter of personal choice.

LITERACY AS DEMOCRATIC IDEAL

While Frederick Douglass's important *The Narrative of the Life of Frederick Douglass, An American Slave, Written by Himself* (1845) demonstrates an individual's alleged personal liberation spiritually and psychologically through reading and writing, the narrative equally forwards a culturally chauvinistic agenda that privileges the printed word. Proposing to show his learned northern abolitionist and primarily white male audience that access to reading and writing transforms him from his perceived animal barbarism to civilized humanhood, Douglass impressively and eloquently details human bondage and his release from it through elaborate rhetorical strategies: symbolisms, ironies, allusions, parallelisms, ambiguities, and repetitions.[3] Indeed, Douglass's liberation from his enslavement comes less from his gaining physical freedom than from his ability to read and write:

> Though conscious of the difficulty of learning without a teacher [his master's wife, Mrs. Auld], I set out with high hope, and of a fixed purpose at whatever cost of trouble to learn how to read. (667)

He learns indirectly from Mr. Auld how threatened masters were of slaves' becoming literate—among other things, they might write their own passes to freedom literally and figuratively—and this knowledge fuels his intense determination to become literate "by any means necessary":

> Mr. Auld ... at once forbade Mrs. Auld to instruct me further, telling her ... that it was unlawful, as well as unsafe, to teach a slave to read. To use his own words, further, he said, "If you give a nigger an inch, he'll take an ell. ... If you teach that nigger (speaking of myself) how to read, there would be no keeping him. It would forever unfit him to be a slave. He would at once become unmanageable, and of no value to his master. (667)

Mr. Auld's warning to his wife is equally one that creates a binary of literacy as a determinant of individual personal power or powerlessness. Unlettered, slaves remained ignorant of the world immediate and beyond. A slave's "unmanageability" and "unfitness" is then directly linked to liberation through literacy. Hence, Douglass's learning to read from Mrs. Auld's instruction and from manipulating little white boys so that he could write what they wrote is fundamental to Douglass's newly realized selfhood. Through literacy and the very act of writing a narrative of his life as a slave, Douglass endeavors to "write [himself] out of slavery, a slavery more profound than physical bondage" (12), argues Henry Louis Gates, Jr., in *"Race," Writing, and Difference* (1985). Gates clarifies the connections between humanity and literacy: "Black people ... have not been liberated from racism by our writings. We accepted a false premise by assuming that racism would be destroyed once white racists became convinced that we were human, too. Writing stood as a complex 'certificate of humanity'" (12). Douglass discovers as well the reality that literacy does not unrestrictively liberate when he is denied a job as a calker because of "prejudice against [his] color" (714).

Still, Douglass's copying—physically mimicking and then performing "white literacy"—speaks directly to the cultural binary that exists between literacy and illiteracy in the Western world. The *Newsweek* epigraph that opens this chapter speaks as well to this binary in its absolute classist and cultural presumption that the quality of one's livelihood is fundamentally connected to one's acquisition of print literacy skills. Although Douglass clarifies that slaves' physical and psychological survival was also connected to slaves "reading" masters' behaviors and motives, as Sojourner Truth announced, he feels completely human and humanized largely because he can read and write. When at the narrative's end Douglass "solemnly pledg[es him]self anew" and "subscribe[s him]self" (719), this act of subscription is his penultimate self-validation and self-proclamation of his humanness. He has rhetorically, psychologically, emotionally, and physically unshackled himself, demonstrating that once he learned to read and write, he understood that "education [reading and writing] and slavery were incompatible with each other" (670). Not only is Douglass able to name himself verbally in this final narrative moment, but his recording this moment as a printed text also signifies "freedom from slavery":

> The ability to utter his name, and more significantly to utter it in the mysterious characters on a page where it will continue to sound in silence so long as readers continue to construe the characters, is what Douglass's *Narrative* is about, for in that lettered utterance is assertion of identity and in identity is freedom—freedom from slavery, freedom from ignorance, freedom from non-being, freedom even from time. (Olney, 1985, 157)

The inherently contradictory language of Douglass's narrative title, *The Narrative of the Life of Frederick Douglass, An American Slave, Written by Himself*, reiterates this connection between identity and literacy. James Olney, in his essay "'I Was Born': Slave Narratives, Their Status as Autobiography and as Literature," from Charles T. Davis's and Henry Louis Gates, Jr.'s *The Slave's Narrative* (1985), explains:

> What typically happens in [slave] narratives … is that the social theme, the reality of slavery and the necessity of abolishing it, trifurcates on the personal level to become subthemes of literacy, identity, and freedom. … There is much more to the phrase "written by himself" … than the mere laconic statement of a fact: it is literally a part of the narrative, becoming an important thematic element in the retelling of the life wherein literacy, identity, and a sense of freedom are acquired simultaneously and without the first, according to Douglass, the latter two would never have been, [hence,] the dual fact of literacy and identity. (156)

As slave narratives worked inherently to boast, bolster, and document literacy as a symbol of civilization and humanness, their idolizing of print literacy sewed the seeds of classist/class and racist identity constructs.

In a broader sense, "formal" education generally and alphabetical literacy particularly have historically been touted within African American communities as keys to African American liberation from economic, social, and political oppression. Violet J. Harris explains in "African-American Conceptions of Literacy: A Historical Perspective":

African Americans hold many of the same views [on the sacred-
ness of education as do white American citizens]; they, too, maintain an unstinting belief in the power of literacy to effect essential
political, cultural, social, and economic change. In the past, and
to some extent now, education was a privilege, albeit a privilege
literally acquired through blood, sweat, tears, and enormous
economic sacrifice. Unquestionably, acquiring access to literacy
for African Americans has involved continuous struggle, in the
face of unrelenting opposition from segments of the planter aris-
tocracy, politicians, clergy, and ordinary citizens. (Harris, 1992,
276)

From these Western cultural scripts measuring personal and social
identities and self-worth by limited literate practices, African Americans adopted consciously or unconsciously these same race and class
biases. Further complicating the literacy binary, Harris (1992) notes
that literacy acquisition has equally served to mark necessary class
structures. Such social circumstances must be taken into account when
commenting on literacy across races and cultures. Harris not only
provides a rudimentary summary of historical realities facing African
Americans in their quest for literacy, but also comments on the fact
that literacy, depending on the nature of what one becomes literate in
or about, can be both "emancipatory and oppressive":

Literacy serves emancipatory functions when appropriated to
reconstruct society and/or provide individuals with the options
needed to participate in all sociocultural institutions. Literacy
functions in an oppressive manner … when curricular materials,
educational philosophies, and pedagogical techniques combine to
inculcate an ideology that denigrates a group, omits or misrepresents the history and status of a group, or limits access to knowledge that would enable the individual or group to participate in
sociocultural institutions. (277)

At best, literacy remained for African Americans an illusion of political, economic, and social equality. Yet, the ideal of literacy has been
historically restricted to the few and not the masses. Hence, class and
race dimensions of literacy acquisition have long been a political tool
to reward or to deny. Gates (1985) further contextualizes such cultural
biases:

Black and other people of color could not write. Writing, many
Europeans argued, stood alone among the fine arts as the most
salient repository of "genius," the visible sign of reason itself. In

this subordinate role, however, writing, although secondary to reason, is nevertheless the *medium* of reason's expression. We *know* reason by its writing, by its representations. Such representations could assume spoken or written form. And while several superb scholars give priority to the *spoken* as the privileged of the pair, most Europeans privileged *writing*—in their writings about Africans, at least—as the principal measure of the Africans' humanity, their capacity for progress, their very place in the great chain of being. (9)

Hence, to connect individual worth and selfhood, as does Douglass, with the ability or inability to read and write—one dimension of literacy—is not uncommon, however problematic, in a Western culture that is, as Harlem Renaissance writer Jean Toomer has claimed, hypnotized by literacy.

According to the 1992 National Adult Literacy Survey, literacy is the ability "to use printed and written information to function in society, to achieve one's goals, and to develop one's knowledge and potential." Buried in this definition is the ideal of literacy as realized personal goals, social worth, and fullest self-potential, implying that illiteracy constitutes failure on any number of personal and social levels. Despite its obvious language bias by specifying "standard" English as the definitive marker, the National Literacy Act of 1991 offers this definition of literacy by adding orality to the equation: Literacy is "an individual's ability to read, write, and speak in English and compute and solve problems at levels of proficiency necessary to function on the job and in society, to achieve one's goals, and to develop one's knowledge and potential" ("Literacy and Life," 2000). Personal goals and social values are again emphasized, and literacy is underscored as a prescribed personal and social ideal and standard. Neither definition, however, acknowledges literacy as a multitude of practices that legitimize realities and communicate diverse and varied experiences. If in fact literacy grants opportunities to achieve various ideals, then those unable to read and write are perceived and treated as socially handicapped and personally burdened. While Nancy N. Rue, in her 1992 volume *Coping with an Illiterate Parent*, maintains that "literacy is not a single skill" (38) and has little to do with the moral and ethical decency of a nonreading individual (19), she nevertheless writes of this issue with extreme pessimism and oversimplification, maintaining that illiterate parents are most often "trapped in a nowhere job, imprisoned by a sense of inferiority, shamed by the inability to give [a child] everything [that child] needs intellectually and socially and emotionally *because* he/she can't read and write competently" (emphasis added, 11). Rue implies that illiterate parents are in some ways less than complete and upstanding social individuals fully capable of maintaining satisfying familial and social relationships and leading productive lives. Even the book title itself—*Coping with an Illiterate Parent*—suggests that illiteracy is a kind of social disease or illness with which a child has to deal until a "cure" or "treatment" is found.

LITERACY IDEALIZED AND MORALIZED

Surprisingly, or perhaps unsurprisingly, few children's texts address the issue of parental illiteracy. The treatment of illiteracy in picture or story books—the focus of this study rather than adolescent and preadolescent chapter books—for those learning to read seems on the surface oxymoronic, perhaps even absurdly risky from the perspective of a publisher wanting to sell books. Indeed, those just approaching alphabet literacy are arguably more easily deceived by a parent's illiteracy than those children who have mastered the fundamentals of reading and writing and are thereby more likely to respond to a parent's inability to read and write with cynicism, condescension, and resistance to parental authority. Hence, the following critiques are not offered to glorify non-reading and nonwriting or to participate in what some literacy police might deem the pitting of literacy against orality and orality against literacy (and white culture against black culture), as if the value of one assumes the illegitimacy or eradication of the other. Rather, the immediate problem revealed in this exercise is that the few texts that dare to broach this recognizably socially and personally sensitive issue of parental illiteracy at all position parental illiteracy as a shameful secret, always to be hidden from the world of the parents' children. Only two children's books, Dolores Johnson's *Papa's Stories*, now out of print, and Vashanti Rahaman's *Read for Me, Mama*, deal specifically with African Americans and parental illiteracy. In these books, the parent/adult-as-teacher role is reversed, and parents are led to literacy by the efforts of and responsibilities to a child. These books idealize literacy and idolize those who can read; literacy also, according to these accounts, allegedly signifies personal and social value and measures adult self-esteem and self-worth. With minimal complexity and minimal compassion for individual circumstances, even for (or especially for) children's texts, these treatments of illiteracy create and sustain artificial, culturally biased binaries that further marginalize those unable to read and write.

Children's texts that celebrate the advantages and luxuries of reading and writing are not problematic in and of themselves. Problems arise, however, when such texts presume that parental illiteracy is simple personal choice and not a series of complicated circumstances almost always beyond individuals' control.[4] In children's texts that deal with the subject of nonreading and writing parents but where the nonreading and writing parents are not in fact the subjects, the circumstances of illiteracy—whether environmental, social, emotional, psychological, visual, or even neurological as in dyslexia ("a disorder that makes learning to read extremely difficult")[5]—are neither addressed nor vaguely alluded to. Instead, literacy is celebrated in these African American children's texts at the expense of parental embarrassment, shame, and even morality.

Literacy is championed with near-religious fervor in Vashanti Rahaman's *Read for Me, Mama* (1997), in which a young seven- or eight-year-old African American boy is the instrument of his mother's "salvation" from illiteracy. Rahaman's story perpetuates class and race stereotypes, equating illiteracy with dirtiness, personal shame, even sin, and literacy with moral cleanliness and spiritual enlightenment. The story polarizes Joseph's ideal school/library experiences and the drudgery and the mundane of his seemingly less-than-desirable home environment. The school librarian—older, wiser, and proportional in weight—is almost God-like because of her professional authority and Joseph's adulation of her; she inspires Joseph with her engaging story reading. In fact, Joseph wants to emulate Mrs. Ricardo as a story reader. While Joseph's mother's storytelling is as exciting as the librarian's story reading, Rahaman's text affords the librarian and literacy an idealized position of power and authority not realized in Joseph's home life.

Race and class stereotyping occurs as well in other textual details. Arguably, Rahaman makes illiteracy the source of these stereotypes. The overweight, late twenty-something African American woman, also a single parent—the text affords no clues to how this circumstance came to be—is trapped financially in two janitorial jobs. She has no independent means of transportation (she rides a bus or walks wherever she goes) and lives in an apartment next to empty lots of garbage and in a neighborhood with broken sidewalks. While these images alone are not distinct class markers, contextually they render this less-than-ideal family unit as limited and existing in less-than-ideal circumstances. Again, images of dirtiness and cleanliness are synonymous with illiteracy and literacy, respectively. The illiterate Mama cleans hotel rooms, dirty dishes, the dirty apartment, and presumably white Mrs. Holder's apartment. These clean/dirty images appear in the illustrations as well. The literate librarian is either a light-skinned ethnic minority or a white person. The illiterate mother is dark-complected.[6] The university student who reads to Joseph at the laundromat is also non–African American. Because of the mother's illiteracy, the text suggests, her participation in society is limited to working two jobs, doing laundry, shopping for groceries, and attending church activities. The implication is that the mother wants more or should want more or deserves more from life than these social rituals afford when, in reality, some individuals, whether literate or not, may be quite satisfied in these circumstances.[7]

While leaving Joseph's mother unnamed in the text affords some degree of character universality in treating this issue of illiteracy, it also suggests that an illiterate parent may not warrant the authority of an identity, a name, not even the ability or opportunity to name herself. Recall that Frederick Douglass's consummate mark of selfhood and manhood comes in his ability to name himself, to "subscribe [him]self Frederick Douglass," suggesting the power and authority of one who can name or possess a nongeneric name. Surely, there is more to this individual's identity than her unnamed motherhood identity, an identity that is neither personalized nor individualized; she could be anyone's anonymous Mama. In contrast, the other literate characters, even the son Joseph, are privileged with a named identity: Mrs. Ricardo (librarian), Mr. Beharry (university student), and old Mrs. Holder. Although Joseph narrates the story and offers no occasion to address or refer to his mother in a more formal way, (il)literacy and (un)named identities are linked when Mama encounters a number of other characters at the laundromat and church, and she is the only character who remains unnamed.

That Joseph's mother finds literacy through her church might easily have been connected in Rahaman's text with the role black churches played historically in educating African Americans during and after slavery. As Leo McGee and Harvey G. Neufeldt note in *Education of the Black Adult in the United States: An Annotated Bibliography* (1985, 92), "[T]he black churches, most noteably [sic] the African Methodist Church, took the lead in providing educational opportunities for blacks of all ages." Yet, this historical note is not revealed in the story but rather it suggests the notion that literacy is a "gift" from God. Just as a mysterious perhaps even a divine presence puts a peace-in-the-midst-of-a-storm symbolic "pot of geraniums ... in the deep hole in the sidewalk" in Joseph's neighborhood, the preacher and the congregation at Mama's church pray fervently to God for her to become literate, and God answers their collective prayers with evening adult reading courses and tutorials for Mama. The timing of the mysterious appearance of the flowers and the almost simultaneous literacy tutorials Mama then receives from the church beg such a symbolic connection of literacy as a divine gift, particularly for this family who the author paints as entrapped by the web of illiteracy. One of the last images in the book shows Joseph and his Mama reading together as though their mouths are reading in unison. This image of open mouths even suggests singing as at Mama's choir practice or church revival service. Indeed, the illustration and the final words—"Slowly and carefully, Mama's voice stepped from word to word, page after page. Mama was reading!"—resound with the religiosity of singing, shouting, and celebration. With Mama's newfound literacy, she is presumably no longer desperate and blinded by personal shame, deception, and inadequacy. She rather cryptically explains her illiteracy before her "conversion": "I have to learn to read. ... My boy *needs* a mama who can read. But I never practiced up my reading, never learnt it good in school, and it all got lost from my mind, all got lost" (emphasis added). Notice that the mother equates literacy with good parenting. Importantly, the book's title, *Read* for Me, *Mama* (emphasis added), rather than *Read* to Me, *Mama* (emphasis added), further suggests that this parent's becoming literate is a response to her son's desperate plea, a plea that goes beyond the son's leisure entertainment: If Mama does not respect herself enough to be literate, then certainly she will become literate for her child. Notice also that Mama's spoken language is mangled and awkward, and presumably once she learns to read, she will be a better parent and will speak correct "standard" English. Indeed, literacy brings light and enlightenment to Mama. In this sense, the final open mouthing might well be the words read or sung of the popular folk hymn "Amazing Grace":

> Amazing grace how sweet the sound
> that saved a wretch like me.
> I once was lost but now I'm found.
> Was blind but now I see.

Rahaman's message associates illiteracy with "wretchedness," being "lost," and being "blind"; literacy, in contrast, is associated with sight and moral purity. While illiteracy may be perceived as a blindness, it is nevertheless one dimension of a person's life experience, not a whole human condition. Hence, although Mama may already know the words to the hymn as she does the hymns she knows well in her church choir, she can now read other unfamiliar verses and other less-familiar hymns.[8] With literacy, the book contends, Mama is a soldier armed to conquer the world. Armed with literacy, the author contends, this mother, and by extension this family, will break from personal and social shackles. Even the book jacket reiterates this religious romanticizing of literacy as "salvation": "Vashanti Rahaman's story of how a mother and son face the challenge of literacy is told with warmth and sensitivity, while [the illustrator's] bold and beautiful oil paintings light the pages with images of hope and love."

Rahaman's message in *Read for Me, Mama* oversimplifies even for a child audience the issue of illiteracy. We see Mama's life of drudgery before she becomes literate and are to believe that her daily busyness as a single parent will either change or cease, and that she will have more time for her son. Indeed, while the mother may not spend time avoiding reading to her son, perhaps too much of the relationship between a mother and her son is connected with her (il)literacy. The message presumes that Mama will not arrive home from work late if her work times are changed because she will be able to read announcements about revised schedules. The story avoids the reality that even literate persons misread or do not always read carefully. And, how likely is it that Mama's workplace would present revised schedules and have no verbal announcement or discussion so that Mama and others might at least hear about the schedule change? The final lesson of the book also suggests that Mama's literacy will change the quality of the relationship between this mother and her child. While reading to a child is an unquestionably important act that can be a bonding experience between a parent and a child, there is no reason to believe that the quality of this family's life overall needs to change significantly.

Although Joseph admits that his mother is a great storyteller— "Mama was the best storyteller in the world. Her voice danced and played with the words. She could make the most ordinary things seem not so ordinary after all"—her storytelling is not really celebrated.[9] The book makes clear that Mama's stories are interesting to Joseph because Mama is an engaging storytelling performer: she uses interesting voices to make stories come alive. But, while Mama is a great storyteller, even better than Mrs. Ricardo and the university student Mr. Beharry, Mama's storytelling—to which Joseph has undoubtedly been exposed long before he goes to school and hears a librarian read to him—ranks second in importance and value to Mrs. Ricardo's, the librarian's, story reading: "Mrs. Ricardo, the librarian, was the best story reader in the world. She could make her voice loud and soft and squeaky and growly. She could sound angry and happy and oh, so very sad. She knew all of the great big words in the books. Joseph wished he could read like that." The librarian, because of her literacy performance, is idolized. Joseph's mother's storytelling performance is as exciting and actually comparable to Mrs. Ricardo's animated performances, yet what distinguishes the librarian from the mother in this context is the librarian's ability to "know great big words." Surely, literacy is more than decoding big words.

Mama's conversion to literacy furthers the primary bias that literacy exempts individuals from limitations and creates false hopes: "Literacy," one source claims, "arouses hopes, not only in society as a whole but also in the individual who is striving for fulfillment, happiness and personal benefit by learning how to read and write. Literacy ... means far more than learning how to read and write. ... The aim is to transmit ... knowledge and promote social participation" ("Quotations about Literacy," 1999, 2). While literacy allegedly "saves" Mama from public and personal shame, *Read for Me, Mama* does little to move what can be the painful realities of illiteracy to a deeper level of understanding. Rather, it maintains and even perpetuates faulty assumptions that illiteracy determines one's self-worth and the quality of one's personal relationships. The text confirms Nancy N. Rue's (1990) assertions that "Illiteracy is considered by our society to be a shameful thing—certainly not something that is volunteered in the course of casual conversation. ... If [adults] tell people they can't read, they're likely to lose jobs, friendships, and even the respect of their kids" (9). That Mama wears a pair of heart-shaped earrings prominently positioned in the illustrations just before her "true confession" to the church congregation and during and after the conversion further presents literacy as a divine gift from God, suggesting again that literacy has a direct impact on the loving relationship between a parent and child.

With the mother's literacy also comes a seemingly newfound church community rallying around the new convert. Was there no community around Mama before this moment? Perhaps Rahaman works too hard to idealize literacy with assumptions that can surely undermine parental authority and individual self-respect. Perhaps she tries too hard to present a "happy-ever-after" ending to a story and circumstance that are more complicated than she realizes or dares to explore. Perhaps the story would achieve greater impact if it explored some possible or probable causes of Mama's illiteracy beyond her cryptic explanation in the church. Perhaps Rahaman's reading audience might be better served by using Mama's illiteracy to discuss the cultural bias and social marginalization of those who do not share the same abilities, talents, opportunities, or even reading levels. The book might have been an occasion to educate both reading parents and children that there are degrees of functioning literate practice, that Joseph's mother's inability to read his library books, her church hymn books, or her work schedule announcements does not mean that she cannot differentiate between cleaning supplies, shop for groceries, read numbers on her paycheck, or pay bills.

Perhaps this children's book might have included some awareness on the author's part of the social, historical, and political history of illiteracy specifically among African Americans since, according to Jonathan Kozol in *Illiterate America* (1985), "[Illiteracy] figures for the younger generation of black adults are increasing. Forty-seven percent of all black seventeen-year-olds are functionally illiterate. That figure is expected to climb to 50 percent by 1990" (2). Although the National Education Association reports that among the total population of adults nonliterate in English—41 percent are English-speaking whites, 22 percent are English-speaking African Americans, 22 percent are Spanish speaking, and 15 percent are non-English-speaking people—"the actual numbers of white non-readers is twice that of the number of African American and Hispanic non-readers, dispelling the myth that illiteracy is not a problem among whites."[10] Despite these actual numbers, prevailing social mythologies and racial prejudice position African Americans, as compared to whites, at the bottom when it comes to demonstrating a mastery of alphabet literacy in school performance and on arguably culturally biased and much valued "standardized" tests. Kozol urges the rightful need to address illiteracy specifically within a particular cultural context of race politics:

> When nearly half of all adult black citizens in the United States are coming out of public schools without the competence to understand the antidote instructions on a chemical container, instructions on a medicine bottle, or the books and journalistic pieces which might render them both potent and judicious in a voting booth, who can pretend that literacy is not political? (92)

While Kozol's comments are fundamentally sound and his call for urgency certainly warranted, perhaps he, too, overestimates the alleged "saving" powers of literacy. Joseph's mother seems not to have endangered her life or Joseph's or suffered any devastating trauma as a result of her inability to read. Nevertheless, the need to historicize illiteracy in any such discussion—forbidden African American literacy during slavery, separate and gravely unequal learning materials and facilities during Jim Crow, and literacy as a means of racial disenfranchisement—is in order.[11] While Rahaman's children's story need not be a history textbook, readers might well benefit from a cursory explanation of the richness of the African American oral tradition represented to some extent in the mother's storytelling, a tradition often less valued by print-literate people. Carl F. Kastle adds the following in his 1991 *Literacy in the United States: Readers and Reading since 1880*:

> For some centuries after the introduction of alphabetic writing, literacy was restricted to a small elite and limited to a few functions.

> ... These early developments took place in the contexts of pervasive oral culture. Oral culture did not atrophy in contact with written culture; rather, the written word modified and extended communication networks. Not only has the great majority of the earth's population been illiterate throughout history, but the great bulk of communication in literate societies is still oral. (6–7)

The artificial and deceptively dated white literate versus oral and African American illiterate dynamic speaks largely to the race and class dynamics more fully understood within the context of social and political history. Kastle (1991) adds:

> On all measures of literacy, at all points during the last century, white Americans have been more literate than black Americans. In 1880, the differences were vast, of course, with American black population emerging from slavery and subject to massive poverty and discrimination. ... A large, durable portion of literacy differences between black and white Americans clearly cannot be explained by measurable economic and family characteristics. In the unexplained portion of the variation lie such elusive but real factors as the effects of prejudice, cultural alienation, discouragement, and differential aspirations, all related to race. (125–126)[12]

In addition, the various ways in which different races, ethnicities, and even genders experience the world have an impact on their learning to read and write. For instance, African Americans, historically and politically denied access to writing and reading, emerge from a folk culture that luxuriates in and defines itself through aural, oral, and visual nonprint expressions often not legitimized to the extent that alphabetical literacy is esteemed and the written word revered. Authors such as Zora Neale Hurston raise the oral rituals of unlettered folk culture to high art. "The white man," according to Hurston, "thinks in a written language and the Negro thinks in hieroglyphics" (1978, 50). Though somewhat flippant, Hurston's comment reiterates the (il)literate binary, choosing to champion—perhaps even romanticize—the lives and rhythmic textures and nuances of southern vernacular language. Her own Bernard training prepared her in the craft of recording and documenting the idioms that allegedly nourished her and legitimized a vernacular tradition of the "speakerly text" fundamental to African American literary and cultural traditions. To offer some commentary that presents parental illiteracy often as the result of varied and complex circumstances is to enlighten readers, young and old alike, rather than perpetuate further ignorance and misunderstanding among the alleged literate.

Dolores Johnson's book on African American parental illiteracy, *Papa's Stories* (1994), comes with mixed and confused messages, again associating illiteracy with parental love for a child and with individual self-love. Even as the book emphasizes folktales, fairy tales, and the rich textures of oral traditions, Johnson's detail of a father's illiteracy seems incidental, not fundamentally connected with the story's inadvertent final message: good storytelling is good storytelling whether the story is read, recited, or improvised.

Perhaps without intention, Johnson has written a book that celebrates folklore and performance. Not only does the narrative engage fairy-tale rhetoric and a young kindergartner, Kari—her father's growing "Princess"—stumbling on her thirty-something-year-old father and mother's secret of his illiteracy, but the story also romanticizes literacy as a middle-class ideal. While Kari's dad does not "read" words in his daily "reading" rituals with Kari, he reads the pictures and creates wonderfully exciting stories from those pictures. In the illiterate father's hands, the culturally familiar stories of Little Red Riding Hood, Snow White, Sleeping Beauty, and Jack and the Beanstalk take on new life for Kari.[13] And since Kari herself is not quite a reader, there is no immediate confusion for her about what she sees on the printed page and what she hears her father reading to her. The father–daughter reading ritual seems complete until the fairy tale's wicked stepmother or witch figure—Kari's older neighborhood friend, Jennifer—disillusions Kari about her whole relationship with her father. Ironically, it seems that Jennifer's literacy threatens the ideal world Kari and her Papa have created:

> Papa settled into his favorite chair, his skin smelling as fresh as fir trees. Kari climbed into his lap and snuggled into the crook of his arm. Then Papa read her a story. … There were times Kari and Papa got so wrapped up in their reading that Mama let supper sit while she joined Kari and Papa on the porch in the moonlight. Or, during winter's chilliest evenings, the whole family would snuggle close together on the sofa and read by the light of the fire. (D. Johnson, 1994)

Although Jennifer's alleged literal reading of the Little Red Riding Hood story affords Kari an opportunity to discuss her dad's illiteracy with him, the story does not clarify why Kari should believe her friend's version over her dad's. The story does nothing to advance an understanding of the issue of illiteracy. That illiteracy seems secondary stems also from the fact that the illiterate father is not presented with any problems particular to his disability: he and his literate wife own a nice house in a pleasant middle-class rural environment, and he presumably has an adequate blue-collar job.

Johnson is not quite sure what her book is about; its focus seems too fuzzy to know what Kari's or Johnson's reading audience is to glean from the details of her father's cryptic explanation of why he is unable to read: "When I was young, I didn't care enough about learnin'. And there was no one who seemed to care about me. When I got older, I didn't love myself enough to even try." Might Johnson have allowed the family to have an honest discussion of less-vague reasons for the father's illiteracy? How young is "young" when this father did not care about learning? Did extenuating family circumstances have an impact on this father's early education? How is learning to read and write fundamentally connected to this father's lack of self-love, and how has this lack of self-love manifested itself in his life as an adult? Did this father drop out of school when he was young? Is it possible for an illiterate individual, a parent even, to have healthy self-esteem? Were the circumstances of this father's illiteracy forced on or "chosen" by him? What specific lessons might Kari learn from her father's reading inability?

Indeed, as Papa reads to Kari, Johnson does not initially make clear that the father is not choosing to improvise. That Kari prefers her dad's improvised, more creative versions of stories accentuates the performative nature of good storytelling, which in this case is not handicapped by the father's illiteracy. When this father learns to read a little from his wife and is able to read the words on the pages of Kari's books, not just the pictures, Kari prefers what might easily be considered sillier revisionist versions where "little boys swallowed magic till they were full of beans, and giants ... were angry because their mustaches didn't fit." At the book's end, Kari makes this request of her father: "Excuse me, Papa. When you finish this book, read it to me again like you always did. I love the extra-special way you read the stories."

It seems odd that Johnson foregrounds her text allegedly about illiteracy in fairy-tale folklore since fairy tales are part of cultural literacy, and even those who may not be able to read them have surely heard of them and know their narrative germs. As folklore, these fairy tales have surely circulated in the father's own childhood whether or not he is the product of a literate family. Just as Kari and anyone else starts the journey toward literacy by inventing stories from pictures, Kari's father has every right to be respected for and confident in his storytelling abilities despite his illiteracy. Are story readers necessarily the best storytellers?

BEYOND THE LITERACY BINARY

Although alphabet literacy and orality need not exist in cultural opposition, many readers and writers take for granted the privilege and authority given those who can do the same. For them, daily tasks such as reading traffic signs, a newspaper or magazine in a doctor's office waiting room, a restaurant menu, telephone books, a child's school progress report, checks, recipes, maps, and medicine bottles are believed fundamental to our social and personal survival. I was starkly reminded of my own middle-class assumptions when I recently assigned to my African American children's literature class an intergenerational oral history midterm project specifically about African American identity and childhood reading experiences. Students were asked to interview two individuals—one at least ten years older than they and another between the ages of five and ten—about their reading experiences as African American children. I had expected to get stories from individuals that allowed students to see how images of African Americans had or had not changed over generations and how early reading experiences had an impact on adult identity formations. While I had assumed that all parents are reading to their children before they are put to bed, the reality of nonreading children and nonreading parents became an issue I had inadvertently overlooked in all of my fairly extensive preparations for teaching the class. When one student submitted his project, his younger interviewee was the only instance of twenty who could not read. The young boy, now age ten and in a juvenile jail until age eighteen for various crimes, was never read to and never learned to read; he still acknowledges no value in learning to read as he is the product of a nonreading adult environment. Another student submitted a project that revealed an eleven-year-old boy's extreme written and verbal giftedness despite having grown up with totally illiterate grandparents. And, just as it is necessary to understand the circumstances of young Johnny's inability to read, it was equally important to understand the circumstances of Johnny's parents' illiteracy since illiterate children become illiterate adults and illiterate parents.

PERFORMING (IL)LITERACY: REDEFINING THE BLACK PARENTAL BODY IN THE CULTURE OF SCHOOLING
BY OLGA IDRISS DAVIS

Schooling represents both a struggle for meaning and a struggle over power relations.

—P. McLaren, "Decentering Culture" (1991)

This commentary problematizes the black (il)literate parental body as a site of contestation through which African American children's books can provide a critical space to interrogate pedagogical constructions of power. The commentary raises three questions to consider: What is the role of African American children's books in creating black parental identity? How does the black parental body craft a space of resistance in transforming the discourse of (il)literacy? How does a healthier vision of literacy inform a culture of schooling that celebrates multiple literacies as a performance of pedagogical possibilities? This chapter, "'Life for Me Ain't Been No Crystal Stair': Readin', Writin', and Parental (Il)Literacy in African American Children's Books," inspires this commentary to envision a literacy that celebrates the black illiterate parental body in its wholeness in learning *and teaching* to "read the world" (Freire and Macedo, 1987). A glimpse at the discursive crafting of parental illiteracy generates discourse that deepens our understanding of the dynamics and complexities of domination. First, a discussion of the role of African American children's books centers black parental identity by creating safe spaces of resistance to pedagogical and hegemonic oppression. Next, transforming controlling images reinvents identity and redefines marginal locations of illiteracy. Finally, the commentary offers for consideration and further commentary a vision of literacy through a critical performance-centered paradigm.

African American Children's Books and Black Parental Identity

The legacy of African American children's literature, traced back to the late 1800s, stimulated liberating change with *The Brownies' Books* (January 1920 through December 1921), articulating the mission to "make Black children familiar with the history and achievements of the Negro race" and "realize that being 'colored' is a normal beautiful thing" (DuBois, 1919, 286). While this mission was among the central tenets of the field, many debates evoked discussion ranging from language usage, to authenticity, to visual literacy, to the pedagogy/literature dynamics (D. Johnson and Lewis, 1998, 7).

In addition to its historical purpose, African American children's literature provided a vehicle for the critical study of ideology, of discursive systems of domination, and of transformative and liberating qualities of African American literature. Its critical quality is what intrigues me most, particularly because African American children's literature creates a *safe space* from which to resist and transform the culture of schooling as a system that perpetuates theories, ideologies, and discourses of pedagogical oppression. The notion of safe spaces resonates with a womanist theoretical perspective that views the world (in this case, the world of parental illiteracy) as a dynamic place where the goal is not merely to survive or to fit in or to cope, but rather to feel owner-ship and accountability (P. Collins, 1991, 237).

I employ womanism as a theoretical perspective in discussing black parental identity and illiteracy for its recognition of African American culture as a culture of resistance—a culture that shapes the private space of home and redefines the public sphere of African American parental illiteracy. In this space, parental illiteracy brings intellectual notions of lived experience and struggles of the nonliterate parent, giving expression to their social, political, and cultural contributions. Revealing the cul-ture and history of nonliterate parents creates safe spaces of survival and wholeness of entire people, both male and female (Douglas and Sanders, 1995, 10; Walker, 1983, xi; P. Collins, 1991, 38). That is, by creating safe spaces, parental illiteracy is seen as a process of self-conscious struggle that empowers women and men to actualize a humanist vision—an experience that celebrates the shared meaning of human community. Therefore, children's literature creates the space to explore black paren-tal identity and authority from the arena of oral tradition and creativity. African American children's books, as safe spaces, explore the notion that there are degrees of literate practice (Lester, 2003b, 14) and craft black parental identity of nonreading parents as humanistic participants in the social construction of culture who maintain a moral discourse, provide a grand respect for life, and affirm their humanity by transcending peda-gogical race politics through the richness of orality.

Reading the Black Parental Body: (Il)Literacy Transformed

Central to the ways in which the black parental body crafts a space of resistance in transforming oppressive discourse is to transform control-ling images of parental illiteracy. As McLaren (1991) notes, "schooling represents both a struggle for meaning and a struggle over power rela-tions" (238). The dominant mythic images of illiteracy include "dirti-ness, personal shame, even sin, and literacy with moral cleanliness and spiritual enlightenment" (Lester, 2003a, 30). African American children's books that reinscribe notions of inferiority and internalize hegemonic structures present images of the black illiterate parental body in specific ways to include "wretchedness," being "lost," being "blind," somehow not a whole person (31). Extending the mythology, such images do not allow a discursive construction of the black parental illiterate body to encompass the whole human condition as a result of the inability to read or write. By asserting and affirming these negative images in African American children's books, the dominant culture of schooling attempts to maintain black parental subordination. These images underscore the Foucauldian notion of discursive structures disciplining, monitoring, and surveilling the black body in the public and private spheres of experience (Foucault, 1977, 25). The absurdity of such images calls for transformation, a space of resistance that redefines the humanity of nonliterate parents and transcends oppressive locations beyond inferiority. From contested roles of urban economic decay to survival in a culture of dominance, African American nonliterate parents redefine controlling images by locating spaces for their creative and intellectual selves to flourish and where their identity and parental authority resonate beyond the marginal and contradictory location of alphabetic literacy—a location of pedagogical and political subordination.

A Healthier Vision of Literacy: Performance-Centered Critical Pedagogy

I contend that a healthier vision of literacy begins with a performance-centered critical pedagogy aimed at transforming society through emancipatory education. Performance is deeply concerned with issues of power and authority. Everyday performances are political and historically situated, thereby presenting a view of ongoing ideological enactments. Performances of (il)literacy are also public events; they are "a site of struggle where competing interests intersect, and different viewpoints and voices get articulated" (Conquergood, 1986, 84). A performance-centered critical pedagogy asks the following:

> How does performance reproduce, legitimate, uphold or challenge, critique or subvert ideology? ... How are performances situated between forces of accommodation and resistance? How do they simultaneously reproduce and struggle against hegemony? What are the performative resources for interrupting master scripts? (84)

The possibilities of disrupting the master scripts of alphabet literacy, the culture of schooling, and pedagogical structures of dominance point to the performance paradigm that by nature is multivocal and counterhegemonic. It counters dominant voices with those that speak from the margins. A performance paradigm claims the body as the locus of subjectivity, rejecting the mind–body Cartesian dualism and rational empiricism that dominate institutional practices in Western pedagogy (Pineau, 2005). By recognizing performance as a public, social phenomenon, African American children's books can interrogate the performance of (il)literacy as political struggle and resistance. In so doing, young readers are learning to engage the world through sociopolitical and cultural circumstances. They learn the politics of the body and explore hegemonic constructions of meaning:

> Ideological hegemony is not realized solely through the discursive meditations of the sociocultural order but through the enfleshment of unequal relationships of power. Hegemony is manifest inter-corporeally, through the actualization of the flesh and embedded in incarnate experience. (McLaren, 1988, 169)

By learning to read the world of the black (il)literate parental body through African American children's books, young readers and nonliterate parents alike create safe spaces of resistance, transform controlling images, and reenvision literacy by celebrating the human community—the body politic, which provides a space for renewal, recovery, healing, and affirmation of our whole being.

TALKING OUT LOUD: IDEAS FOR DISCUSSION

1. Which knowledges are privileged in African American children's literature? How are certain knowledges privileged in African American children's literature? In other words, what are the guiding epistemologies and ontologies in African American children's literature?
2. During the DuBois era of the development of *The Brownies' Books*, the first recorded published African American children's periodical, the mission of African American children's books/literature was to provide a history of the race and to promote self-esteem. Over two centuries later, what now in the twenty-first century is the mission, the role, the purpose of African American children's literature?
3. Scholar Patricia Hill Collins (1991) points to several guiding principles of black feminist thought. One tenet of this theoretical perspective is the interdependence of thought and action. What is the relationship between thought and action relative to literacy, orality, and oral tradition?
4. In what ways is the notion of "naming" a recurring theme in African American children's literature? What is the significance of the act of naming in black communities as well as in children's literature? What is the rhetorical value of naming?
5. Theoretical and methodological principles guide our research and scholarly ruminations. From a conceptual framework, how can the

study of parental (il)literacy craft a new paradigm for understanding the culture of literacy in African American communities?

6. Regarding the black parental illiterate body, what are the social, political, and cultural constructions that marginalize it? What are specific aspects of the social construction and of the performance of the black body that illuminate the study of black parental illiteracy?

7. Barbara Christian, in her germinal article "A Race for Theory," argues that African Americans have always theorized but in different ways than do their white counterparts. How do black parents theorize? In what ways does a culture of orality, oral tradition, and literate/nonliterate inform ways of knowing and of making meaning in the social world of black parents?

8. What contributions to the study of black parental illiteracy can a performance-centered critical pedagogy offer? How are parents transformed? How are young readers transformed through performance and critical pedagogy?

9. To what extent do children's texts define and celebrate multiple literacies?

10. To what extent does our Western culture devalue certain literate practices?

3

"STICKS AND STONES MAY BREAK MY BONES"

Airbrushing the Ugliest of Ugly in African American Children's Books[1]

It is in the early days of rollicking boyhood that the revelation first bursts upon one, all in a day, as it were. I remember well when the shadow swept across me. ... In a wee wooden school-house, something put it into the boys' and girls' heads to buy gorgeous visiting-cards—ten cents a package—and exchange. The exchange was merry, till one girl, a tall newcomer, refused my card—refused it peremptorily, with a glance. Then it dawned upon me with a certain suddenness that I was different from the others; or like, mayhap, in heart and life and longing, but shut out from their world by a vast veil.

—W. E. B. DuBois, *The Souls of Black Folk* (1903)

Misery is when your very best friend [white] calls you a name she really didn't mean to call you at all.

Misery is when somebody [white] meaning no harm called your little black dog "Nigger" and he just wagged his tail and wiggled.

—Langston Hughes, *Black Misery* (1969)

I realized instantly that I had wandered embarrassingly into the wrong bathroom, the "children's bathroom," it was later clarified, when I noticed above the toilet of the elegantly decorated room an elaborately

framed black and white print of about thirteen half-naked preadolescent black boys feverishly climbing a broken wooden fence, implicitly
trespassing to take a swim in a lake or pond. The bold caption below the
picture read: "Last one in's a nigger." I forgot nature's call and immediately reflected on the conversation I was just having with my upper
middle-class, professional white male host, whose previous home my
wife and I were purchasing, about getting our children together for
future play dates. At the time, we had our two-year-old daughter with
us, and he and his wife had two youngsters and a newborn. The three
older children were playing voraciously in a nearby corner. When I
returned from the bathroom as flush as a medium brown-skinned person can be flush, I felt betrayed and angry at my own surprise, embarrassment, and naïveté. I said nothing in the presence of my hosts and
only mentioned the discovery to my wife on the way back to see our
new home. That happened in Birmingham, Alabama, in 1991.

Just over two years ago, as I sat quietly one morning on my backyard balcony reading a text for the day's class, I was interrupted by a
group of neighborhood white boys, probably between the ages of ten
and twelve—en route to school and unaware of my presence—casually
commenting about "some nigger doing something." I was as stunned as
I was during my house-buying, bathroom experience some years ago. I
did not naïvely think that overt black–white racism did not also exist in
Phoenix, Arizona, as in Birmingham. Nevertheless, in both instances,
I had innocently eavesdropped on and witnessed firsthand the publicly
private spaces of white racism. Had I not gone to the "wrong bathroom,"
the one on the left downstairs rather than the one on the left upstairs,
or been sitting unassumingly on my balcony, I would have never
grasped the extent to which my previous and present predominantly
white "professional" neighborhoods could at any moment transform
themselves from safe, familiar environments into a minefield wherein
my then nine-year-old son and twelve-year-old daughter might easily
become the emotional casualties of my "neighbors'" casual and careless
racism.

To (mis)advise a child responding to peers' verbal mockery and
name-calling that "sticks and stones may break my bones, but words will
never hurt me" is not to realize the gravity of one's own parental naïveté.
Words attack and wound. As parents of any child visibly marked with
the sociohistorical "almighty one drop of black blood," a peculiar and
particular circumstance can leave us powerless to protect our little ones
from verbal attacks by young white racists-in-training who learn early
on, directly or indirectly, that "nigger"—the most "racially potent word
in the American language" (Ross, as cited in Rollins, 1967, xvi)—can

instantly degrade, offend, wound, even emotionally and psychologically maim a black child.

As an African American father of two youngsters, I recognize the ever-present difficulties of creating and sustaining a strong sense of self-worth and self-pride in a dangerously aggressive racist society. As well, I acknowledge that while many of the overt and physically violent manifestations of American racism of the recent past have mostly vanished, use of the word *nigger* by whites in their attacks on blacks is one of the few remaining overt signs of the persistence of racism in our society. In such an aggressively racist culture that can launch attack missiles without warning and in the most unexpected circumstances, mine are not feelings of paranoia but rather the feelings of any caring parent whose children of color exist in a society that continues to challenge or threaten his and his children's legitimacy racially and culturally. Living not necessarily by choice as much as by circumstance in a predominantly white society, in the predominantly white state of Arizona, in a predominantly white upper middle-class professional neighborhood, with my children attending predominantly white public schools, I anxiously await their return from school or play each day, dreading their first personal encounter with the word *nigger*, a word that immediately snatches away innocence and thrusts African American children into the adult world of America's lingering racial divide. If they were somehow able to get through their childhood years without personal racist humiliation, then I wonder if and when they will encounter the potential white boyfriend or girlfriend who tells them that their parents will not allow them to be friends with, let alone date, a nigger. Of course, my assumption here is that they have not already had this experience and were not too embarrassed or uncomfortable to talk with my wife or me about it.

How does one protect his or her child from the possibilities of such a racist attack? We teach our children physical self-defense strategies like taekwondo and karate. We bundle them up with scarves, sweaters, and gloves to protect them from bitter cold in parts of the country. In the Sonoran desert, we even slather brown-skinned children with gallons of sunscreen to protect them from the merciless summer sun. How do we help protect them from or teach them how to deal with the eventuality of being called a nigger? Does talking about the word *nigger* demystify it or render it more powerful to offend? While I am not ignoring the politics of political correctness or the reality of commercial market force both from the publisher's and consumer's perspectives, it is imperative that there be frank and open treatments of the word *nigger* in literature to which children and parents can turn in coping with attacks via the word black prosecutor from the infamous O. J. Simpson trial, Christopher Darden, called "the filthiest, dirtiest, nastiest word in the English language" (Margolick, 1995, Y13). As well, we acknowledge that *nigger* is a "white-created word expressly designed to show maximum contempt for black people [and that] no definition of the word—no synonym, no lexicographer's phrase—can come anywhere close to the insult of the word itself." (Raspberry, 1995) Kenneth B. Noble, in his commentary, "The Simpson Defense: One Hateful Word," summarizes:

> "Nigger" is an almost universally known word of contempt. … It is as if all the country's tangled legacy of racial animosity, brutality and fear has been bottled up in two ugly syllables. The despair and anger simmers without them, but when those two syllables find their way into the open air, the explosive power of old emotions is unleashed, and that power can sweep rationality, wisdom and even common humanity out of its path.
>
> It is part of the treacherous rhetoric of race in America. … The word "nigger" occupies a place in the soul where logic and reason never go. (Noble, 1995, 1, 4)

Certainly, erasing the word *nigger* from dictionaries or airbrushing it with more "universal," non-racially specific meanings like "lazy" or "ignorant" does not remove its social and historical association with blacks no matter the gender, age, education, skin tone gradation, or socioeconomic background. The National Association for the Advancement of Colored People (NAACP)'s objection to Merriam-Webster's first definition of nigger as "a black person" and only secondarily as "*perhaps* the most offensive and inflammatory racial slur in English" is in order (emphasis added). However, removing the word from print does not erase its public use or its presence in the American public and private consciousness. Sandra Evers-Mahley, president of the Beverly Hills/Hollywood NAACP, comments on efforts to censor experience by erasing the word *nigger* in print:

> We can't get rid of *nigger* anymore than we can get rid of racism. But we need to deal with it head-on. When I am called a nigger, I use reverse psychology or I get into heated debates. … We need to have people tell their stories. By erasing a word, you don't erase a history. If *nigger* could be banned, it still wouldn't get rid of the attitudes that it symbolizes. We need to create an environment for dialogue about the word's purposes and problems. (Hamilton, 1994, 56)

How do individuals and society unlearn racist behavior and racist attitudes that inform racist language? In defense of not deleting the word from dictionaries, Frederick Mish, editor-in-chief of Merriam-Webster, reasons: "We do not believe we can make offensive words go out of existence by leaving them out of the dictionary. People do not learn these words from the dictionary, nor would they refrain from using them if we left them out." (Epstein, 1995, A15) While Mish is correct that pretending that the word does not exist does not make it go away, he fails to acknowledge or admit the social and psychological problematic in a dictionary definition that makes *nigger* synonymous with "a black person." This kind of lexiconic debate further highlights what African American author Gloria Naylor asserts about written and spoken language: "Words themselves are innocuous; it is the consensus that gives them true power" (1994, 380).

LIFE IMITATING FICTION?

When I happened upon the 1994 HBO Family Playhouse video *Whitewash* (Sporn, 1994) a few years ago, I was pleasantly surprised to see that Ntozake Shange had written such a powerful piece for children about black–white racism. I was already aware of Shange's writings about her childhood in her semiautobiographical novel *Betsey Brown* (1985). Through her thirteen-year-old female narrator, Shange highlights a child's first experience with overt racism:

> Susan Linda's mother didn't like the colored, so the three girls had to be gone before she got home from [working] … at the twenty-four-hour breakfast place, … "For Whites Only."
> … Susan Linda put a dab of perfume on everybody and asked them to leave quickly cause her mother'd be walkin in the door any moment and weren't no "niggahs" 'sposed to be in the house.
> Betsey knew there was something wrong with that. She and Charlotte Ann always let Susan Linda come over to their houses. Veejay scoffed at them. "Y'all so dumb. Don't you know bout prejudice? It's when white folks don't like Negroes. Didn't you hear that gal call us niggahs. Now, that there is a bad word. My mama tol' me don' 'ssociate wit nobody callin me no niggah, not even colored what does it." (40–41)

Although Susan Linda is not attacking her young black friends, Veejay understands the power of the word "niggah" to separate and to belittle. Although they may not fully comprehend the gravity of the word in adult black and white race relations, both the black girl and the white girl know that "niggah" is a "bad word." Whereas Susan Linda echoes her mother's derogatory use of the word, Veejay's mother's lesson to her young black daughter about this word is one of warning and offense. This same parental concern about a child's encounter with the power of "niggah" recurs in the novel when Betsey's politically conservative mother, Jane, expresses angst about her daughter's "integration" into a new white school:

> But now, with the buses and the new schools, God only knew what miseries her children would have to endure with all those peckerwoods out there. Jane was disheartened. She felt a collapsing of her spirit akin to despair. She had no idea where half these places the children were going to go to school were, much less how to get them there. Would there be the ugly crowds of thin-lipped rednecks throwing tomatoes and bottles at her children? Would she have to go up to the school every day on account of some poor racist child who didn't know niggah is not the same as Negro? (Shange, 1985, 90)

Jane's anxiety is that of any black parent, particularly in a racist society where a black child's world can be disrupted by a white person's casual or aggressive use of a single word. I continue to search for a single racist word for whites that transcends gender, class, age, religious affiliation, educational background, and sexual orientation; a single word that registers the same emotional and psychological intensity as "nigger" for a people whose legitimacy has been historically denied by those who wield power politically, socially, and economically. Surely, "redneck," "honky," "whitey," "ofay," "peckerwood," and "cracker" do not come close.

In the 1979 interview "A Colored Girl: Ntozake Shange" with New York Shakespeare Festival producer Joseph Papp, Shange details her earliest brush with the word *nigger* when entering a new elementary school in upstate New York:

> Any black child who was raised between 1948 and the present had a peculiar childhood because two different kinds of eras were going on. Up until I was eight years old or so, there were certain places black people could not go and then all of a sudden—in the middle of my life—you were supposed to go to these places. [White] people would ask me things like "You're not a nigger, are you? You're Greek, aren't you?"

As a result of these early awakenings to America's adult racial dilemmas, Shange, as a child, understood that walking outside her intensely race-conscious family environment did not and could not shield her from the confusion and hurt of external racist attacks. In this same interview, Shange's mother recalls the young Shange's confusion soon after entering the new white school: "One day, shortly after being introduced to the classroom, she came home and asked, 'Mommy, am I colored?' She held out her hands and asked, 'Mommy, am I colored?' I knew immediately what had happened." Even Shange's mother, at least in this interview, avoids naming what she instinctively as a black parent "knows" and "feels" happened to her little girl.[2] From these childhood experiences with racial bigotry from other children, Shange insists that she is very comfortable teaching and writing about "stuff [her black and white students] don't know about or are not willing to admit. I'm able to write with some clarity about things that we [blacks and whites] don't discuss because we are allegedly so integrated." Shange's video names the unnamed and says the unsaid for a children's audience.

Hence, with my fairly extensive knowledge of Shange's work, I was not surprised that Shange had written the screenplay *Whitewash* (1994), a children's cartoon about racism—past and present—in its most blatant forms: physical and verbal assault. As anyone who has read her work knows and expects, she does not censor lived experience or mince words when the deliberate rawness of her language and imagery intends to "make you swoon, stop in yr tracks, change yr mind, or make it up"; the characteristic nitty-grittiness of her language and imagery means to "happen to you like cold water or a kiss" (Shange, 1977, 72). So as I watched the video, I once again applauded Shange's daringness to show African American youngsters baptized in what Toni Morrison insightfully deems "the nastiness of life" that is American racism (1987, 23).

Based on the true story of the January 1992 hate crime against a twelve-year-old sister and her fourteen-year-old brother in the Williamsbridge section of the Bronx, *Whitewash* details a vicious attack on a fourth-grade African American girl and her preadolescent brother by a gang of white teens en route from home to school. While the supercool and comical brother is robbed and badly beaten and subsequently embarrassed that he was unable to defend himself and protect his younger sister, the story ultimately focuses on the "trauma" of the young girl—having her face spray-painted white and being called "nigger" several times by the aggressive thugs. Helene-Angel, long after the assault, refuses to leave her room and to return to school until coaxed by her supportive, courageous multiracial classmates. Although Mauricio's physical pains go away and the white paint is washed from Helene-Angel's face, the video highlights this moment as a grave life lesson for the young girl and her schoolmates. Her brother's embarrassment deliberately pales in light of Shange's characteristic focus on this female character.

Although the *New York Times* account, "Sadness and Shame in the Bronx" (10 January 1992), describes the Bronx incident as "a particularly cruel and unforgivable racial attack" and recognizes the gravity of the attack on children—"young victims of prejudice can be left with permanent scars"—Lynda Richardson, in her *New York Times* (28 January 1992) coverage of subsequent "acts of violence" in New York City, dismisses unnamed "racial slurs" as less hurtful than physical attacks. Poet Nikki Giovanni, in her 1996 introduction to a recent edition of Eve Merriam's 1969 book *The Inner City Mother Goose*, takes issue with such a naïve claim, insisting: "Sticks and stones are easily forgotten; it is the words that stay with us. The hurtful words make us less than human; the words used to describe Black Americans. ... Words will always be stronger than swords because swords can only harm our bodies. Words can harm our souls" (3). Indeed, while the white paint can be cleaned from Helene-Angel's face, it becomes more challenging to heal her emotional and psychological wounds.[3]

Despite educators' accolades heaped on this twenty-minute "Teaching Tolerance" video intended for grades four through eight—it received the 1995 Carnegie Medal and the Silver Apple Award—in reviews of *Whitewash*, the only specific detail given of Helene-Angel's trauma generally involves having "her face spray-painted by a racist gang." Purposely vague and suggestive, the word *racist* in this comment means to capture the full impact of being called something too nasty or vile to print in *School Library Journal*'s "Notable Films/Videos, Recordings and Computer Software, 1995" (April 1995). Fay L. Matsunaga's review of the video for *School Library Journal* (May 1995) is even more elusive, describing it as "a story of violence and racial prejudice based on actual events in the Bronx in 1992" (65). "Violence and racial prejudice" does not draw specific attention to the thugs' repeated use of *nigger* in their violent attack. Phyllis Levy Mandell's brief comment on the video in *School Library Journal* (April 1996, 62) and *Peace Review*'s listing of "Recommended Videos" (June 1999, 353) mention the spray painting but only that the attack on Helene-Angel and her brother is by "a racist gang." Joanne Kaufman, noting in *Family Life* (June–July 1998) that the video is appropriate for ages four through nine, again describes the face painting but merely adds that the video is about "a young black girl's run-in with racism" (110). A part of me was surprised at the consistent and deliberate omission of the word *nigger* as a specific part of these youngsters' experience. And, if the word is repeated at least three times in the video during the attack and echoes in Helene-Angel's daydream when she psychologically revisits the event, why is it not mentioned in these reviews? Is it too vile to mention, too vile to print? The only reviewer who comes close to saying the unsayable word is Nancy McCray, whose review in *Booklist* (1 April 1995) mentions the face painting along with the black children being subjected to a "horrific mugging and racist remarks" (1432). "Racist remarks" may or may not include nigger.[4] Although Diana West's review for *The American Spectator* (July 1995) finds the video problematic because it teaches that "white racism lurks around every corner" and brings about an unnecessary "heightened awareness of each other's skin color" (65), her comment actually speaks to the reality too many black parents continually face: the fact that white racism *does indeed* lurk around every corner. In such a comment, West demonstrates her total unawareness of parental dread of his or her child's first encounter with the word *nigger*, a reality that can assault any brown or black child in America at any time, anywhere, and be perpetrated by any white person of any age, gender, or class.

When the picture book version of *Whitewash* appeared a few years after the video, I was curious to see how—not if—the publisher would deal with the racist language that had struck me so powerfully in the video. In the glossy pages of Helene-Angel's experiences with the gang, there is no mention of the gang's assault with *nigger*. In fact, whereas we hear the thugs explicitly calling Helene-Angel and Mauricio "niggers" in the video, the book, from Helene-Angel's perspective, says that the thugs called them "mud people":

> One asked if we spoke English, pushing my brother out of the way. I heard Mauricio shouting to me: "Run! Run, Helene-Angel! Run now!" But how could I? I was scared to death.
>
> I only remember a little of it. Something about doing me a good deed, then about "how to be white" or "American." I don't know. I just know for sure I felt this stinging cold on my face and around my ears and neck.
>
> I was dripping white. Really itchy, stinging white paint covered me wherever my brown skin used to be. I couldn't understand. Why were these boys doing this to me? Why were they laughing as they walked away?

That Helene-Angel in the print version forgets some of this event in a retelling not long after the experience lacks credibility. Indeed, that she recalls being called "mud people" undermines the gravity of the experience when the thugs' specific use of the word *nigger* is a significant part of their assault and of her emotional and psychological response to the attack. Surely, Helene-Angel is not so traumatized by the experience that she cannot remember being called nigger. Indeed, I have no doubt that the book publisher decided for both Shange and Helene-Angel that this specific, age-old racist label could not pass before delicate children's eyes and into their parents' sensitive hands. In short, the publishers played it safe but in doing so missed a perfect opportunity to arm parents of black children with another tool for dealing with a very specific dimension of racial intolerance. Although the *School Library Journal* book reviewer, Marie Wright, notes the importance of the book—"Adults could use this story for a lesson in tolerance, resolving unanswered questions, and preparing young children for some of life's cruel realities"—Wright adds that "the full-length award-winning video is probably the better medium for this story, but the book will be available to a wider audience" (1998, 125–126). Wright makes no mention of the specific racist verbal attack on the black children. That the book is more available to a wider audience than the video perpetuates the myth that protecting our children from racism means censoring or trying to censor the experiences to which they are often exposed.

Differences between the print and video versions go beyond genre or formatting; the video demonstrates the blatant absence of a violent reality from which black children are seldom protected. Would reading the word *nigger* cause or encourage youngsters to use the word? Another reviewer in *Notable Children's Trade Books in the Field of Social Studies, 1998* recognizes the social significance of the story but makes no mention of the racist language that is clearly part of the assault: "Based on a series of true incidents, this is a moving story of a young African American girl who is *traumatized* when a gang attacks her and sprays her face white" (Raspberry, 1998, 6; emphasis added). Is it problematic to include that the gang members are white to clarify the racial specificity of this attack? Indeed, including *nigger* in Shange's book may be an opportunity for a parent to teach children about the power of hurtful words, presuming an adult is either reading the book to or with the child, or is otherwise aware of the child's independent reading and takes full advantage of this "teachable moment."

Although I am not a specialist in language acquisition theory, my sense is that children who dare to use this "real" word and others deemed unprintable—at least in a children's picture book—do not "learn" and then use them from reading books. As well, surely children who assault brown children with the word *nigger* are not picking up this word from a dictionary or any other print text, but are hearing it in their immediate environment from peers, older brothers and sisters, parents, neighbors, and relatives who use this word deliberately and without caution. Why not use children's books as tools to combat violent language just as we use children's books to explain death and dying, divorce, child molestation, sexuality, disease, poverty, gang violence, stealing, disobedience, bullying, physical disabilities, gay parents, intraracism, and parental illiteracy? Does not the deliberate absence of *nigger* in print give it more power to wound and cripple our young? When, after all of our parental nurturing of our young ones toward developing healthy identities racially and otherwise, will we include this particular verbal violence in our lessons about life? Not one of the ten sections of Richard Wright's autobiographical essay about his physical survival specifically as a black male child in the 1930s and 1940s segregated South, "The Ethics of Living Jim Crow" (1938), deals specifically with the label "nigger" he was repeatedly called by white adults and children during his various "learning" experiences. Yet the spiritual, emotional, and psychological impact of such a childhood experience involving the assault of the word *nigger*, especially from another young child, is succinctly present in Countee Cullen's three-stanza poem "Incident," which suggests the loss of innocence and the power of memory. An eight-year-old, happy to be traveling by train to Baltimore, smiles at a peer:

> Once riding in old Baltimore,
> Heart-filled, head-filled with glee,
> I saw a Baltimorean
> Keep looking straight at me.
> Now I was eight and very small.
> And he no whit bigger
> And so I smiled, but he poked out
> His tongue, and called me, "Nigger."
> I saw the whole of Baltimore
> From May until December;
> Of all the things that happened there
> That's all that I remember. (1971, 98–99)

The devastation of this assault on this youngster is unquestionable and immediately overshadows pleasant moments the black child may have experienced prior to and after this unprovoked attack. Indeed, the impact of this moment lasts well into black adulthood and conjures the same emotions in each conscious or unconscious recollection. Using the video of Shange's screenplay and the book in combination specifically to address the word *nigger* as a racist label would benefit both the young children who might use the word without full awareness of its grave implications and the youngsters who might be victimized by this word.[5]

Benjamin F. Chavis recognizes the urgency of candidly dealing with such racially motivated attacks, and he challenges socially responsible adults to acknowledge the reality that "children are exposed to this dangerous virus [of racism] at an early age and as a consequence become either victims o[r] perpetrators." His honest and substantively detailed account of the actual Bronx, New York, incident in *California Voice* is a deliberate effort to awaken readers with a quick, symbolically meaningful poke in the eye:

> A recent racial attack near the Whalen Intermediate School in Bronx, New York is but another shameful example of how racism infects growing numbers of children in the nation. Two African American children attempting to walk to school were attacked by a group of white male children. The African American youths were brother and sister, age 14 and 12, respectively. The attack occurred at 8:00 a.m. in full public view on Boston Road, only a block from the school. The group of white male youths approached the African American youths from the rear screaming, "Niggers, niggers, niggers." They first grabbed the little girl, beat her and then cut her hair with a box-cutting knife. Then the African American male was attacked and punched to the ground. His sister was then thrown down beside him and the group robbed them of their lunch money. The attackers then began to spray white paint in the face and hair of the two beaten children shouting, "You Blacks are turning white today."
>
> Thanks to the efforts of an unidentified passing motorist, the attackers were chased away. *The physical and psychological trauma that this brother and sister have had to endure is cause for moral outrage. ...* There are some who ask, why do we persist in raising these [unpleasant] issues? It is not because we prefer to, but because *we have a responsibility to expose the painful realities of America's race problem in order to encourage more effective strategies to find a cure for this systemic disease. As a society we can ill afford to deny the gravity of the problem of racism. The children and youth of the nation deserve a better chance for a life free from racial discrimination and hatred.* (Chavis, 1992, 3; emphasis added)

Hence, if we are to give children and parents alike the tools with which to counter others' narrow thinking, why censor an experience that cannot be wished away or erased from America's historical past and immediate present?

MISSED OPPORTUNITIES?

African American adult literature has always offered adult perspectives on African American childhood baptisms into racism. To consider in an African American children's text the word and experience of *nigger* as a realistic part of the racial and social violence that is American experience is to arm children and parents with defensive strategies before the verbal bombing. Furthermore, including the word in African American children's books in the context of complex black–white race relations might well educate white children to the harms of the word despite their adult racist environments. For instance, televised documentaries of 1960s racial upheaval often present the reality of white racists screaming *nigger* and other insults at black protesters or printed on picket signs. Still, in Robert Coles's *The Story of Ruby Bridges* (1995), we are denied historical accuracy in knowing specifically the names Ruby is called when she integrates a white elementary school amid aggressively hostile white resistance. Coles's book includes illustrations of angry white adults taunting the little girl as she walks courageously into the segregated Mississippi school, yet the racist verbal attacks are conspicuously absent: "A large crowd of angry people … carried signs that said they didn't want black children in a white school. *People called Ruby names; some wanted to hurt her*" (emphasis added). Wherein lies the danger of including racial epithets? And why does the author assume that being called names is not as hurtful as any physical attack? Just as youngsters are not formally taught to say "dirty" words or to cuss, white children are not necessarily formally taught to use the word *nigger*. Its use is part of a familial culture the child absorbs before he or she realizes it. White journalist James T. Adams admits this kind of racist absorption:

> If you grew up in the South in the 1950s as I did, you are undoubtedly intimately familiar with the "N-word." The polite term for African-Americans then, and especially among more educated whites, was "colored," as in "colored folks" or "colored people." But the "N-word" was always there. In fact it was so pervasive in the white culture in Alabama that I was in the sixth grade before I realized the word spelled N-e-g-r-o was actually pronounced "Nee-grow."
>
> Until then, my teachers had routinely replaced the word "Negro" with the "N-word" whenever it appeared in textbooks or conversations.
>
> But even as a child, I was aware of the emotional impact of the word when used by whites in the presence of blacks. (1995, C1)

Including the word *nigger* in a children's book will not introduce white children to or encourage them to use a word they have most probably already heard in some familiar segregated setting. Consider that the word continues to be part of some white children's segregated play, and imagine the immediate discomfort of the African American adult or child witnessing the ritual with black and white children innocently at play. Robert G. O'Meally, in his Afterword to the 1994 edition of Langston Hughes's *Black Misery* (1969), writes:

> To the black child [,] ... the world [can] seem a prison-house of color-coded language. ... The black child feels it ... when one of his white friends unwittingly uses a counting rhyme with the sharply racialized history: "Misery is when you start to play a game and someone begins to count out: Eenie, meenie, miney, mo [Catch a nigger by the toe. If he hollers, let him go. Eenie, meenie, miney, mo"]. (1994, n.p.)

If white adults encountered the word *nigger* in their childhood through such early racist lore as the "Seven Little Niggers" poem from the *San Francisco Examiner* (1905)—"Seven little niggers playing tag with bricks, one was hit 'most all de time, den dey was six. ... Six little niggers fooling 'round de hive. ... One little nigger in de scorchin' sun. Soon dey was de smell of smoke, and den dey was none" (Riggs, 1989)—there is no reason African American children's authors should euphemize or shy away from this nearly universal African American childhood experience. While current political correctness monitors such early boldly racist public performances, political correctness does not prevent this sort of verbal attack on black children today. In her popular autobiographical essay "Mommy, What Does 'Nigger' Mean?" (1994), Gloria Naylor reiterates the emotional and psychological gravity of this specific racist verbal attack on potentially every African American child and her parent:

> I remember the first time I heard the word nigger. In my third-grade class, our math tests were being passed down the rows, and as I handed the papers to the little boy in back of me, I remarked that once again he had received a much lower mark than I did. He snatched his test from me and spit out that word. Had he called me a nymphomaniac or a necrophiliac, I couldn't have been more puzzled. I didn't know what a nigger was, but I knew that whatever it meant, it was something he shouldn't have called me. This was verified when I raised my hand, and in a loud voice repeated what he had said and watched the teacher scold him for using a "bad" word. I was later to go home and ask the inevitable ques-

tion every black parent must face—"Mommy, what does 'nigger' mean?" ...

So there must have been dozens of times that the word "nigger" was spoken in front of me before I reached the third grade. But I didn't "hear" it until it was said by a small pair of lips that had already learned it could be a way to humiliate me. That was the word I went home and asked my mother about. And since she knew that I had to grow up in America, she took me in her lap and explained. (380–383)

Such a moment further highlights the immediacy and the inevitability of dealing with the labyrinth of American racism in as many ways as possible to serve and to protect the innocent on both sides of the color divide. Ironically, however, the more allegedly integrated we become racially, the easier it becomes to censor the very experiences that give legitimacy to our lives and to our world.

Yet, in today's climate of political correctness and alleged social tolerance and cultural sensitivity, African American children's books deliberately steer away from racially specific hate speech. Whereas we have African American adult accounts of their childhood encounters with such early verbal assaults, very few of these testimonials are directly rendered from a child's perspective and addressed to a child reader. Even when a book's subject matter affords the opportunity for candid and frank treatment of this sensitive issue, readers are denied the fullest legitimacy of what is all too frequently experienced. Marybeth Lorbiecki's *Sister Anne's Hands* (1998), for example, tells of a white seven-year-old's introduction to racist implication and behavior by her father and by her all-white second-grade class, respectively, when her school gets its first black teacher. Paired with her father's implicitly racist comment about Anna's new teacher—"I don't know how *a woman of her color* is going to survive" (emphasis added)—is an unidentified classmate's prank of throwing a paper airplane across the teacher's desk with the enclosed message: "Roses are red, violets are blue. Don't let Sister Anne get any black on you." The teacher uses this incident to show her young students the horrific consequences of discrimination based on skin color, ultimately giving them a lesson in race relations and American history:

Sister Anne had plastered the room with pictures of black people, poor or dying, some hanging from trees, others shot and bleeding. We saw signs over water fountains saying "Whites Only," and people marching with posters: "Go Back to Africa."

As the teacher exposes her students to what she terms "the colors of hatred," her lesson on Jim Crow's segregation and the physical violence African Americans have endured throughout American history might easily have extended to verbal violence, especially since she displays on the classroom bulletin boards pictures of angry white crowds with placards protesting 1950s and 1960s racial integration. Expectedly, the story ends happily with Anna discovering value in human difference, and with the author missing an opportunity to address racial slurs that were indeed integral to the historical moments Sister Anne candidly exhibits for her students.

Evelyn Coleman's *White Socks Only* (1996), another story about the racially turbulent Jim Crow past, offers no clues about the verbal violence to which African Americans were subjected in their struggle for social and political equality. In this story-within-a-story, a grandmother tells of her earliest childhood encounter with white bigotry. As she recounts a verbal attack from a white man because she publicly drank water from a "Whites Only" fountain, we are given very little with which to "hear" the white man and his white cohorts' shouting—shouting that leaves the little girl threatened, afraid, and in tears:

> The big [white] man with the bandanna kept right on yelling. His face got red as fire. He was snorting through his nose like a bull does when it's gon' charge. Other white folk came up and started yelling at us, too.

Although the narrative relates the white man's threat to "whup [the youngster and her black supporters] 'til [they] can't sit down," we have no details of the specific verbal racist attack that is surely part of this disturbing encounter. What are the angry whites yelling at the crowd of resistant blacks, aside from threats of physical violence?

Based on Rosa Parks and the Montgomery bus boycott incident, William Miller's *The Bus Ride* (1997) shows a black child's face-to-face brush with American racism. Young Sara emulates Rosa Parks's civil rights protest by sitting at the front of a public bus in the segregated Southeast, thus encountering the wrath of white adults. As the little girl and a crowd of African American adults take a stand for their civil rights, we witness a "loud and angry" white crowd "call[ing] Sara ugly names." These "ugly names" are neither identified nor discussed although they are part of the angry mob's aggressive behavior. From archival footage documenting the civil rights movement of the 1950s and 1960s, we know that use of the word *nigger* was pervasive in whites' verbal attacks on blacks. Particularly in the above three texts, a discussion of the power of the word *nigger* could easily be part of these children's lessons on racial bigotry. Such discussion is considerably important given the fact that, unlike dated references to African Americans as colored or Negro, the word *nigger* as a racist attack cannot be restricted to temporal historical boundaries.

Verbal violence can mar and cripple both adults and children. As socially and historically conscious adults, we cannot allow political correctness to take a front seat to arming youngsters with appropriate tools to address racism on the playground, in the classroom, or at the neighborhood hangout. African American mother Patricia J. Williams, in her essay "Racism Explained to My Son"—commenting on the importance of Tahar Ben Jelloun's collection *Racism Explained to My Daughter* (1999)—posits:

> Children—even, or should I say particularly, very young ones like my son—are hungry for some logic to explain the irrationalities of being marked and mocked. Their questions are too often greeted with deflections, silence, or sunny, universalizing cover-ups. Too many adults, I think, diminish the significance of playground racism by denying the degree to which little ones have already absorbed, like sponges, some very unbecoming attitudes from the world around them. ... [Racism], with increasing age, tends to become increasingly emotionally laden for most people. Many adults have difficulty deciphering the complexities of prejudice for themselves, never mind for their children. (85–86)

Discussing verbal abuse becomes as much of a parental responsibility as telling our children to avoid strangers and to be home from play by dark. Just as white youngsters absorb the weapons of racist attack, black youngsters absorb the hurt and pain that come from early racist experiences, emotionally painful experiences parents themselves do not always want to discuss. One such personal testimonial of the impact of early brushes with racism, Allison Hamilton's essay, "Nigger, Please," in *Image* (October 1994), reveals the immediate need to heal young victims:

> I was in the first grade, and my friends and I were walking home from school. We walked by a group of older white guys, and one of them said, "Look at those niggers." I knew they said something bad, but I didn't know why, so I asked my mom what it meant and she said it was a bad word, like a swear. It has a bad connotation; it's derogatory; it can mean lazy, shiftless, subservient, submissive, undeserving of the label "human being." It's a fighting word. (16–17)

Others in Hamilton's piece reiterate that "nigger" is "a derogatory word that will always have a powerful historical meaning," and that it is "really a negative, hateful word" when used in a black–white social context. In a society in which race has always mattered and continues to matter personally, economically, politically, legally, socially, and professionally, it is vitally important to equip black children and their parents with strategies to combat racist verbal attacks that rupture childhood innocence emotionally, psychologically, and intellectually. Only with honesty and directness, not paternal censorship in this particular matter of verbal violence, can we come closer to changing what African American comedian and political activist Dick Gregory, in his autobiography *Nigger* (1964), calls "a system where a white [person] can destroy a black [person] with a single word. Nigger" (209).

NIGGERS OLD AND NEW

BY JOSEPH L. GRAVES, JR.

"Sticks and Stones" insightfully calls our attention to an ongoing danger deeply entwined in the lived experience of American racism. Today, as in our past, our youth are unprepared to deal with a particularly hurtful form of verbal abuse associated with the social construction of race. The abuse is enjoined by use of the word *nigger*, which can be applied by any person of non-African descent to instantly insult a person of any detectable African descent. This word retains its power as a weapon of mass destruction regarding the African American psyche. The word *nigger* is so deeply engrained in our social consciousness that African Americans have coopted it for our own goals. Comedian Richard Pryor crafted much of his reputation by infusing the word throughout his monologues, once remarking: "They've got the Vietnamese in army camps teaching them how to say *nigger*." Pryor said that the instructors chanted, "Nigger, nigger, nigger …". To which the students replied: "rigger, rigger, rigger. …" The punch line was: "If you get your ass kicked, then you know you got it right!" (Pryor, 1975).

In the 1920s, a person of African descent could have routinely expected to be called a nigger. Today, the epithet is so controversial that some misguided but well-meaning authors and editors of children's literature actively censor the word. It has been removed from film and literary texts in ways that make little sense. Furthermore, parent groups have stepped forward to protest the reading of classics in American literature such as *The Adventures of Huckleberry Finn* due to the references to African Americans as niggers throughout the text.

These individuals have three very different motivations. Some individuals simply fail to understand the damaging power of the verbal abuse entailed in this particular racial epithet, simultaneously underestimating the residual racism still present in American society. By misunderstanding its power, they believe that by the simple act of censorship, they can prevent harm. They see no need to prepare youth to resist its impact, either as the perpetrator or as the target. Still others fear that by allowing the word to appear in such texts, they themselves are introducing young minds to it and thereby encouraging its use. And some of these authors and editors are historical revisionists, taking on the role of sanitizing both the emotional and physical violence that pervades the history of European American racialized social dominance in this country. Historical revisionism eliminates the guilt of the perpetrators by removing the evidence of their wrongs from public view. It also cools the furor of the victims by denying that they have anything to be angry about.

The writings of the nineteenth-century social theorist Alexis de Tocqueville help to illustrate why racialized historical revisionism is so popular today. He argued that the social integration of the descendents of African slaves into America would be impeded by their physical differences with the socially dominant European population (*Democracy in America*, 1835, Vol. 1). He suggested that European slaves had managed social integration into European nations because of their physical similarity with their former masters. However, in a country in which the slaves and rulers differed "racially" and in which rules against intermarriage were enforced either officially or by social convention, the mark of servitude would forever remain on the progeny of those enslaved.

Nigger, as a derogatory epithet used by people of European descent against those of African descent, retains its power because American racial relations are fundamentally unaltered. Virtually every measure of social and material well-being favors Americans of European descent, including net worth, educational attainment, and even mortality and morbidity. Recent research on health disparity suggests that African Americans are not only allegedly deficient in intellect, but also have an inherently weak genetic constitution. In other words, this alleged genetic inferiority of African Americans accounts for their earlier morbidity and mortality, as opposed to the toxic social environment they have been forced to endure in American society.

If European Americans do not or refuse to see the mechanisms of discrimination, then for them they do not exist. This situation creates further discord because African Americans live the oppression of American society daily. Cognitive dissonance dominates any serious conversation between African and European Americans because the former cannot understand the insensitivity of the latter, and the latter cannot accept the anger of the former. Humans have a tendency to avoid controversy; thus, as the disparity between these groups grows, they separate from each other. The persistent wealth differential between these groups also supports residential segregation. Market forces driving housing prices up and discriminatory lending practices make it harder for minorities to purchase homes in "white" neighborhoods. Indeed, even in cities where minorities can afford equivalent housing and thus attend the same public schools as affluent whites, whites move their children to private schools to avoid integration. Probably the most illustrative example of the ongoing potency of America's racial discord is that Sunday mornings still are the most racially segregated hours of the week. For example, Christians who espouse a doctrine of universal brother/sisterhood, even within the same denomination, are still actively separated by race regarding place of worship.

Some revisionists believe that we as a society cannot move forward unless we bury the cultural practices of the past. For them, eliminating the word *nigger* from the language results from their emotional repulsion to past injustice (see, hear, and speak no evil). We do know that we previously occupied a world without such racism. Indeed, racial theories of social hierarchy against people of African descent did not exist in ancient Europeans (Graves, 2001, 15–22). Furthermore, racist behavior could not have been a feature of the archetypical human mind. There is general scientific agreement that anatomically modern humans evolved in Africa around 180,000 years ago. These humans arose in one limited geographical locality and thus could not have exhibited the sorts of external physical variation associated with modern human diversity. They most likely had the same dark skin color and anatomical proportions similar to modern eastern Africans. More important, the behavioral templates that make us modern humans must have already been in place before any subgroups of our species left Africa. Hence, it would have been impossible to have evolved behavior to distinguish and discriminate against other humans based on features we currently associate with modern conceptions of race.

Despite centuries of misconception, the Neanderthals were not our ancestors and soon went extinct after modern humans arrived in Europe. There is some debate regarding whether Neanderthals passed genes to modern humans, but all genetic analyses to date invalidate that possibility. This results from the fact that they lived in Europe, and since Europe has more archaeologists than Africa, Neanderthals have been more extensively studied. Popular culture still depicts Neanderthals as if they were human ancestors, and European society still has difficulty representing their ancient human ancestors with African features. We do not know how our long-limbed, dark-skinned ancestors perceived the short-limbed, light-skinned inhabitants of Europe. If the word *nigger* can be taken to mean intrinsically inferior, did they see them as the niggers of Europe? After all, Neanderthals were intellectually slow and had physical and cultural differences from modern humans. Did they ignore them, or did they make war on them and enslave them because they were different? If any Neanderthal genes ended up in modern humans, was it because the intrinsic superiority of the *Homo sapiens* males allowed them to raid the hapless Neanderthal camps and steal and enslave their women and take their sexual liberties with them? We do know that the Neanderthals died out, in part due to their inability to compete with the dark-skinned new arrivals from Africa. If racial theories of hierarchy existed at this time, then they would have been the opposite of how we now view them. In fact, we know that even in recorded history, racial theories of *nigger* have been different from the American tradition.

The use of derogatory epithets to belittle and control the socially subordinated is not unique to American society. Japanese master race theorists use the term *junketsu no minzoku* to describe themselves as a pure-blood people. The implication is that non-Japanese are not pure blood and, by such lack of purity, inferior. This ideology supported the invasion and subjugation of much of East Asia in the 1920s, including Korea. During World War II, Japan impressed much of the Korean population to its service, including women as "comfort" girls (girls forced into prostitution) and men as soldiers. The narratives of many allied prisoners in Japanese prison camps suggested that the Korean guards were more brutal than the regular Japanese army (Graves, 2004, 55). In Rwanda during the Hutu/Tutsi conflict, both sides developed ethnically based rhetoric debasing the other (Janzen and Janzen, 2000, 179–183). Thus, it seems that as long as social subordination is at play, ideological justification for it shall be developed, and one consequence of that is the production of linguistic shorthand in the form of racial/ethnic epithets, empowering the users and dehumanizing the target.

TALKING OUT LOUD: IDEAS FOR DISCUSSION

1. Compare and contrast the rationales for removing the word *nigger* from films and literary texts. Are these rationales fundamentally different? Do they achieve the same result even when motivations differ?
2. To what extent is the word *nigger* historically and nonhistorically specific?

3. Check multiple dictionaries for definitions of *nigger*. Explain the similarities and differences.

4. List and discuss comparably racially charged and derogatory words used for whites and other groups. Are these words based also in class, gender, and sexual orientation? What other childhood ditties and rhymes or popular culture include references to "nigger," such as Brazil nuts' being called "nigger toes"?

5. Examine nineteenth-century American blackface minstrel tunes for their use of the word *nigger*. How does this use compare to the prevalence of the word *nigger* on commercial products, for example? Consider such minstrel songs as *Disney Favorite Children's Tunes* "Dixie," "Oh! Susanna," "Polly Woddle Doodle," and "Jim Crack Corn."

6. As another instance of how lines blur between the personal and the political for people of color and other nonmainstream groups, Dr. Graves explains that just in the summer of 2005 his then eleven-year-old son and he were called niggers while walking through the parking lot of their public library in New Jersey. He and his son looked at each other, did not respond to the verbal assault, and walked away calmly. What do you imagine their immediate feelings were at this insult? How might their behavior be perceived by the name-caller? Was their choice of response defensible, morally or politically? Should they have confronted the name-caller? What impact would being called a nigger have on his young preteen son and on him as a professional African American fifty-year-old man?

7. This chapter gives examples of how denying the existence of ongoing racial discrimination against African Americans has become commonplace in the past decade. Can you provide further evidence of this reality? How does this denial by both the perpetrators and victims of racism influence the ongoing psychological impact of racial epithets? What social changes need to occur, and how long will it take to dismantle fully the power of the word *nigger* in the minds of the oppressed and the oppressors?

8. Discuss the television show *Boston Public* episode based on Randall Kennedy's book *Nigger* (2002). What does the show achieve? Who is the episode's and the show's audience?

9. To what extent does African American appropriation of the word *nigger* affect its derogatory intent and impact?

10. Discuss the importance of the documentary, *The N Word: Divided We Stand* (2004), written and directed by Todd Larkins, and the

Ebony editorial by Bryan Monroe, "Enough! Why Blacks—and Whites—Should Never Use the 'N-Word' Again" (February, 2007). What is the impact of this conversation on the word by "some of today's A-list celebrities, journalists, historians, and every day people commenting on their personal history with and society's use of the 'N' word"?

4

NAPPY EDGES AND GOLDY LOCKS
African American Daughters and the Politics of Hair

Oh give me a perm
Where the waves all roam firm—
And the style and the body will stay.
While seldom is heard—
A bad, blasphemous word
As my scalp becomes toxic sauté.

—Anonymous, to the tune of "Home on the Range"

Soft & Beautiful Just for Me! By Pro-Line: America's #1 Children's Relaxer ... The Answer to a Mother's Prayer. A New Formula for Coarse Hair! Try the new Just for Me Coarse Relaxer today ... created in part by mothers, especially for their daughters!

—Hair advertisement, *Jet* (27 October 1997)

Until the birth of our daughter, Jasmine, some seventeen years ago, I had never given head hair much thought. Whenever my wife (Italian and Argentinian) and I (African American) were out with our baby daughter, we were almost always complimented by blacks and whites alike on our daughter's hair.[1] Whites generally commented on how "nice" or "pretty" Jasmine's hair is. More like my wife's hair in terms of texture, length, and grade than mine, Jasmine's is now about midback in length, bouncy, thick, and in ringlets. While complimenting, whites almost always impulsively touched her hair, presumably to feel if its texture is more like her dad's or her mom's. African Americans generally described Jasmine's hair as "good" hair. Our daughter's friends, both black and white, loved playing with her hair. One of Jasmine's then seven-year-old black girlfriends, whose own hair was processed chemically and about shoulder length, always commented that she wished she had hair like Jasmine's. As Jasmine and her hair grew, some blacks even asked if Jasmine wears a hair weave. When our second child, Jared, was born three years after Jasmine, this emphasis on his head hair as "good hair" resurfaced. Jared's hair, like Jasmine's, is fluffy and in big, loose curls. In fact, because of Jared's abundance of curls, many assumed him to be a baby girl.

Nearly all my life, my mother has worn wigs. Though her own hair is short and somewhat thin, she has never experienced problems with balding or hair loss. She maintains that she is not very creative with her hairstyling, and that wigs allowed her more styling options. What is interesting to me even now as I reflect on these early years at home, the 1960s and 1970s, is that neither my mother nor any of her many wig-wearing women friends owned Afro or braided wigs or wigs anywhere close to black hairstyles and textures. Their wigs were always straight, long, and flowing.

As a first-year college student in the late 1970s, I had my first white roommate, whose admittedly limited contact with African Americans had been with his family's housekeeper; one of the first things he wanted to do as we were getting to know each other was touch my hair. He was noticeably surprised to discover that my short Afro hair did not feel like steel wool. My wife, before we dated and married, requested and concluded the same.

In graduate school in the early 1980s, I experimented with relaxing[2] my hair. I, too, wanted the smooth, slicked-back Billy Dee Williams look and experienced the scalp burns and physical discomfort often necessary in obtaining it. I concluded, though, that the physical and psychological gain was well worth the physical discomfort and pain,[3] an experience not unlike Malcolm X's with conk, which he details vividly and even humorously, but not with any less emphasis on the extreme physical discomfort:

> The congolene just felt warm when Shorty started combing it in. But then my head caught fire. I gritted my teeth and tried to pull the sides of the kitchen table together. The comb felt as if it was raking my skin off. My eyes watered, my nose was running. I couldn't stand it any longer; I bolted to the washbasin. I was cursing Shorty with every name I could think of. (1964, 53)

An embarrassing moment associated with my hair and its care occurred during my first year of professional teaching, 1987, at a small predominantly white university in the southeast. As mostly white faculty members underwent physical exams required for health insurance, we were each connected to an electronic monitor that measured our body fat percentages as we reclined on a leather cot. After I was tested and off the cot, a white health attendant wiped a greasy spot from the headrest before the next (white) faculty member reclined. At that point, it occurred to me that my embarrassment was a variation on W. E. B. DuBois's notion of blacks' "double consciousness" in *The Souls of Black Folk* (1903): seeing our black selves though the eyes of dominant white oppressors with contempt and pity. Rather than accept the episode as a kind of cultural ignorance on the part of the white health attendant, who technically should have covered the headrest for each faculty member, I felt ashamed because of a necessary scalp-greasing ritual of hair care for many African Americans, a ritual quite the opposite of whites' hair care, and a ritual of which whites are generally unaware and by which they are simultaneously surprised and repulsed.

When I decided for various spiritual and I suppose sociopolitical reasons to get rid of the flat top, military fade I had sported for over ten years and to grow dreadlocks, the move created quite a stir for my parents, grandparents, and a minister uncle, who all insist to this day that dreadlocks are not "professional." And that was a concern for me when, in the early knot stages of dreadlocking, I was on the job market. While my children and their little black friends thought the twisted knots all over my head were the funniest looking things they had ever seen, white children and adults generally just stared curiously at my head. My black professional friends assured me that since I was not in "corporate" America, my dreadlocks were "way cool" for a college English teacher, many adding that they personally did not have the nerve to try something as allegedly "daring" as dreadlocks. As I was sitting browsing books at a multicultural children's book festival recently, a little three- or four-year-old white boy came over to me and began lifting my dreadlocks with his hands and playing with them. While I was amused at his curious boldness, his mother was mortified and unnecessarily apologetic.[4]

This consistent attention to hair offered connections with what I had in earlier years dismissed as insignificant and trivial. These occurrences now, however, signify for me continuing racial and gender biases about head hair both within and outside black cultural perceptions. Competing mythologies around something as deceptively insignificant as hair still haunt and complicate African Americans' self-identities and their ideals of beauty, thus revealing broad and complex social, historical, and political realities. The implications and consequences of the seemingly radical split between European standards of beauty and black people's hair become ways of building or crushing a black person's self-esteem, all based on the straightness or nappiness of an individual's hair.

TAKING NOTES FROM HISTORY

Within African American culture, head hair is a big deal—so many choices in hairstyles: dreadlocked, "natural," curled, faded, braided, twisted, straightened, permed, crimped, cornrowed, and even bald. Hair is also big business. Madame C. J. Walker (1867–1919), honored as the first self-made woman millionaire, made her fortune with her 1905 capitalizing on the straightening comb and other black hair care products that "revolutionized the [black] hair care industry" (Chappe, 1997, 50). Hair care for "ethnic" (commercially translates as African American) folks' hair is a multimillion-dollar industry. When my then seventy-eight-year-old grandmother visited my family and me for two weeks, she flat out refused to socialize or sightsee after arriving until she had gotten her hair "fixed." We shopped around and found a hairdresser, spent well over two hours at the hairdresser's, and paid a whopping $68 for this service. She later lamented that she would need a "retouch or touch up"[5] in about two weeks and that would cost about $35. African Americans know that African Americans are seriously preoccupied with hair—less with hair coloring than with hair textures, grades, and lengths. African Americans, even within families, rate each other and themselves on the good and bad hair scale, where "good hair" is perceived as hair closest to white people's hair—long, straight, silky, bouncy, manageable, healthy, and shiny—while "bad hair" is short, matted, kinky, nappy, coarse, brittle, and wooly. Author Veronica Chambers (1999) further clarifies:

> Because I am a black woman, I have always had a complicated relationship with my hair. For those who don't know the history, here's a quick primer on the politics of hair and beauty aesthetics in the black community, vis-à-vis race and class in the late twentieth century. "Good" hair is straight and, preferably, long. Think Naomi Campbell. Think Whitney Houston. For that matter, think RuPaul. "Bad" hair is thick and coarse, a.k.a. "nappy," and often short. Think Buckwheat of the Little Rascals. Not the more recent, politically correct version, but the old one, in which Buckwheat looked like Don King's grandson. (171)

This Western ideal of beauty connected specifically with hair occurs as early as biblical times. For instance, 1 Corinthians 11:14–15 establishes this Eurocentric ideal of female beauty: "Doth not even nature itself teach you that if a man have long hair, it is a shame unto him? But if a woman have long hair, it is a glory to her." Martin Luther, in *Table Talk* (1569), claims that "The hair is the finest ornament women have. Of old, virgins used to wear it loose, except when they were in mourning. I like women to let their hair fall down their back; 'tis the most agreeable sight" (Evans, 1968, 297).[6] Intraracist ideals of good and bad hair are rooted in the African American slave past. With forced miscegenation rampant on plantations, not only did blacks' skin tones and complexions become more variable, but differences in hair textures occurred as well. As Willie Morrow's docudrama "Four-Hundred Years Without a Comb: The Inferior Seed" (1989) and Naomi Sims's *All About Hair Care for the Black Woman* (1982) explain, slave women's ease at grooming masters' children's hair often led to internalized feelings of inferiority about the texture and alleged manageability of a mother's own hair. Such feelings of inferiority were sometimes overt in their rejection of their own children's hair and in their wearing of kerchiefs to shield their perceived aesthetically displeasing hair from their white superiors. And, since lighter-complected slaves closer to masters' skin color had "good hair" that was closer to straight, these slaves were perceived and treated as "privileged" house slaves. Darker-skinned slaves with "bad hair" were relegated to allegedly less-desirable field work. When slaves were not born with "good hair," some used axle grease and lye to make their hair straight, slick, and subsequently longer, a transformation that brought them closer to their perceived white ideal of beauty. This caste system based on skin color and hair demonstrates far-reaching psychological and social manifestations when some historically black churches and other black civic organizations used the brown paper bag test for skin tone and the fine-tooth comb or soda can test for hair length and texture to admit or reject members.

There is no shortage of head hair references and treatments in African American folklore, literature, and popular culture. However full of racist stereotyping, Richard M. Dorson's *American Negro Folktales* (1956), for instance, includes the tale "Why the Negro Has Kinky Hair," explaining that because blacks were late—they were devouring watermelon—when hair was being given out at the world's creation, "The only hair that was left was what the other people didn't want—they stepped on it. [Gesture of twisting foot into the ground.] So the colored people had to put on kinky hair ... while the other people, Chinese and Japs and whites, put the hair on and smoothed it down" (176). There are also many "snaps" — a ritual of insults based in the history of blacks' self-fashioning through language performance rituals — that diss "yo mama for havin' hair so nappy she needs painkillers to comb it." Others include "yo mama's hair so short and nappy that when she plaits it, it looks like stitches" and "yo mama's hair is so nappy, when she combs it, the teeth bleed." These rituals of insult are intracommunal ways alleg-edly of appropriating and redefining negatives associated with black people's hair as positive. Eldridge Cleaver's satirical critique of Euro-centric aesthetics of beauty centers particularly on hair in "As Crinkly as Yours" (1962), in Alan Dundes's *Mother Wit from the Laughing Bar-rel: Readings in the Interpretation of Afro-American Folklore* (1990).

Among academics, black feminist theorists bell hooks ("Straighten-ing Our Hair," 1992) and Michele Wallace ("Anger in Isolation: A Black Feminist's Search for Sisterhood," 1990) have written extensively on the cultural, racial, and gender-specific communal rituals around hair straightening among black women. The chapter "Hair: The Straight and Nappy of It All" is included in Kathy Russell, Midge Wilson, and Ron-ald Hall's *The Color Complex: The Politics of Skin Color among African Americans* (1992). Noliwe M. Rooks's *Hair Raising: Beauty, Culture, and African American Women* (1996) is one of the most comprehen-sive scholarly treatments of the hair issue. Authors Tina McElroy Ansa (*Baby of the Family*, 1989); Gwendolyn Brooks ["To Those of My Sisters Who Kept Their Naturals (Never to Look a Hot Comb in the Teeth"), 1983]; Ed Bullins ("Street Sounds: Dialogues with Black Experience," 1973); Lorraine Hansberry (*A Raisin in the Sun*, 1958); Zora Neale Hur-ston (*Their Eyes Were Watching God*, 1978); Tayari Jones ("An Open Letter to Syria Who Recently Stopped Straightening Her Hair," 1999); Adrienne Kennedy (*Funnyhouse of a Negro*, 1988); Dominique LaBaw ("Bad Hair," 1994); Melissa Linn ("All That Hair," 1995); Benilde Little (*Good Hair*, 1996); Audre Lorde ("Is Your Hair Still Political?" 1990); Dudley Randall ("On Getting a Natural, for Gwendolyn Brooks," 1973); Dori Sanders (*Clover*, 1990); Natasha Tarpley ("Haircut," 1991); Alice Walker ("Oppressed Hair Puts a Ceiling on the Brain," 1998); and George C. Wolfe ("The Hairpiece," 1987)—to name a few—write hair politics into their explorations of African American culture generally and of African American women's realities specifically.

Even late nineteenth- and twentieth-century minstrel and plantation songs written by whites mockingly imitating blacks for the entertain-ment of whites include details of "nappy," "kinky," or "wooly" hair as a common tactic for ridiculing blacks. For instance, Sidney D. Mitchell's "Mammy's Chocolate Soldier" (1918) includes the line "Come and lay your kinky head on Mammy's shoulder"; Clarence Williams's "Ugly

Chile (You're Some Pretty Doll)" (1918) includes the line "Your hair is nappy, who's your pappy"; and Sam M. Lewis's "Underneath the Cotton Moon" (1913) includes the line "You's ma little black boy wid a turned up nose,/ An' a little bunch o' wool upon yo' head/ ... You's ma little bit o' wooly headed brown-eyed gal." African American songwriter Gussie Davis even cashed in on the popularity of minstrelsy and black folks' alleged nappy hair problem with his minstrel song, "When They Straighten All the Colored People's Hair" (1894):

> Oh, you jolly little "nigger," you make a funny figure.
> For your wool kinks up just like the letter "o."
> And you seem to be happy, although
> your head is nappy.
> But then never mind, 'twill always not be so.
> They have a new invention, and
> they say it's their intention,
> To experiment on darkeys everywhere.
> Oh, your face it may be dark, but
> you'll be happy as a lark—
> When they straighten all the colored people's hair.

Notice how the song's narrator assumes nappy hair is undesirable, furthering the presumed black nappy/white straight polarization.

More recently, African American drag queen, actor, and talk show host RuPaul celebrates black hairstyles and styling with rituals of community in the tune "Back to My Roots" (1993). Spike Lee includes in his movie *School Daze* (1988) a musical number called "Straight and Nappy: Good and Bad Hair," wherein hair type, texture, and length are intricately connected with intraracism and discrimination within black communities on the basis of skin tone. Commenting on the impetus for that segment of the movie in *Uplift the Race: The Construction of School Daze* (1988), Lee offers a personal testimonial:

> When [black people] say "straight and nappy," we refer to a criterion which Black people use to defeat or praise; we use it as a weapon, have used it very effectively over the years, and will continue to, as far as I can see. ... When I was growing up, I thought white people had good hair. I thought they didn't have to do anything to it, just get up in the morning and walk right out the door, while we have to struggle with trying to get the comb through our hair without breaking all the teeth out. (147)

Finally, Middleton A. Harris's *The Black Book* (1974) presents historical notes on and pictures of products used to bleach black people's skin and to straighten their hair. To show how early on blacks embraced the ideal of straight hair, he cites the following report from the *New York Times* (9 February 1859):

> Hodgon, the Great African Hair Unkinker, invented a process to straighten hair and expected great financial rewards. He ... invited all sons and daughters of Ham to a live demonstration. ... A dishpan with a mysterious concoction was put over a gas burner, and when the potion got warm it was applied to one side of a wooly head. What had been tight curls was suddenly "straight as a coon's leg; as glossy as a wet beaver's back; and several inches in length." (Harris, 1974, 190)

Racist interpretations of the Bible—the curse of Ham allegedly explains why blacks were enslaved—combine with the popular coon image to reiterate the anti-African beauty ideal and to underscore this perpetual quest for the straight and narrow.

LESSONS FROM LITERATURE AND REAL LIFE

Black folks' hair as a complex and simultaneously personal and political issue has not been dealt with so prolifically and to the same extent in children's texts, although much African American adult literature deals with little black girls coming to terms with their hair in the face of culturally competing beauty mythologies. African American women have, in both personal autobiography and fiction, exposed this complicated struggle for little African American girls. Maya Angelou's youthful persona Marguerite, in *I Know Why the Caged Bird Sings* (1971), imagines her nappy hair replaced with the perceived ideal of straight blond hair:

> Wouldn't [the folks in Stamps, Arkansas] be surprised when one day I woke up out of my black ugly dream, and my real hair, which was long and blond, would take the place of the kinky mass that Momma wouldn't let me straighten? ... [Actually,] I was really white and ... a cruel fairy stepmother ... was understandably jealous of my beauty, ... and turned me into a too-big Negro girl, with nappy black hair. (2)

And Pecola in Toni Morrison's *The Bluest Eye* (1970) internalizes her familial and communal racial self-hatred, praying fervently for the blue eyes that in her perception create the idealized white world of Father, Mother, Dick and Jane, Greta Garbo, Shirley Temple, Mary Jane candy wrappers, and Ginger Rogers: "Adults, older girls, shops, magazines, newspapers, window signs—all the world had agreed that a blue-eyed, yellow-haired, pink-skinned doll was what every girl treasured" (20). Among the physical attributes that define beauty and ugliness in both accounts is hair.

While there are acknowledged bonding social rituals between black girls and women during these rites of passage from "natural" to straight hair, the common thread of personal and social inadequacy for many little African American girls is very real. In her essay "The Pain of Living the Lye" (1993), journalist Kim Green confesses her rage, anger, and shame, even as a black child, that her hair was one of the things that negatively marked her social difference:

> I grew up mad at my hair because it wasn't "pretty" like the swinging manes of the white children who surrounded me. It was short and petrified. It stayed where I put it and even where I didn't. It refused to move *with* me and fought against me. That was how my rage was born.
>
> The shame came subtly, but it was the hardest to bear. The shame of my hair started with me watching my mother struggle to gather money to send me to the hairdresser. As a young child, I grew through Afros and cornrows. I suffered the grueling embarrassment of being the only Black child in a sea of blondes, helpless and unable to answer the gaping questions and comments of those who wanted to touch and understand the seasons of my ever-evolving hair. They wondered why it was that on some days my hair was "straight" and just weeks later it was lackluster and no longer "moving." I was wondering the same thing and felt rage toward a God who wouldn't explain it for me. (38)

Rapunzel's, Goldilocks's, and Barbie's long, flowing, blond, straight hair[7] and television commercials about innocuous detanglers for little white girls' hair offer striking contrast to the potentially dangerous chemical relaxers recommended and celebrated in television commercials and in *Essence* and *Ebony* advertisements aimed at African American mothers and their preadolescent daughters. One such ad proclaims the relaxer as a natural part of a mother's nurturing of her preadolescent daughters: "Mommy says PCJ Pretty-n-Silky with Nutrient Sheen Conditioner will keep our hair strong and healthy as we grow!" The rhetorical construct of the ad posits silkiness as prettiness, nonsilkiness as ugliness. Deceptively, the language implies that relaxed hair is stronger and healthier when in fact hair that has undergone chemical treatments such as this is often weakened, stressed, and dried. The ad continues to address the mother of the daughters:

> Everything about your daughter is growing and changing. Especially her hair. That's why she *needs* PCJ Pretty-n-Silky No-Lye Crème relaxer. It is the only children's relaxer with … an intensive treatment that replaces moisture to the hair immediately after the relaxing process, leaving hair silky and bouncy. And to keep hair shiny and silky between relaxer touch-ups, use PCJ Pretty-n-Silky styling products. Nothing beats how PCJ Pretty-n-Silky straightens beautifully while she grows. (*Upscale,* February 1999; emphasis added)

Clearly, the repetition of "silky" renders it an ideal, and the ad implies something quite natural in a mother's desire to make this product part of a young daughter's natural maturation. Indeed, the rhetoric urges that a young black girl's beauty—her prettiness—is fundamentally connected to her hair, and that straightening and processing it is as natural as tending to her changing hygiene needs. Although *Essence* and other black readership magazines do include regular attention to the complexities of African American identity as it relates to beauty ideals and hair—for instance, Stephanie Stokes Oliver's "Word from the Editor" (*Heart and Soul,* October–November 1995) and "A Hair-Raising Story" (*Essence,* February 1997)—the sentiments of Whoopi Goldberg's young black girl persona when she discards her pretend "long, luxurious blond hair" and eventually accepts her own short, matted dreadlocks even if they don't "cas-sca-sca-dade down her back" ("Blonde Hair," HBO, 1985) or "blow helplessly in the wind" (Chenzira, 1984) have not found extensive treatment in books written specifically for child audiences. The *Upscale* ad's focus on growing and "changing" is at the root of the double consciousness many blacks associate with their hair. Veronica Chambers offers a personal testimonial of this unhealthy childhood need for "transformation":

> I knew from the age of four that I had "bad" hair because my relatives and family friends discussed my hair with all the gravity that one might use to discuss a rare blood disease. "Something must be done," they would cluck sadly. "I think I know someone," an aunt would murmur. Some of my earliest memories are of Brooklyn apartments where women did hair for extra money. These makeshift beauty parlors were lively and loud, the air thick with the smell of lye from harsh relaxer, the smell of hair burning as the hot straightening comb did its job. To this day, the sound of a hot comb crackling as it makes its way through a thick head of hair

makes me feel at home; the smell of hair burning is the smell of black beauty emerging like a phoenix from metaphorical ashes: transformation. (171)

Chambers (1999) echoes with irony the multitude of messages sent to little black girls and their mothers about the necessity of accepting and then "transforming" themselves, however temporarily, into someone else's cultural image of beauty. The transformation also involves taking away a childhood innocence often associated with freedom and resistance, changing it into something more womanly and grown-up—tamed and orderly.

As for attention to the hair issue in early children's books particularly, it is not at all surprising that Augusta Goldin's *Straight Hair, Curly Hair* (1966) includes two drawings of brown children with curly hair but affords no attention to the cultural and racial specificity of textures and grades and the particular cultural dynamics operating on many levels within black communities. Among African American children's texts, Camille Yarbrough's *Cornrows* (1979) explores the fine artistry and ancestral history of this special braiding of a little girl's hair, Alexis De Veaux's *An Enchanted Hair Tale* (1991) celebrates the mysterious wonders and creative imagination associated with a little black boy's dreadlocks, and Tololwa M. Mollel's *The Princess Who Lost Her Hair* (1993) is an Akamba legend that speaks to the damage wrought by vanity on a young African girl's hair.[8] The *Rapunzel* of Fred Crump, Jr. (1991) recasts the long, blond, silky-haired and fair-skinned Rapunzel as a brown Rapunzel with long braids that are more ropelike and easier for a prince to climb than silky straight strands even when plaited. In the now-defunct "In Living Color" (FOX, 20 September 1990) parody of the always blond and white Rapunzel, a skit from "Uncle Joe's Fairy Tales and Barbecue Recipes" replaces Rapunzel with an African American female named Betwinda Malika Hightower, Jr., who wears a hair weave that comes off as the African American prince tries to climb the hair ladder.

While not about hair as a subject, Alile Sharon Larkin's revisionist video story *Dreadlocks and the Three Bears* (1991) is about a "cinnamon brown girl" named Nimi who lived on an island in the Caribbean. Nimi had "lots and lots of African curls on her pretty little cinnamon brown head. Nimi had curly-curly-kinky-curly-nappy-curly hair. Nimi had curly-curly-kinky-curly-nappy-curly locks and twists called dreadlocks, so simply divine that everyone just called her Dreadlocks." Still, Angela Hunt's *If I Had Long, Long Hair* (1988) shows that even little white girls with their already straight hair fantasize about having Barbie's long waterfall of hair. Loretta Littlefield, the story's seven- or eight-year-old character, already with shoulder-length stringy hair, wants "long, long hair" to put into braids for jumping rope with friends. She wants hair that cascades behind her down stairs like "majestic, royal robes," hair that spills over her bed and covers her bedroom floor, hair that "streams behind her" in a parade.[9] When Loretta realizes that "long, long hair" can be heavy atop her head, and that it can be easily tangled and messy with her active life of play, she accepts her own straight, shoulder-length hair as fine. Indeed, when Loretta emerges from her fantasy world, she returns to an image of herself that is not fundamentally connected to beauty ideals she can never naturally and permanently realize. In contrast, the "transformation" of little black girls' hair from its nonchemicalized form to a processed state that lengthens the hair as it straightens it is most often not without complex political, personal, and social implications.

CHILDREN'S TEXTS AND ADULT RESPONSES

Aside from bell hooks's picture book, *Happy to Be Nappy* (1999),[10] which celebrates clean-smelling and sweet, billowy soft, frizzy and fuzzy, twisted and plaited, brushed and braided nappy hair and nappy-haired little "girlpies" in their various skin shades and hairstyles, Natasha A. Tarpley's *I Love My Hair!* (1998), which poetically celebrates the versatility of a little black girl's hair with a decidedly apolitical stance; and Nikki Grimes's *Wild, Wild Hair* (1997), which makes a little black girl's Monday morning haircombing and braiding ritual a family game of hide-and-seek ("wild" may be an implicit euphemism for "nappy"), Carolivia Herron's *Nappy Hair* (1997) is one of the most controversial and effective treatments of the complex nuances of the gender and race politics of hair, rendered within a matrix of rich African American folk traditions.[11] Autobiographical, the book is "based on the fun [Herron's] own family poked at her nappy hair when she was a girl" (book jacket). While the book revises notions of black female beauty, it also teaches and entertains as it celebrates African American storytelling.

Framed as stories within stories, the book opens with a storyteller—self-consciously aware of the art of storytelling—preparing to share the story of Brenda, a "sweet" and "cute little brown baby girl," probably between five and eight years old, who has some of the nappiest hair the family has ever seen. After an announcement of narrative intention, the storyteller, Uncle Mordecai, becomes a preacher launching into Brenda's story through folklore, rap—"It's your hair, Brenda, take the cake, And come back and get the plate"—American history, and the Bible. As the preacher/storyteller presents Brenda's story, the other listening family members chime in spontaneously to offer a common and familiar southern black church service call-and-response ritual; the text then becomes a sermon recreated rhythmically and performatively to celebrate the richness of African American cultural traditions. To African American hair, Herron attaches a folkloric and spiritual texture that, according to her, is achieved and sustained through communal fellowship and individual and collective redefinitions of identity and ideals of beauty.

Brenda's story is also her family's, as the storyteller/preacher takes them through Brenda's and their own ancestral slave history of being brought from Africa to America, and of the horrors of family separations at the slave block—"sold your momma for a nickel [or] a buffalo" and "your daddy for a dime." The subsequent social and political resistance of African Americans in the New World is also recreated as Brenda aggressively challenges—even as a child—any efforts to restrain or straighten her nappy hair: "the kinkiest, the nappiest, the fuzziest, the most screwed up, squeezed up, knotted up, tangled up, twisted up, nappiest ... hair you've ever seen in your life." Brenda's hair is itself African American resistance and rebellion, life and survival, "an act of God that came straight through Africa," precisely why it will not and cannot "be permanently hot-pressed or relaxed into surrender" (Wolfe, 1987, 22). Rapper KRS-1 Parker, in "Ya Strugglin'" (1990), comments on the dilemma faced by many African Americans trying to create a positive and healthy sense of themselves amid prevailing and celebrated European aesthetics of beauty: "Africa is so strong that once she puts a stamp on you, four hundred years of cold weather, lye and frying your hair shall not disguise you. As a matter of fact, she's so strong that no matter what chemical you put in your hair, she will come back and snatch it out." Chemical processes to control naturally growing hair are, as the rapper insists, often futile, costly, and frustratingly temporary.

As Herron offers this text (1997) specifically with little black girls in mind, since hair and beauty ideals plague them in ways from which little black boys are exempt,[12] she offers it as well to the parents of those little black girls who feel the need to straighten and hot-comb their daughters' hair to make it manageable and attractive. With bold warning labels on relaxer kit boxes, manufacturers recognize the safety factor with their products both in terms of potential eye injury, immediate scalp burns, and irritation from leaving the chemicals on the head too long, and in terms of hair loss and damage with repeated usage. The warnings on children's relaxer kits are the same ones found on adult relaxer kits; interestingly and ironically, all the warnings state boldly: "Keep out of the reach of children." While the necessary message of keeping harmful chemicals away from children is clear, it is intriguing that this warning appears on such a common nonmedicinal, noncleaning product that so many young black girls encounter long before they are able to make a decision for themselves about its use.[13] One response to a question regarding the safety of pressing a child's hair addressed to an *Essence* beauty consultant, directly expresses Herron's extended concern in her book:

> It's difficult to pinpoint a specific "safe age" when you can be sure you can press your child's hair without causing damage. The texture of a child's hair doesn't develop fully until around the age of six or seven. ... However, what's more important to realize is that pressing the hair can be a traumatic experience for youngsters. The very procedure of tugging on the hair with extreme heat can frighten a child and implant in her negative thinking about her hair. Therefore you need to take into account your reasons for wanting to press your child's hair. Why are you pressing it? Do you want more control of the hair, or just a straightened look? There are easy and stylish alternatives to pressing to achieve both. ("Beauty Answers," 1993, 18)

Still, the black hair care industry is saturated with products marketed specifically for preadolescent and adolescent daughters. One such television commercial and a printed advertisement for the same product picture two long- and straightened-haired, light-complected young girls, presumably between the ages of six and nine, playing dress-up with lipstick and mascara and exclaiming that they are "beautiful *because* they use PCJ Relaxer" (emphasis added). The commercial presents this product as a sure way for little black girls to be the female beauty ideal—to have hair that is "soft and silky and manageable." Another commercial, Pro-Line's Just for Me No-Lye Relaxing Crème, also marketed for young African Americans daughters, promises to give their hair "style, body and shine." With this product, "combing and styling [will be] worry-free" since the child's hair will be "soft, silky and free." Luster Products' PCJ "Original" Relaxer claims to leave young girls' hair "soft, silky and so manageable." PCJ No-Lye Conditioning and Crème Relaxer Kit allegedly allows a young black girl to have "silky easy care hair she can move, bounce, toss and twirl." *Nappy Hair* (Herron, 1997) is a direct challenge to individuals and to an industry insisting as does one *Ebony* advertisement that "Mommy gives us PCJ Pretty-N-Silky No-Lye Conditioning Relaxer *because* she loves us!" (emphasis added), and another from *Essence* (February 1997) for the relaxer Beautiful Beginnings, which claims:

> A Wonderful Start for Beautiful Hair. There's no doubt. Beautiful Beginnings Children's No-Lye Relaxer is the safest, gentlest children's relaxer you can buy. Only Beautiful Beginnings is made with Comfort Plus, a safeguard ingredient that helps prevent scalp irritation and damage. And with Beautiful Beginnings maintenance products, her hair will be softer, silkier and more manageable than ever before. Whether it's curls, twists, ponytails, or braids, Beautiful Beginnings from Dark & Lovely is a wonderful start for beautiful hair. The safest, gentlest Children's Relaxer. (125)

The ad's repeated emphasis on safety and gentleness invariably highlights the fact that the chemicals are dangerous and harmful. Notice also that there is no guarantee against scalp irritation and damage. And, although different young girl styles are listed—twists, ponytails, or braids—the ultimate goal of the product is to achieve softness, silkiness, and manageability, traits not generally associated with nonchemicalized African American hair.[14]

Herron offers in Brenda's story an alternative to negative perceptions of black people's hair in its untreated state. Brenda's family sees Brenda's nappy hair as a manifestation of a unique spiritual and cultural identity. Brenda's story is then a loud shout for revisionist thinking among black people who turn so often, quickly, easily, and unthoughtfully to alternatives to nappy. In contrast, there are no chemical hair care products marketed for white children. Only little black girls are indoctrinated early in the tyranny of achieving the beautiful hair ideal. White girls are usually teens before they are bombarded with the "need" to alter their hair chemically through coloring or perming. Commercials and advertisements marketed toward little white girls and their white mothers importantly deal with innocuous hair detanglers rather than with chemical straighteners.

Herron's text of Uncle Mordecai's story is framed as a revival sermon intended to bring lost souls back into the fold. His sermon, which might easily be variously called "Happy Nappy," "Nappy Happy," "Happy to be Nappy," "Nappy and Happy," or "Bein' Thankful for Whatcha Got," challenges each listener and reader to rethink negative perceptions of black people's hair and to reexamine blind subscription to traditions that mock black people because of hair textures and styles, especially as they relate to little black girls subjected to adult standards of black female beauty. Herron has, in this book, done more than write a children's story. Since we never get any sense of Brenda's own attitudes *about* her hair one way or the other—the story is presented as a parable about Brenda and her hair—the book is as much about the adults who need to be "saved" from their own misperceptions about themselves and others who look like them. From the opening announcement of its subject or sermonic text to its improvisational call-and-response and final shout of "Ain't it the truth," *Nappy Hair* "builds, its spirit draws you in, rolls you around, and doesn't let you go" (book jacket). Herron catches us up in the spiritual energy of a church revival that, in the words of poet-play-wright Ntozake Shange, is a celebration of life and living: "the roots of your hair/ what turns back when we sweat, run, make love, dance, get afraid, get happy: the tell-tale sign of living" (*Nappy Edges,* 1978).

That Brenda's hair is crown-shaped further reiterates the book's message of Afrocentric celebration. The shape of Brenda's hair even forms the silhouette of an African woman's headdress. This gathering of Brenda's family members, black people of different shades of brown and with Afrocentric hairstyles from braids to dreadlocks and Afros, is a celebration laced with humor in familiarity, revisionist history, and with emphasis on black community dramatized, revitalized, and sustained through talking, storytelling, preaching, and teaching. Importantly, *Nappy Hair* addresses both young and old and boys and girls in one historical, cultural, and rhythmic moment. It is a spiritual and cultural revival that provides a strong foundation for Brenda's self-identity as a young black girl bombarded with gender and racial ideals that exclude her. And if Brenda's family can resist the cultural aggressions that endeavor to dictate standards of female beauty, especially for little black girls, it is likely that Brenda is armed with a positive sense of her racial identity to resist an environment that seeks to deny or negate for little black girls—and black adults making decisions about little girls—the fact that beautiful, proud, and happy can be synonymous with nappy.

Veronica Chambers offers a sobering emotional note suggesting that change in social, political, and personal perceptions of the black hair ideal is taking place slowly:

Sometimes I see little girls, with their hair in braids and Senegalese twists, sporting cute little t-shirts that read HAPPY TO BE NAPPY and I get teary-eyed. I was born in the sandwich generation between the Black Power Afros of the sixties and the blue contact lenses and weaves of the eighties. In my childhood, no one seemed very happy to be nappy at all. (171)[15]

Indeed, Carolivia Herron's *Nappy Hair* does not claim to make hairstyle or texture a mirror of any individual's identity politics; it is nevertheless another important move to make adults more conscious of the urgent need to nurture the natural in its earliest stages. Herron's message of cultural celebration and self-acceptance rings loudly and proudly in my former student Isis Jones's unpublished poem "Nappy Hair" (1998):

Nappy hair, Nappy hair, Nappy hair!
Nappy hair holds the secrets to the recipes of life
Like plants hold the oxygen you breathe.
My naps seize all positive energy.
You don't hear them when they be speaking silently,
Telling me to do things life-saving.
My naps be paving the way for new kings,
Creating Gods and Queens
Praising Black things.

...

Nappy hair, Nappy hair, Nappy hair!
Nappy hair holds the secrets to the recipes for living.
While you spending your time on weaves and wigs,
My nappy hair gives me the self-esteem
That you look for in blonde images that do
nothing for ebony skin complexion.
Do you see your reflection in my knots?
Some know the power of locks
And refuse to damage them at any cost.
Nappy hair, Natural hair, Nappy hair, Natural hair!
I dare you to stand up and to stop being mute!
Get back to your roots!
While you be spending all your loot on chemicals,
I'm soaring, speaking telepathically with myself,
Inheriting my true wealth.
The secret is that
Nappy hair is Natural hair,
Nappy hair is Natural hair,
And natural hair is the key to the recipes for life!

(Isis Jones, 1998; used with permission)

THE HAIR DILEMMA: CHAOS OR ORDER?

BY VINCENZA MANGIOLINO

The history of the world shows us that hair has always been a powerful symbol, sometimes associated with religion, sometimes with mysticism, and sometimes with politics. Orthodox Jews, for instance, do not cut their children's hair until the age of three. In the Talmud, the Shalos Utshuvos Arugas Habosem explains that "A person is compared to the tree of the field" (Devorim 20:19). Just as it is forbidden to benefit from the fruit of a tree for the first three years because the fruit is considered Orlah, so too we do not cut the hair of a male child until he is three years old. According to legend, Hercules lost all of his formidable powers after an untimely haircut. In prerevolutionary France, the women of the upper classes favored elaborate hairstyles piled high on their heads. In Africa, the manner and style of the hair indicated not only religion and status but also wealth and origins.

In recent American history, hairstyles have been mandated more by the fashion industry than by political or socioeconomic reasons, with the exception of the 1960s. The era of free love was illustrated in the musical *Hair* (Rado and Ragni, 1968), in which hairstyle was political protest. Hippies, those the government loved to call radical left wing extremists, wore their hair long and as little cared for as possible in order to thumb their noses at the "establishment." Of note, Afros were also popular then as a symbol of the growing civil rights movement.

However, as we Americans have evolved, hair has become not only a fashion trend but also newsworthy. Dorothy Hamill scored high points in the ice skating competition of the Olympics not only for her performance but also for her perky new bob. Let us not forget how white American women viewers waited with bated breath each season to see Jennifer Aniston's new hairstyle and to be the first on the block to copy it. The current craze for flat-ironed hair has girls and women of all ages frying their hair to get that smooth, silky look. This is the good hair look of today. Billions of dollars are spent each year by American women (and men) to avoid bad hair days.

I firmly believe that the question of "good hair" transcends all cultures and races. I conducted an informal survey of about 58 women, with fairly equal representation of Caucasians, Hispanics, African Americans, and Asians. These women had hair types ranging from pin straight to the tight curls of an Afro. All of the women had issues with their hair: too curly, too frizzy, too dull, too coarse, or too straight. However, all responded, when questioned, that their vision of the perfect hair was a crown of silky, straight, glossy hair. Even the Asian females thought their hair was neither straight enough nor shiny enough to suit their tastes.

I tend to think that this ideal of "good hair" emanates from two sources: our innate desire to have order and our willingness to belong. Smooth silky hair is hair that is controlled. Frizzy, nappy hair is chaotic and perhaps gives us an unsettled feeling, contributing to the entropy in our universe. In addition, if we all conform to the ideal, we can all be a part of the greater community. This also gives rise to more order by eliminating diversity. Is this a good thing? Can we eliminate prejudices and biases by eliminating our diversity? Or, are we actually creating more bias by reneging on what is an integral part of our identities? The nagging thought in my head as I see innumerable clones of flat-ironed coiffures on the streets of New York is that we are losing ourselves in being slaves to this ideal. Perhaps we need the hippies back.

TALKING OUT LOUD: IDEAS FOR DISCUSSION

1. In his essay, "Black Hair/Style Politics" (1987), cultural critic Kobena Mercer maintains that natural hair is a social construct:

   As organic matter produced by physiological processes, human hair seems to be a natural aspect of the body. Yet hair is never a straightforward biological fact, because it is almost always groomed, prepared, cut, concealed, and generally worked upon by human hands. Such practices socialize hair, making it the medium of significant statements about self and society and the codes of value that bind them, or do not. In this way hair is merely a raw material, constantly processed by cultural practices which thus invest it with meaning and value.

   Discuss the meaning and validity of Mercer's statement. Does it challenge meaningfully our thinking and talking in oversimplified hair binaries—good and bad, black and white, beautiful and unattractive?

2. What is the prevalence of straight hair in African nations?
3. To what extent does hair have a gender-neutralizing dimension in theory and practice?
4. At what point do social prescription and expectation take away individual choice in hairstyle?

5. How do discussions of little girls and hair ideals inherently involve little boys?
6. What parallels do you recognize between the significance of hair among African Americans and perceptions of hair within other cultures and groups?

5

ROOTS THAT GO BEYOND BIG HAIR AND A BAD HAIR DAY
Nappy Hair Pieces

Although there is no single definition of *nappy*, words like *kinky* and *wild*[1] are often interchangeable with nappy but without the loaded historical baggage for African Americans; the term's impact is markedly different depending on the social contexts.[2] African American linguist Geneva Smitherman, in *Black Talk: Words and Phrases from the Hood to the Amen Corner* (1994), identifies nappy hair as kinky hair: "extremely curly hair, the natural state of African-American hair, curled so tightly it appears 'wooly.'" Clarence Major's edited *Juba to Jive: A Dictionary of African American Slang* (1994) offers that nappy hair is synonymous with kinky and wooly hair. Most generally, nappy hair resists a fine-tooth comb's easy movement through it. Acknowledging hair as one of the central components of discrimination within African American communities, African American poet Maya Angelou offers this comment:

> A hundred years ago, … there were churches in Philadelphia, in Virginia and in New Orleans which had a pine slab on the outside door of the church and a fine-tooth comb hanging on a string. And when you tried to go into the church you had to be able to stand beside that pinewood and be no darker than that, and take that fine-tooth comb and run it through your hair without snagging. That's how you could get into the church. ("Intra-Racism," 1)

Hair has long been a social marker of gender, race, and even class. African American author and educator Carolivia Herron's controversial children's book *Nappy Hair* (1997) focuses on an African American female child's "nappy hair," as detailed in her family's ritual of story-telling. Through Uncle Mordecai's narration and the family members' participation in the storytelling, Herron's text "performs" African American cultural identities of resistance and of individual and collective cultural affirmation.

In early 1998, when one of my undergraduate students and I read *Nappy Hair* as a duet at a youth session of the Arizona Alliance of Black High School Educators Conference, the mostly teenage black audience was ecstatic. They laughed and smiled and understood that the book celebrates an aspect of African American culture not often talked about in academic settings, presented in a way that is accessible and fun. In fact, after our reading, wherein the student and I alternated the calls and responses—an African American oral performance ritual involving a leader and a respondent—as typographically formatted in the book, several students wanted to know where they might purchase copies of the book. I used Herron's book to demonstrate how pursuing a formal academic interest in African American studies is a way of exploring the complexities of African American experience, specifically pointing out how Herron takes something traditionally perceived negatively by blacks—nappy hair—and challenges her readers to transform the negative into positive thinking and positive talking. My student then read one of her own original poems, also called "Nappy Hair," as a companion to Herron's book's celebratory message. The student's autobiographical poem challenges and invites African Americans to luxuriate in the mystery and wonderousness of nappy hair, even when family and friends insist that she do something about those kinks on her head. Her poem concludes: "Nappy hair is natural hair and natural hair is the key to the recipes of life." Students laughed and cheered the attitude of resistance and self-acceptance.

During the final moments of the session, I asked students to share a "snap"—an intraracial ritual of insult—that deals with black people's hair, an exercise that had students and myself rolling out of our chairs with laughter, not self-mockingly, but as a celebration of the art of storytelling and redefinition. One student offered, "Yo momma's hair is so nappy, she has to take painkillers to comb it." Another chimed, "Yo momma's hair is so short and nappy, her head looks like it's full of stitches." The students understood the exercise of snapping (also termed dissing, cracking, or playing the dozens) as a display of verbal gymnastics. They also understood that somehow the act of "dissin'" about hair was one way of appropriating a negative image from a Euro-centric culture that does not value nonstraight, non-European hair and making that the source of a celebratory communal storytelling ritual.

Having had such a positive response to the book from this youth audience and just previously with my own two children, then ages six and nine, I left the session and the conference even more excited about what Herron's book had achieved politically, aesthetically, and cultur- ally. When a whirlwind of controversy surfaced in national headlines in the United States the fall of 1998, these headlines told the story of anger, criticism, and upheaval:

"After Objections to a Book, A Teacher is Transferred" (*New York Times*)

"Author Defends *Nappy Hair* Book" (*Columbia Missouri Tribune Online*)

"Chancellor Says Parents Were Misguided in *Nappy Hair* Epi- sode" (*New York Times*)

"Fallout from *Nappy Hair* Furor" (*New York Times*)

"Flap over *Nappy Hair* Book Leads to Teacher's Transfer" (*Educa- tion Week*)

"*Nappy Hair* Teacher Gets Complaints at New School" (*New York Post*)

"New York Teacher Runs Afoul of Political Correctness" (*Kansas City Star*)

"N.Y. Teacher Runs into a Racial Divide" (*Washington Post*)

"Queens Parents Happy with *Nappy Hair* Teacher" (*Boston Herald*)

"School Officials Support Teacher on Book that Parents Call Racially Insensitive" (*New York Times*)

"Teacher Threatened over Book Requests Transfer" (*San Jose Mer- cury News*)

"Threatened Over Book, Teacher Leaves School" (*New York Times*)

"White Teacher Accused of Racism Fears for Life" (*Arizona Republic*)

"White Teacher, Black Parents, Unthinking Condemnation" (*San Jose Mercury News*)

I was stunned. I was shocked that parental objections to the book had led to threats of violence against Ruth Sherman, a white teacher who had shared the book with her black and Latino third-grade students in Brooklyn, New York. As I read headline after headline dealing with the controversy, it was clear to me that the problems some black parents had with the book were politically, historically, and psychologically bigger than Ruth Sherman and Herron's book.

For one, some parents had problems with Herron's use of the word *nappy*. Perhaps the white teacher was unaware of the political, historical, and emotional baggage still connected with a word that Raymond S. Ross includes in his 1967 list of "Racially Potent Words" alongside other racially offensive and loaded words like "the n word," darkie, Sambo, Mammy, and spook. What had not occurred to me was the extent to which some African Americans have been unable to redefine as positive that which has been traditionally perceived as negative, as unattractive, and as ugly. The controversy highlights fundamental connections between language and perception and between language and identity, demonstrating how certain words consciously or unconsciously carry with them loaded emotional and psychological responses. As controversy over this book reveals, some words have a history bigger than the historians and the students of history.

That Ruth Sherman is not black was for many a major issue here. As an African American, I could have probably gone into that third-grade classroom as I did at the Arizona youth conference and read the book, recreating its rich lyrical cadences and rhythms without parental resistance. Because of the ever-present tensions between European standards and African American realities—everything from standards of physical beauty to "standard" English—Ruth Sherman never really had a chance with this book as a public performance of multicultural celebration. When the reality of the book's title and subject along with the white teacher reading the text in its vernacular format reached some black parents, those offended could see only a white teacher imitating black folks talking and laughing at black folks' hair. In fact, my guess is that her white face reading aloud in the black vernacular of Herron's text became for some an echo of 1800s minstrelsy, when whites who mocked and ridiculed blacks through burnt-corked face, exaggerated language, behavior, and gesture. To draw a parallel about real and perceived cultural and racial territorial claims, I offer this example. At my predominantly white university and in my predominantly white department, I have an office decorated with black "Americana"—racist memorabilia from pickaninny and mammy dolls to coon and Uncle Ben advertisements and Aunt Jemima pins—that I use in my multimedia, interdisciplinary teaching of African American literature. I cannot imagine my white colleagues, who also teach African American literature but not without suspicions from many students, getting away with an office decorated as and proudly proclaimed as my "colored museum." Indeed, in any black–white race dialogue, lines of privilege and authority are for some clearly drawn and fiercely policed.

That offended black parents and community members launched an attack on Herron for writing the book is intriguing; she admits receiving a death threat via e-mail. This hostile public response from some echoes the backlash against Spike Lee after he aired gritty linens of African Americans' intraracist cultural perceptions and discriminatory practices in his movie *School Daze* (1988). Along with Lee's comments about the absurdity of African Americans treating each other better or worse based on the hue of brown skin, the degree of hair straightness or nappiness is also central to this public behavior and individual self-perception. In Sherman's case, her students loved the book and wanted pages to read and take home. To my knowledge, no criticisms of the book have included actual negative responses from Sherman's students. The third graders' excitement over Herron's book parallels that of my youth conference audience. In a March 1999 intergenerational interview, part of the midterm project in my African American children's literature course, a seven-year-old African American girl cites *Nappy Hair* as her favorite book: "I just got *Nappy Hair* and I like it. It's my favorite [book]. It is funny and the hair is funny. I like the pictures too." In a companion interview, the child's African American mother shares her excitement about the book as well: "I bought *Nappy Hair* for my kids after I read it myself. I liked the pictures, thought they were colorful. And [my daughter] loves that book. She won't put it down."

Not surprisingly, the national attention generated by this controversy dramatically increased the sales of the book. Yet, what intrigues me is that at the root of this controversy is hair's lingering racial, emotional, and psychological pain, of which some African Americans cannot rid themselves. Even after the 1960s "Black Is Beautiful" movement, there persists an intracultural tendency to rate African American adults and children on the "good" and "bad" hair scale: "good" hair is perceived as hair closest to white people's hair: long, straight, silky, bouncy, manageable, healthy, and shiny. "Bad hair" is short, matted, kinky, Brillo pad-wooly, coarse, brittle, and *nappy*.

Certainly, *Nappy Hair* is one of the richest contributions to this important and ongoing intraracial discussion of hair politics as it relates to gender and racial mythologies of beauty.[3] Autobiographical, the book is "based on her experiences as a Visiting Scholar at Harvard Divinity School and on the fun her own family poked at her nappy hair when she was a girl" (book jacket). While the book revises notions of black female beauty, it also teaches and entertains as it celebrates African American oral traditions.

The orality rituals of traditional black churches ground Herron's book. From the preacherly Uncle Mordecai's opening announcement of his "text"—Brenda's nappy hair—the book becomes a moment in a church service full of "talkin' back" to the preacher. With vocal responses rhythmically punctuating the preacher/storyteller's words about Brenda and her hair, the family members, as the vocally responsive church congregation, become integral to the performance of the tale, forming a necessary symbiosis between the storyteller and his audience. As the sermon is preached, the family audience-as-church congregation members acknowledge and embrace Brenda's story as their own, the storyteller taking them through Brenda's ancestral slave history of being brought from Africa to America and through the horrors of family separations at the slave block ("sold your momma for a nickel [or] a buffalo" and "your daddy for a dime"). The subsequent social and political resistance of African Americans in the New World is also recreated as Brenda boldly challenges—even as a child—any efforts to restrain or straighten her nappy hair: "the kinkiest, the nappiest, the fuzziest, the most screwed up, squeezed up, knotted up, tangled up, twisted up, nappiest … hair you've ever seen in your life." Brenda's hair becomes a metaphor of her resistance: she speaks "good" and "bad" English and refuses to be shackled by others' perceptions of her beauty. The illustrations of Brenda and her family exude confidence, self-knowledge, and historical awareness.

Regarding how Brenda ended up with this nappy hair, the preacher-as-storyteller dramatizes, improvises, incants, and draws on folklore to challenge Western mythologies that God favored those with white skin, blue eyes, and long, stringy hair. Herron's revisionist text presents a presumably Afrocentric God who, in moments of creating the world, wanted very specifically to have nappy hair on the earth. As brown angels approach God to discover "Why [he] gotta be so mean, why [he] gotta be so willful, why [he] gotta be so ornery, thinking about giving that nappy, nappy hair to that innocent little child," Herron presents a God who creates a child with hair that symbolizes spiritual completion: "Napping up her hair, five, six, seven, maybe eight complete circles per inch. … I'm talking about eight complete circles per inch." Herron draws on Afrocentric philosophy that emphasizes circularity of existence rather than linearity, fluidity rather than stasis, orality rather than literacy, ritual rather than ceremony. Symbolically, Brenda's hair is resistance and rebellion against Western servitude. It is also life and survival, "an act of God that came straight through Africa," that will not and cannot "be hot-pressed [or relaxed] into surrender" (Wolfe, 1987, 22).

Herron's 1997 book is also about family; the family has gathered to commune and fellowship, and a common activity at such gatherings is to laugh and share stories that they all know and love to hear, to tell and to perform again and again. It is also about familiarity with black folk rituals of talking, from the pulpit to the picnic. As Herron offers this book with little black girls in mind—hair and beauty ideals plague them in ways from which little black boys are exempt—she offers it simultaneously to little girls' parents who feel the need to straighten and hot-comb their daughters' hair, allegedly to make it more manageable and attractive.

As a speakerly text, *Nappy Hair* is meant to be read aloud with multiple voices that highlight the performative high art and drama of traditional southern black church services. Herron's use of black vernacular allows the rhythmic cadences and textures of black speech to define, create, and decorate African American identity. The detail that Brenda can "talk the king's English [and] the queen's English too" perhaps addresses national debates regarding the legitimacy of Ebonics in black children's education process. Clearly that debate, erupting during the same year as Herron's book publication, was not about teaching African Americans vernacular English in the classroom, but rather about legitimizing the language and experience some African American children bring into classrooms from a family environment that is just as legitimate as the academic school environment. That Brenda communicates effectively with those who speak a different "standard" of English does not hinder on any level her ability to learn and master standard English simultaneously.

Illustrator Joe Cepeda's rich dark colors (browns, oranges, golds, greens, and pinks) make this book especially inviting to kindergarten and elementary school youngsters, and his decision to make Brenda's hair almost crownlike reiterates the book's message of Afrocentric and queenly celebration. The shape of Brenda's hair even forms the silhouette of an African women's headdress. Cepeda also pays attention to variations of black people's skin tones and hairstyles: Brenda's family members are different shades of brown and have braids, dreadlocks, and Afros. With its visual appeal, its cultural celebration laced with humor in familiarity, its revisionist history, and its emphasis on black community sustained through talking, testifying, storytelling, preaching, and teaching, *Nappy Hair* appeals to young and old and boys and girls in one historical, cultural, and rhythmic shout.

In a conference session I moderated with author Carolivia Herron as a special guest,[4] not long after the publication of *Nappy Hair*, Herron outlined what she perceives as the three components of the controversy over her book: the fact that parents received photocopies of selected pages from the book, and pictures of African Americans do not photocopy without dangerously darkened distortion; the fact that the teacher reading the black-voiced book was white; and the fact that many African Americans are still very sensitive about the word *nappy*, both interracially and intraracially. For her, she added, what has been missing from all the controversy is the reality that the children to whom Ruth Sherman read the book enjoyed it tremendously. The children, according to Sherman's account to Herron, responded to Sherman's calls with big gestures, creative body movements, and funny voices. They then begged Sherman for copies of some of the pages. Perhaps African American adults offended by the book should witness children's responses. Relates Herron:

> All the children I've talked to love the book. ... I talked with a fourth grade in Washington, D.C., one hundred percent African-American. When I came in and said "I'm going to read you a book called *Nappy Hair*," they all went "Huh!" Within an hour, they were competing to see who had the nappiest hair. ... In Binghamton, New York, that's all white, there were two or three black families with two or three black girls. We chanted the story back and forth, with everyone getting into it. You should have seen the look on the three black girls' faces as they looked at their own kind—all happy about nappy hair—and then at the white faces all enchanted about how wonderful this hair is. It's about pride and respect. Everybody was speechless. They couldn't even talk after that.

Surely through talking and testifying about it, hair can cease to be the marker that continues to divide, to reward, or to attack.

DISGUISED AS NICE

BY C. A. HAMMONS

Pains

Pain is the body's reaction to stress, illness, and injury. Pain is a relative state. A "little pain" implies degrees that can be amplified to a teeth-grinding, eye-popping implosion. Black women have accepted suffering for the sake of appearances as inevitable in the pursuit of fleeting physical beauty. The hot-comb method utilized for routine hair-straightening treatments during the 1950s and 1960s imbued in me an intimate acquaintance with the levels and varieties of pain that accompanied attempts to convert my nappy hair.

For a black girl in the postmodern era, the path to integration, assimilation, and finally acceptance started at the top of her head—always. To imply that the mind was neglected would be a disservice. Three-hundred-plus years of being African American females was distilled for young mental consumption by impressing on girls the necessity of being prepared to interact with whites—more pain. If your hair was in its natural state, you were not prepared to be and therefore could not be a "nice girl." The infrastructure of "niceness" was a complex system of deportment, which had at its apex the mandate always to present yourself to the world "shining like a new penny" and with vinyl-straight, shining hair. The discomfort that accompanied hair pressing was inevitable. Acquiescence often depended on liberal administrations of an expeditious and highly effective "rod." Life in ultraconservative Phoenix, Arizona, found us an obedient, undistinguished multitude with our patent leather toes always walking a fine line.

Of necessity, to subdue the unruly requires physical force. The foremost enemy of the legions loosed by Madame C. J. Walker focused its considerable might and ingenuity on an equally formidable genetic enemy: nappy hair. My grandmother was a zealous foot soldier, with many a slick pate under her belt. I imagine how the Walker objective of sustained employment autonomy would have been of greater pragmatic attraction to her. Like Madame Walker, she had little education and performed physically demanding, low-paying work; both were Mississippi girls. What my grandmother could not empathize with was "bad hair." Clottee Annie Laurie Henry was the daughter of a young black girl and an Irish superintendent of schools who had access to as many thirteen-year-old black girls as he could reach. While my grandmother did not have the red hair and green eyes that her eight half-sisters inherited, she was endowed with flowing, raven-black hair in her youth. To add further to an already smoldering confluence of explosive subjective factors, my grandmother was Catholic. Madame C. J. Walker held near patron saint status in our lives.

Preparations

Before one could arrive at the hair-straightening moment of truth where metal met protein, there were meticulous stages of excruciating preparation. In black households all over America, the battlefield was the kitchen. The kitchen sink would have been commandeered for shampoos on Saturday morning, and no food was prepared until the last head was rinsed. Because my hair is especially thick, I would kneel with my head under the bathtub spigot while the water ran full force, the resistant Prell shampoo ebbed and rebubbled. The pain of finally being able to stand and straighten my back and neck was exquisite.

This was the only small portal where we felt and saw our "real" hair. The wind blowing through my wet hair has always been an acutely delicious sensation. My grandmother would have been mortified.

The "breaking" phase of hair pressing was just as odious as the word implies. This involved parting and combing the hair into workable segments. The area of merchandising Madame Walker overlooked was the manufacture of part-making appliances and combs for thick, nappy hair. The combing out often diminished to forcefully dragging the comb through the hair until it tore. It was usually at this juncture that the switch, the belt, the shoe, the hand, or a stern word would have been introduced to restore the (girl) sitter to "her right mind." Since I was the youngest of four girls (and with the most hair), patience was nonexistent by the time I took my turn in the hot seat.

The principal cudgel wielded by the Walker Agents was the pressing comb, tempered metal with closely spaced teeth, which darkened with time and use. The kitchen was the source of ammo for nap assaults because of the heat provided by the full-open flame of the gas range; the site where *discomfort* merged with *danger*. The comb did not have a thermostat, leaving the absolute control of the heated comb to the presser. A slight variance in the determination of "hot" and "too hot" has often been pitiful.

The nice girl transformation began in earnest when the comb was literally on the fire. The hair from scalp to ends was generously coated in a petroleum dressing: Dixie Peach, Hy-Beaute, Bergamot, Sulphur 8, Alberto VO5, Posners, or just good old Vaseline, which was purchased by the tub. Pressing creams were later developed for a more "natural" (white) look.

Pronouncements

The pressing combs had smooth wooden handles that in short order became slick; simple rubber grips would have been an innovation. The ears and kitchen (nape of the neck) would inevitably sustain burns and battle scars; the hot grease would often melt along the hair and burn the scalp of the sitter and the hands of the presser. The grease or damp hair would sometimes make a sizzling noise, which caused the sitter to flinch involuntarily and sustain another stinging burn and more recriminations. Sometimes, my grandmother would give my hair a hard pull because I was not holding my head in the position she wanted and she was just too weary to tell me again. Predictably, early on in the process, she would be "tired of talking." Often, as the pressing comb was pulled away, the limp hair would fall across my arm or face; those burns did not raise marks. Madame Walker would have probably done well manufacturing asbestos capes and gloves, too.

The hot grease raised a smoke and odor comparable to a solemn high mass. The smoke would get in my grandmother's eyes until she was driving blind. "I can't see, I can't see," she would say, still working the comb through my hair. Some of the most fervent prayers I ever said were made in the hot seat. My family thought that I was asthmatic as a child, a condition I "grew out of." I wonder how many attacks resulted from gulping frying hair. That the physiology of the hard-working Walker Agents was uniquely suited to the work of hair-straightening is a given: the work ethic involved in the daily use of bare hands to perform near-impossible feats is not for quitters. In addition to burns, I imagine the hazards for Walker Agents would be eye, respiratory, hip, back, neck, foot, and hand and wrist ailments. The last head pressed can never expect the level of styling finesse that the first or even second enjoyed.

During those long hours spent in the pressing chair, my grand-mother would harangue my "bad hair" and other deficient aspects of my physique and character, often tapping the tip of the hot comb on my scalp for emphasis. Those burns would rest under the hair to be revived daily by a brush or the adjustment of a plait, where the pain sharply announced that it was still there.

The air around our relationship was always as thick and heavy as that smoky kitchen. I was a delicate little girl routinely assaulted. To imagine the amount of what we now consider child abuse, multiply the number of every little black girl you ever saw with unnaturally straight (or long) hair times the frequency that hair was manipulated, and they will each have a story about pain.

Pride and Prejudice

When the wind blew and my pressed hair retained the odor of smoke, a wave of melancholy often came over me. Sometimes, I was a very sad little girl, indeed.

My grandmother was especially proud of her "hard press." A hard press is arrow-straight and can only be accomplished by double or tri-ple pressing. My older sisters despaired it. They would go to their rooms and immediately rub a towel over and through their hair as if they were drying it again in a futile effort to degrease it. Because the straightening procedure was so arduous, we were fastidious about keeping our hair dry. I am sure we missed out on the fun and freedom of swimming, but we could not let our edges (hairline around the face) nap up and endure that process without making an effort to avert it. I swear I could outrun the rain. It might seem that grease would repel the water, but even bathtub steam would fray our edges and cast us back into the hot seat.

I never thought pressed hair contributed to my cuteness. I would never be blue-eyed, but a lot of people were not. I would never have blond hair (until I got older). Even fewer people had blond hair and blue eyes, and I was okay with that. In my little Catholic school, there were plenty of people who were worse off lookswise than I. Being cute was not a dilemma that ever complicated my childhood. I never equated pressed hair with attractiveness. My pressed hair was a disguise that announced to the world that I came from a family as cultured as white folks, and that I was an especially "nice" colored girl.

TALKING OUT LOUD: IDEAS FOR DISCUSSION

1. From the early 1900s until about the mid-1960s, hair pressing became a booming economic national phenomenon. Aside from the technical training Walker Agents received, how were they able to matriculate into black communities to establish shops and acquire property and status in Western states that were not as densely populated with African Americans?

2. By all accounts, Secretary of State Condoleezza Rice is an example of the evolution of a nice African American girl. During the 1950s and 1960s, examples of nice and attractive young African American women were generally only found within the girl's family or sphere of travel. There were not many opportunities for young girls to see black entertainers, and it is not likely many of them would have withstood scrutiny under the terms of nice criteria. As a result, our image role models were white public figures like Natalie Wood, Annette Funicello, and Audrey Hepburn. Has this imaging of female beauty changed along race lines, and whose hair and overall style do young African American girls (5–18 years old) most admire and emulate today?

3. In her popular 1980s dance tune, "Vogue," Madonna claims: "Beauty is where you find it" and that "it makes no difference if you're black or white/if you're a boy or a girl." To what extent is Madonna's tune a study in contradiction in terms of both gender and race?

4. Are African American girls still being raised with a system of what is nice? Has the emphasis shifted significantly from appearance (hair) to something else?

5. Torture victims have often described the cessation of the actual pain(s) as bearing a pleasurable intensity. What were the likely effects of such frequent exposure to pain on the conduct of the girls that endured hair pressing?
6. Read the directions and warnings on a home relaxing kit. Do these instructions highlight contradictions and ambivalence on any levels?
7. To what extent is a discussion about hair of black girls and women also a discussion about hair of black men and boys?
8. Poet and playwright Pearl Cleage has written and performed at the 1990 National Black Arts Festival at Spelman College (Atlanta, GA), a piece called "Hair Piece," wherein she laments with humor and biting cynicism the loss of precious hours, days, weeks, months, and years "obsessing" over her hair before accepting her own nappy-headedness. Discuss Cleage's poem and the multilayered and nuanced complexities that connect race, gender and class.
9. Analyze the lyrics of songs about hair overall or songs that make passing references to hair. Which tunes celebrate or challenge or perpetuate stereotypes about beauty? One example is India.Arie's "I Am Not My Hair," from her 2006 album *Testimony: Volume 1, Life & Relationship.*

6

DON'T CONDEMN WHITE TEACHER OVER
NAPPY HAIR
(AN EDITORIAL)

As a white teacher, perhaps Ruth Sherman was unaware that within African American culture head hair is a big deal. Surely, there was no way for her to expect that reading Carolivia Herron's *Nappy Hair* (1997) to her third-grade black and Latino students in Brooklyn, New York, would lead to public outcries of racism, threats of violence, and her subsequent departure from teaching at that school.

National reaction to this teacher's innocent act of celebrating a dimension of African American experience reveals the continued preoccupation, perhaps even an unconscious obsession, with hair care, as well as with hair textures, grades, and lengths.

Painfully real even today is a cultural tendency to rate African Americans—even within families—on the "good" and "bad" hair scale. Good hair is perceived as hair closest to white people's hair: long, straight, silky, bouncy, manageable, healthy, and shiny. Bad hair is short, matted, kinky, coarse, brittle, woolly, and nappy.

Treatments of head hair abound in African American folklore, literature, and popular culture, from racist minstrel songs of the 1800s to African American folktales like "Why the Negro Has Kinky Hair."

Yet, the black folks' hair issue has not been dealt with much in children's texts, which is ironic since much adult African American literature deals with little black girls coming to terms with their hair amid culturally competing beauty mythologies.

The long, straight blond tresses of Rapunzel and Barbie and television commercials about innocuous detanglers for little white girls contrast with the potentially dangerous chemical relaxers celebrated in commercials and black magazine ads aimed at African American mothers and their preadolescent daughters: "Mommy gives us PCJ Pretty-N-Silky No-Lye Conditioning Relaxer because she loves us!" and Pro-Line's Soft and Beautiful Just for Me is "America's #1 Children's Relaxer—The Answer to a Mother's Prayer, A New Formula for Coarse Hair!"

Nappy Hair is one of the richest contributions to this ongoing intraracial discussion of hair politics as it relates to gender and racial mythologies of beauty.

It celebrates the uniqueness of black people's hair within the context of rich African American cultural traditions. While the book revises notions of black female beauty, it also teaches and entertains as it luxuriates in African American oral traditions: storytelling; rap; folklore; the performance nature of traditional black church services.

Herron's book is about family. Members of Brenda's family have gathered to share stories that they all know and love to hear repeated and performed. It is also about familiarity with black folk rituals of talking from the pulpit to the picnic.

Autobiographical, the book is "based on the fun [Herron's] own family poked at her nappy hair when she was a girl." Writing specifically with little black girls in mind, Herron addresses little black girls' parents who feel the need to straighten and hot-comb their daughters' hair.

The book beckons Herron's readers to reexamine the psychological and spiritual implications behind the negativity associated with nappy hair. Herron offers in Brenda's story an alternative in family perception—Brenda's family sees Brenda's nappy hair as her uniqueness, as their spiritual and cultural identities—and a call for revisionist thinking among black folks who turn so quickly and easily to alternatives to nappiness.

As a kind of revival sermon, *Nappy Hair* intends to bring lost ones back into the fold. As a parable about Brenda and her hair, the book is as much about the adults who need to be saved from their own misperceptions as about themselves.

Clearly, Herron has done more than write a children's book. She has challenged people to rethink negative perceptions of black people's hair. From the opening lines of the sermonic story to the final "Ain't it the truth," *Nappy Hair* catches us up in the spiritual energy of a church revival. Indeed, Carolivia Herron, Ruth Sherman, and others know the psychological, emotional, and even spiritual healing power of this children's book. Let the church say "Amen!"

AT THE RIGHT TIME, IN THE RIGHT PLACE: HAIR GROWING IN ALL PLACES

BY KIM CURRY-EVANS

Ruth Sherman just happened to read a book at the right time, in the right place. A white teacher presenting a topic about diverse cultures certainly is not new, but Sherman came under fire from the African American community for presenting a book about a black girl coming to terms with the natural texture of her hair, which speaks to sensitive topics about race that still lie just below the surface for generations still dealing with the stereotypical misrepresentations of their heritage. The resulting fallout from the Brooklyn, New York, community became a country-wide lightning rod. In particular, it was an opportunity for the black community to turn the mirror on itself and address long-standing issues of self-perception through the lens of a Eurocentric view of beauty. In addition, it was an appeal to understand that an acceptance of multiple voices—not just one specific voice, paired with an ethnically appropriate face—can shed light and enlighten our youth. This chapter defends Ruth Sherman's innocent attempt to provide a great story for her elementary school classroom.

What Lester touches on in this chapter—and what needs to be empha-sized—is that Carolivia Herron's book *Nappy Hair* (1997) is actually a call to African Americans to abandon the good and bad hair syndrome, yet another way to divide an already-fractured community based on skin tone and hair textures, but instead revise its perceptions and accept that good hair comes in all types, not just the long, straight, and flowing tresses that typify mainstream beauty ideals. Since slavery, African Americans have been conking, pressing, dyeing, straightening, and relaxing their hair to look like something that naturally it is not. Why? The explanations are abundant and range from ease and manageability in daily maintenance, to wanting to make a different fashion statement. Indeed, for too long, African Americans have been beholden to what W. E. B. Dubois coined as *double-consciousness*, a "sense of always looking at one's self through the eyes of others." Through *Nappy Hair*, Herron attempts to show that blacks need not go to great lengths to be beautiful, that they are beauti-ful because of the unique nappiness of their tresses. The white teacher, Sherman, was simply advocating for the cause by reading the book to her largely African American and Latino class.

But, context is everything. A white woman reading a book about a black girl's hair, with the lilt of the gospel church in the voice—in accordance with the way the story is written—can still cause a black community to be uncomfortable. For African Americans, the perception is not that far off from the early twentieth-century minstrel shows, in which whites purposely denigrated African American characteristics for entertainment purposes. Ironically, altering the scenario so that the teacher is black instead of white immediately creates an image of calm, whereas before it was one of unease and angst. The African American Brooklyn community outraged by Sherman's book choice was unconsciously tapping into those historical reserves that dictated that whites taking on the voices of blacks should tread lightly since the damage has already been done. After all, how can a white person know and understand the struggles of African Americans, particularly when it comes to their hair? William Styron suffered a similar argument after writing the story *The Confessions of Nat Turner* (1967). Black Americans took issue with whether a white man, this time an author, could authentically create the voice of his main character and narrator, a black slave, regardless of the fictitious nature of the novel.

As an art curator, I have seen firsthand how a white interpretation of African American material can create discord among blacks. In 2001, the Scottsdale Museum of Contemporary Art exhibited the work of nationally known African American artist Beverly McIver, whose paintings are typically self-portraits in black clown makeup, which is also frequently taken to be minstrel blackface. Many of the museum's black visitors were visibly upset and enraged, wondering if the museum was poking fun at a sensitive issue within the black community (minstrelsy) and incorrectly assuming that the artist was white. The museum realized that they had missed the boat by assuming that their audience, which was largely white, would automatically understand the artist's message, which was really about growing up poor and black in North Carolina, loving the freedoms that clowns have to express themselves behind the mask of paint, and coming to terms with being an African American female. A museum that typically catered to a white audience realized that a more sensitive approach, which included more interactive dialogue and plenty of explanatory signage, was necessary to convey McIver's distinctly African American voice properly to the museum's black and white audience. Again, however, context is everything. McIver's paintings were recently exhibited at the 40 Acres Art Gallery, centered in the inner-city community of Oak Park, Sacramento; the audience for the gallery is primarily African American. Unlike the reception in Scottsdale, Arizona, the reception to McIver's work was one of widespread acceptance and emotional release.

In the guise of a children's book, Herron's *Nappy Hair* (1997) is actually a warning cry to the black community, using hair as a means to review its own notions of beauty. Regardless of who or what becomes the vehicle for that cry, whether it is a black author or a white teacher, the least a community can do is take the time to hear and understand the message. *Nappy Hair* is about how the identities of African American girls can be shaped based on an acceptance of their natural beauty; it is up to the community to support that message, regardless of the messenger.

TALKING OUT LOUD: IDEAS FOR DISCUSSION

1. Why and how are blacks still sensitive about whites' perceptions of them?
2. Marlon Riggs's 1987 documentary, *Ethnic Notions: Black People in White Minds*, is about the prevalence of negative images associated with blackness and black people in literature and popular culture: film, magazines, newspapers, commercial products, and music. The documentary looks at images from slavery and minstrelsy through the 1970s and 1980s. Having viewed the film, discuss whether the film's narrative perspective is or is not limited to black victimization. To what extent are blacks challenging or absorbing negative perceptions of blackness? Extend the film's discussion to the twenty-first century. Are such images still present, and if so, where and why?
3. What advice would you give Ruth Sherman to avoid such a controversial moment in her future teaching to diverse student audiences?
4. How might *Nappy Hair* be considered a "black" text? What makes it a black text? Does a teacher talk about this children's text any differently than any other children's text?
5. What is the difference between a white's oral performance of *Nappy Hair* and a black's performance of this same text? Why and how does this difference emerge?
6. If *Nappy Hair* is Brenda's story of self-acceptance of her nappy hair, where is her voice in the story? Have the family members silenced her in their storytelling? Can they speak for her? Is their telling of the story as much about their own racial self-acceptance as about Brenda's?
7. How does the narrative of *Nappy Hair* connect to other African American oral rituals such as playing the dozens and sermons?
8. How is this book's story like a blues song? How does the story mirror some rap performances?
9. During this national controversy, we heard from Ruth Sherman and from the concerned parents. What were the children's voices, and where were they in the controversy?

10. Analyze the messages of other children's books about hair. How do the messages of these books compare to and contrast Herron's? One such book is bell hooks's *Happy to Be Nappy* (1999), published after *Nappy Hair*. Why is hooks's book not as controversial as Herron's? Do the books convey parallel messages about race, gender and beauty ideals?

7

ANGELS OF COLOR
Divinely Inspired or Socially Constructed?

i'm
gonna put black angels
in all the books and a black
Christchild in Mary's arms i'm
gonna make black bunnies black
fairies black santas black
nursery rhymes and
                    black
ice cream

—Mari Evans, "Vive Noir!" (1973)

Whenever my wife and I decorated our Christmas tree, we were annu-
ally reminded that finding angels of color as ornaments or on Christmas
cards[1]—or even a Valentine's Day Cupid that is dark-complected—is
as futile as finding a black clown to complete our then infant son's circus theme nursery. This near absence of non-white angels in popular
culture[2] and literature (both adults' and children's) signals far broader
political, social, and cultural implications. Are our Western sensibilities
violated when we imagine a black Jesus, a black Adam and Eve, and even
angels of color?[3]

The subject of numerous articles and books,[4] inspiration for at least
five mail-order companies, a bimonthly journal about angels (*Angel-
Watch*), and the Angel Collectors Club, angels continue to hold mys-
tic fascination. Indeed, while we propose to know about their divine

functions and purposes, their alleged interventions into human affairs, and their appearances in both male and female forms, we often fail to imagine and to image them as possessing anything but Caucasian skin tone. Is it inherently contradictory to conceptualize angels as anything but light and white?

African American actor-playwright Ossie Davis, in his telling exercise on the King's English, "The English Language Is My Enemy!" (1967, 18) simply examined *Roget's Thesaurus of the English Language*, comparing connotative positive and negative associations of "whiteness" and "blackness." His findings revealed that of 134 synonyms for whiteness, 44 are favorable or pleasing (e.g., purity, cleanness, immaculateness, bright, shining, ivory, fair, blond, stainless, clean). Of the 120 synonyms for blackness, 60 are decidedly negative (e.g., sinister, deadly, dirty, foul, evil). It is no stretch to link our past and present associations of angels with whiteness not only in their usual white robes, but also with their usually white skin. The antithesis of angels' whiteness is blackness.

The Bible[5] and Milton's *Paradise Lost* (1674) offer extensive commentary on the complexity of the angelic orders, and not surprisingly, their angels are always imaged as white. Does imagining black angels that are not fallen or devils shake the very foundation of our Western cultural aesthetics? Does relying on Western images limit our ability to perceive non-white angels? When questioned about why the needlepoint selections of angels in *Holidays Remembered* (1993) are all pink-fleshed, Consumer Sales representative Judy Millard responded: "Our needlework adaptations … were charted from antique post cards and ornamental scraps" (letter to author, 22 April 1993). As if to settle the matter with her response about the authority of the past, she reassuringly added that another of their books, *Christmas Portraits* (1991), does present a black Santa.

In African American adult literature, black angels are imaginable and have been used to attack the Southern racist social order that many "Christian" whites allegedly believe will be reinstated in the heavenly hereafter. For instance, Ralph Ellison's short story "Flying Home" (1944), presents a fantasy in which an elderly black man, Jefferson, endeavoring to teach an intellectually arrogant and culturally detached young black man about the glass ceiling of racism that prevents him from active duty as a military pilot, imagines dying and going to heaven. Jefferson explains his celebration of heavenly equality with white angels as an escape from the restrictive existence of blacks in the Deep South:

I went to heaven and right away started to sproutin' me some wings. Six good ones, they was. Just like the white angels had. I couldn't hardly believe it. ... I went and found me some colored angels—somehow I didn't believe I was an angel till I seen a real black one, ha yes! (in Emmanuel and Gross, 1968, 260-261)

While Jefferson is using his story to attack American hypocrisy, the angels symbolize black soldiers, like himself, unable to pilot planes in World War II. His metaphor further extends to encompass the very nature of a racist heaven created by the same hypocrisy and bigotry of racist white Southern Christians.

Jefferson then details how heaven was full of Southern racists who, in their efforts to maintain their heavenly order, insisted that black angels wear harnesses when they flew. Jefferson, as a black angel, is a threat to the alleged harmony of the white heavenly community when he demonstrates his finesse at flying without a harness, using only one wing, and with incredible speed. Consequently kicked out of heaven for "speedin'" and sentenced to live on earth in Jim Crow Alabama, Jefferson rejoices in his experience and power, however short-lived: "While I was up [t]here I was the flyinest sonofabitch what ever hit heaven!" (262).

Langston Hughes's vignette, "Golden Gate," from his *Simple* volume, *Simple's Uncle Sam* (1965), presents a black militant and deceptively simple Jesse B. Semple who, contemplating turning the Devil black and having him live in the Jim Crow South for a few days as the ideal Christmas present for the Devil, also dreams of dying and going to heaven. In his dream, Semple appears before the golden gates in his winged splendor and threatens to whip a black St. Peter unmercifully if he does not allow him to enter heaven through the front entrance. The fantasy presents Gabriel as black and God not far removed from Uncle Sam. Semple also finds that heaven is governed by the "down home" governor of Mississippi-Alabama-and-Georgia. That dream soon becomes a nightmare when he sees a kennel of police dogs beside the Jordan River and "For Whites Only" signs by the milk-and-honey counter. In frustration, Semple "ghosts" back to earth, concluding that when that Day of Judgment comes, he will demand his rightful place around the heavenly throne, and that white Southern racists will be greatly surprised and dismayed that heaven will not be run according to Jim Crow practices.

Both Ellison and Hughes use black angels as direct attacks on Southern white racism, an institutional racism resting on a foundation of sin, moral corruption, and hypocrisy. To present black angels at all is to empower these authors who challenge Christian and Western ideals of social order.[6] Poet Priscilla Hancock Cooper, in her poem, "Gone and Found Me an Angel (for Larry)," responds to Aretha Franklin's Motown hit, "Angel," with an imaged brown angel:

Well Sis. Retha,
just want you to know
that I found my angel.
and he has no wings,
no long white robe,
no peachy cherub's face.
nope,
my angel ...
has nappy black hair,
a matching moustache and beard
(most of the time)
warm, smooth tan skin
and a pair of the deepest, darkest most loving brown
eyes
i have ever looked into. (1993, 33)

And, Essex Hemphill, in his poem, "The Tomb of Sorrow (for Mahomet)," speaks of black gay men as angels:

When I die,
honey chil', my angels will be tall
Black drag queens.
When I die, my angels,
Immaculate
Black diva drag queens,
all of them sequined
and seductive,
will come back
to haunt you,
I promise honey chil'.[7] (1992, 81-82)

Yet, what happens when some whites create and present black angels? To what extent have whites conceptualized and presented black angels as racist stereotypes?[8]

Perhaps the most celebrated presentation of black angels, a colorization of biblical scriptures, is a play (1930) turned movie (1935), *The Green Pastures*, by Marc Connelly. Adapted from white southerner Roark Bradford's book, *Ol' Man Adam An' His Chillun Being the Tales They Tell about the Time When the Lord Walked the Earth Like a Natural*

Man (1928), Connelly's *The Green Pastures* dramatizes the scriptures as a black minister tells biblical stories to a black children's Sunday school class. With an all-black cast, both the play and the film represented a historical milestone in its employment of some fifty-plus actors and in its bold move to conceptualize the Bible Afrocentrically. From the Sunday school room opening, with its theme of God's career, "from that first shiny heaven, full of his angels, all sinless and hungry for fish-fries, songs and innocent pleasures," blacks are presented as simple, typically docile, wide-eyed and grinning innocent creatures who only want to eat, drink, dance, and fight (Brown, 1993). With quaint, exaggerated dialect and Stepin Fetchit mannerisms, the black cast reaffirmed Southern white racists' stereotypes about black life and experience. Not surprisingly, a white reviewer, Stark Young, celebrated both Bradford's and Connelly's depiction of black folks:

> We have too many of those portrayals of the Negro for his primitive color and impulses, his sexual powers, his alluring animality—too often writings that only insult the subject and, what's more, reflect the repressions and complexes of the author. It is high time we heard more of their fancy, humor and patience, their devotion, easy temper, and rich sensuous gifts, their easy and imaginative love of life and their simple natural goodness. (Young, 1948, 120)

White critics—and not a few black ones—were "amazed" that such a play as *The Green Pastures* could be rendered so accurately by "a white man, a sophisticated New Yorker" (Cripps, 1979, 19-21), and praised Connelly for his efforts to capture black experience authentically: Connelly allegedly "read dialogue to the [black] field hands for their approval" and visited black churches (19). Bradford's own "works of fiction and folklore were based on his childhood's contacts with African-American preachers, musicians, and storytellers in his father's plantations" ("Roark Bradford," 24 September 2006). Thomas Cripps's more recent attention to Connelly's play seems to justify its racist and stereotypical presentation and reveals Cripps's own unconscious patronizing:

> *The Green Pastures* ... [is] an American classic, an event that memorialized, celebrated, romanticized, and embalmed lost values while offering them as the foundation of the present. It presented Afro-Americans as interracial ambassadors of goodwill whose charming flaws of dialect and naivete allowed white audiences to admire their unthreatening dignity under duress. (21)

Cripps concludes quite confidently:

Connelly has taken an element of Negro religion and reshaped it into a sympathetic portrayal through which whites glimpsed the darker [pun intended?] side of their arrogant history, and blacks derived racial pride from his sentimental treatment of their culture. (36)

Yet playwright Lorraine Hansberry, in her essay addressing the subtle and overt manifestations of racism in American theater, "The Negro in the American Theatre," recognizes the absurdity of the praise lavished upon Connelly's stereotypical presentation:

Marc Connelly … [n]ever dreamed that he was writing a racist document in *The Green Pastures*. Rather, it is a matter of a partially innocent cultural heritage that, out of its own needs, was eager to believe in the colossal charm, among other things, of "childlike" peoples. (1965, 166)

The Green Pastures ran five years on Broadway with 640 performances, and had five national tours.[9]

Concerning her efforts to find a publisher for her first children's book, *Alabama Angels* (1989), Montgomery, Alabama, author Mary Barwick recalls: "New York publishers thought it was a regional book. Southern publishers thought it was a national one (Reeves, 1990, 1F). That Barwick's *Alabama Angels* and *Alabama Angels in Anywhere, L.A. (Lower Alabama)* (1991) have received such acclaim in her native state of Alabama is not surprising given the state's scholarly and public efforts to celebrate its own authors, particularly those who write about Alabama. Given the distinctly regional focus of these books—the South—it is also not surprising that Barwick's books have found their place in the Southern History and Literature Archives of the Birmingham Public Library and in practically all of the local Christian bookstores. They have been endorsed enthusiastically by the *Birmingham News* and Barwick's hometown newspapers, the *Montgomery Advertiser* and *Alabama Journal*. Garland Reeves of the *Birmingham News* describes *Alabama Angels* as "something of a publishing phenomenon," (1990, 1F), citing the printing and selling of about 8,000 copies in three printings, evidence that a market for Barwick's books exists. This overwhelmingly positive reception of the *Alabama Angels* companions seems to signal the values and attitudes of a very specific reading audience for which the books are written: conservative white southerners who continue to romanticize a particular slave past that, fortunately for African Americans, is "gone with the wind."

Alabama Angels went into its fifth printing, selling about 20,000 copies. As the phenomenal success of Barwick's books reveals, residual stereotypes and misrepresentations of African Americans as "happy" slaves and pickaninnies by a dominant white culture linger. Barwick's allegedly "heart-warming text[s] and charming pictures" (Land, 1989, 1F) should give pause to parents, black and white, who are looking to these books as socially appropriate for their impressionable youngsters.

Most problematic about Barwick's *Alabama Angels* series are the actual illustrations of the black childlike angels and of the black people themselves. Reeves insists that Barwick's angels are "the cutest little angels you ever did see," that "they are black, yet beyond any particular race" (1F). What Reeves means by the angels being of no particular race is unclear since, in America's history, African Americans have been the only race represented derogatorily and quite intentionally as happy slaves and as pitch black, unattractive pickaninnies. What Reeves (1990) describes as and Barwick intends to be "cute" is everything but cute to black Americans, who historically have been and continue to be dehumanized and misrepresented in what is euphemistically called "Americana" or Southern folk art: the blacker-than-black-faced lawn jockeys, fishing boys, and train conductors holding lanterns that decorate many white southerners' lawns, and the mammy and Amos figurines that smile and rest quaintly on many white southerners' kitchen counters and shelves. Indeed, Barwick's angels are not brown or even shades of brown; they are black, literally as black as night. Their facial features are obliterated; their hair sticks out like wheel spokes and is adorned with myriad small colorful bows. Such images recall historically racist depictions of black children as pickaninnies. The blackness of the angels also echoes the American minstrel tradition of the 1800s, prompted by Thomas D. Rice and his "Jim Crow" (1832) creations, when whites, and later blacks, blackened their faces with burnt cork to mock and ridicule black people. Even when Barwick tries to make the angels brown, the brown is so dark that it seems black, and the angels' facial features remain absent. These consistent renderings of blacks in both *Angels* books cannot be attributed to the printing quality; these are high gloss, well-produced books.

Not only do the illustrations give reason to pause, but also the narratives and the story settings are not far removed from the documented plantation days, and the angels themselves are not far removed from slaves. Even the character of God bears a striking resemblance to a white plantation master. Set in the rural South amid cotton fields and with blacks living in cabins, the action in *Alabama Angels* (Barwick, 1989) involves a young black girl, Alethea, who prays to a benevolent

God to help her overburdened parents with their farming chores. God, who addresses the blacks almost condescendingly and patronizingly as "His good children," "my Alabama folks," "those good folks," and "dear family," sends black angels (Bubba, Sara, Emily, and a host of other "southern" angels) to do the farm chores. They pick cotton, wash and iron clothes, feed animals, rock the baby, pack tomatoes for shipping, gather flowers, and do odd jobs around the St. John's Holiness Church of Deliverance. After these "gentle exploits" (Reeves, 1990, 1F), the angels travel throughout Alabama (Mobile, Gadsden, Selma, Eufaula, Slocomb, Tuskegee, Opp, Scottsboro) providing whatever services others need. When they return to heaven, they celebrate their ability to service others. Nineteenth-century slave narratives, minstrel songs, and even popular culture (advertisements for household products, for example) document such misrepresentations of slaves and later freed blacks, who allegedly felt personally rewarded and spiritually fulfilled through their service to masters specifically and to whites generally. Barwick insists that her angels' rural realities grow out of her "[love for] history, and the gentle cultivation of Southern life [that] was assigned to black people" (as quoted in Kemp, 1991, A6). Slave narratives and historical documentaries, however, clarify the threatened and tortured existence of slaves in the New World as anything but "gentle" and reason for celebration. Indeed, Barwick's presentation falls disturbingly in line with the sentiments of Frank Dumont's minstrel ditty, "The Alabama Blossoms":

> Far away down south in Alabama, Where the darkies plant the cotton and the corn;/In that land where bloom sweet magnolias, In that paradise us darkies we were born./Old Massa, he was kind, and little Missus too, They'd be amused to see us jump and dance,/Oh! they called us Alabama blossoms, And we're going back whene'er we get a chance. (Weir, 1929, 31)

And, while Barwick does not resort to the stereotypical mocking black dialect of minstrel songs, she attempts to give the language of Alethea's prayer the flavor of black vernacular by arbitrarily omitting the final *g*'s from her pronunciations of the verbs: "tendin'," "washin'," "ironin'," "doin'." This move seems awkward and is inconsistent ("listening" and "talking" remain standard) and renders the language perhaps more southern than black.

Alabama Angels in Anywhere L.A. (Barwick, 1991) involves basically the same narrative as Barwick's *Alabama Angels* (1989). God sends Mr. Willie, a black farmer, angelic help (Bubba, Emily, Sara, and their entourage) to save his farming community from the "big highway." In their mission to save God's "dear people" in Anywhere, L.A., the angels pick and shell pecans, catch fish, make quilts, care for sick animals, deliver flowers, and pack wagons and trucks with goods to be shipped. Though this story is less problematic than that of *Alabama Angels*, the illustrations of blacks remain disturbing.

The popularity of Barwick's books in the Southeast generally (Georgia, Mississippi, Tennessee, Florida) and in Alabama specifically speaks to a readership that continues to romanticize "the good ole days" of the faded South, the sentiments in Dan Emmett's celebrates "Dixie['s] Land" (1859)—not coincidentally a "lively" minstrel song:

> I wish I was in de land ob cotton,
> Old time dar am not forgotten.
> Look away, look away, look away, Dixie Land. (8–9)

That Barwick's books are written for children is particularly disturbing given these visual images and representations of blacks. Any socially conscious and concerned adult should be cautious in exposing impressionable youngsters to books that perpetuate racist stereotypes under the guise of rural and racial quaintness and religious innocence.

There seems to be no reason that Barwick's *Alabama Angels* (1989) are angels of color. The very depiction of these angels as blacks, given the illustrations and the storylines, suggests a dehumanizing association with a white racist image of blacks as "good darkies." This is particularly disappointing since non-white angels are rarely depicted in Western culture, a real grievance Barwick might have used this opportunity to redress.[10] A more satisfying presentation would include black, white, red, and yellow angels in a depiction of heaven as a place where racial integration and harmony abide.[11] Had this been the case, it is doubtful that the reception of these books among conservative southerners would be as enthusiastic, especially since white angels would be "serving" black people. Yet, this is precisely the type of courageous, groundbreaking move that all children need: one that does not maintain the status quo and extends it to such a utopian ideal as heaven.

Unquestionably, Barwick falls into this social and political trap largely because of the South's specific history of tense race relations. In fact, Barwick's publisher, Randall Williams, who admits having reservations about the angels' presentation, submits that "carefully analyzing the book for all its 'social implications' ... [is not] the way the 'fairy tale' should be read" (Land, 1989, 1F). Yet these social implications are particularly important since these are children's books with images and ideas that will inevitably help form and influence social attitudes. Furthermore, Barwick does illustrate white angels who are not featureless and not chalk white. Her white angels appear in Lucy Blount's devotional, *Letters to the Precious Group* (1990). The illustrations of black angels in this work are significantly less stereotypical, although they are almost consistently adorned with small colorful head bows, pink cheeks, and red lips. And, while they do have distinguishable facial features, their overall visual rendering is not as conscientiously human-like as that of Barwick's white angels.

Indeed, not all efforts to present angels of color in children's books have been either politically charged or socially constructed. While Charles Tazewell's *The Littlest Angel* (1946) is about the trials of a young white male angel, Tazewell and illustrator Paul Micich include both adult and child angels of color thoughtfully and conscientiously. One of the most refreshing images of an angel of color is presented in Michael J. Rosen's *Elijah's Angel: A Story for Chanukah and Christmas* (1992), about the friendship and shared religious notions between an elderly black man, Elijah, who is a wood carver, a barber, and Christian; and a Jewish youngster, Michael. Michael's Chanukah present to Elijah is a menorah, and Elijah's to Michael is an angel he has carved: "Elijah's angel is ... one foot tall. Its wings are polka-dotted. Its eyes are diamonds. Its robe sparkles with glitter"(1). Elijah's angel is smooth-brown complected, has short, nonstraight hair, and is as colorfully splendid as a butterfly. Rosen's illustrators, Aminah Brenda and Lynn Robinson, render the colorisms of blacks in the book quite appropriately and nonstereotypically. In addition, Anita Rodriguez's *Jamal and the Angel: An Aunt Martha Story* (1992) is the story of a young black boy, Jamal, whose turbanned adult black male guardian angel guides him to a job for money to pay for a guitar he desperately wants. Jamal's angel has shoulder-length, coiled black hair and wings that are pastel blue, white, and pink. The angel's robe is also rainbow-colored. While the blacks in this book are presented in different shades of brown, their pastel pink lips are distracting. Mary Hoffman's splendidly balanced *An Angel Just Like Me* (1997) seems to answer the question driving my earliest exploration: Where are the brown angels that look like me and my brown children? In Hoffman's book, the young Tyler raises these profoundly provocative questions:

> Why do angels all look like girls?
> Can't boys be angels?
> Why do they all have gold hair?
> And why are they always pink?
> Aren't there any black angels?

I'm going to get a new angel [to replace the broken female white
    one] for our tree.
One that looks just like me.

Tyler's questions further underscore racialized representations of all
biblical characters, and even Santa Claus. Hoffman's is a satisfying
narrative of a young African American boy who ultimately gets as a
Christmas gift, an angel made in his brown image. His multicultural
schoolmates then desire angels like them, underscoring the powerful
message that if we can imagine alternative realities, those realities can
be actualized.

    Another example of a book with brown angels is Diane Stortz's
The Always-Late Angel (1993). While highlighting the exploits of a
young red-headed female angel who is never with the angelic choir
when she should be, *The Always-Late Angel* includes images of
brown angels, both male and female. That the nativity scene which
forms the basis of the narrative action is peopled with characters
that are white lessens the potentially positive impact of this would-
be multicultural text. As well, Margot Zemach's controversial *Jake
and the Honeybunch Go to Heaven* (1982) seems, for some, to flirt
too closely with racial stereotypes about African Americans as care-
free and free-flying, even as angels. For instance, when Jake enters
heaven, he zips around with two left wings and is nearly as disrup-
tive of heaven's tranquil environment as is the "crazy mule" Honeybunch. While the atmosphere of leisure that includes cooking and
eating, frolicking, and enjoying the juke joint borders on stereotype, the presentation ultimately images a heaven with a black male
God and black angels of both genders, all ages, and all shapes and
sizes. The book's final image of a flying Jake clearly challenges the
restrictiveness of black flight in Ralph Ellison's "Flying Home," and
echoes the African American folktale of flying Africans and slaves,
who had the inner power to transcend their shackled existence in a
racially oppressive Western society. It is unclear whether Zemach's
multiple references to "great green pastures" intends to applaud or
to attack associations with Connelly's and Bradford's highly contested presentations of black angels. That the book's narrative is a
fable explaining how and why we see stars in the sky at night can
be read as an effort to imbue the tale with a gentle positivity and a
cosmic mysticism.

    Julius Lester's brilliantly hued *What a Truly Cool World* (1999) offers
a culturally diverse heaven with a "sextillion voices Hallelujah Angelic
Choir," a black male God, and a quick-talking and fashion-conscious,

take-no-mess leading female angel "in charge of everybody's business." God's efforts to make the world more exciting are prompted by a persistent Shaniqua, who is determined to make the world more beautiful. Their heavenly efforts, along with black male secretary Bruce, result in heavenly music whose notes fall to earth and create flowers. Butterflies are then created to keep the flowers from being lonely. Similarly positive images are found in Jan Spivey Gilchrist's illustrations of brown children and adults accompanying Eloise Greenfield's poems in *Angels* (1998), a celebration of human kindness and uplifting spirituality, which are elegantly sketched in graphite. These illustrations reinforce the powerful message of seeing goodness in ourselves and those around us. Lastly, Walter Dean Myers's *Brown Angels: An Album of Pictures and Verse* (1996) uses angels as a metaphor to present narratives on lives of black children: "These pictures speak to me of hardworking people—of tenant farmers, porters, and teachers of the 'colored' schools—who celebrate the lives of their babies as have all people before them and since." The antiquated black and white photographs underscore Myers' celebration of brown angels—the "dark and precious," the "sweet and brown," the "pretty little black girl," the "pretty little tan girl," the "pretty little brown girl," and the "pretty little coffee girl."

To insist that her black angels are "divinely inspired" and imaged accordingly is to invite curiosities concerning the nature of the God that inspires Mary Barwick. Might her inspiration also come from other white southerners who share her quaint romantic visions of black experience in the past, an inspiration that has led to much regional fame and not a little financial success? In fact, the latest additions to the "Barwick Library" include "an Advent calendar," a limited edition set of prints from the first *Alabama Angels*, a "Bubba Knows Books bookmark, and the illustrations for a forthcoming book-tape children's lullaby package" (*New Titles for 1992–1993*, n.p.). I will not be surprised by Mary Barwick's next "divinely inspired" black angel project (perhaps Christmas cards and tree ornaments?) or by the sweeping popularity of such a project in the Heart of Dixie.

While the president of Angel Watch Network, Eileen Elias Freeman, alleges that "angels transcend every religion, every philosophy, every creed" (Woodward, 1993, 55), not many recognize the implications that angels rarely transcend race. Indeed, the popularity and prevalence of angel lore and our cultural preoccupation with and belief in angels continue to maintain the ideological, social, and aesthetic boundaries that disassociate people of color from yet another Eurocentric ideal.

SLANTED AND ENCHANTED

BY BEN CLARK

As I read the chapter, "Angels of Color: Divinely Inspired or Socially Constructed," the thought that kept returning to my mind was the ease and enthusiasm with which we, as Americans today, erect and accept barriers that insulate ourselves from the reality of the world around us. The focus of Lester's chapter concerns how African Americans are either excluded from literary and media representations of angels or are depicted in terms of racist and stereotypical archetypes (i.e., "picka-ninny" imagery). He notes that angels, both historically and presently, have been presented as white, red-cheeked cherubs, thus transmitting the unspoken message that whiteness is synonymous with virtue and holiness. The deleterious effects of all-white imagery on the psyches and self-esteem of black youths has been well documented, but Lester points out that even more "inclusive" texts can be offensive as well. The *Alabama Angels* (Barwick, 1989) children's book series, for example, features African American children who are "black as night" with poorly drawn faces and hair with pink bows and whose dialogue in the text seems evocative of Jim Crow-era minstrel shows.

The dearth of non-white angels in Christmas cards, children's books, film, and television merely reflects unexamined prejudices of America's dominant race, which blithely assumes that God's messengers must be the same color that they are. Moreover, most readers of the *Alabama Angels* series probably accept the books' racist depictions of black children because they conform to a worldview with an unspoken belief that black children are cute, precious, silly, and inferior to white children. In both cases, images are accepted because they do not attempt to puncture the misbegotten perceptions of their audiences. This brand of thinking can be extended to nearly any social or political event where there is a significant disconnect between reality and the ways that the actors in the situation choose to countenance that reality. That is why I believe it is possible to make a connection between Lester's chapter "Angels of Color" and the current sociopolitical climate within the United States.

In his chapter, Lester rhetorically asks, "Are our Western sensibili-ties violated when we imagine a black Jesus, a black Adam and Eve, and even angels of color?" For many, such images violate the subcon-scious assumption that all that is heavenly is white; to suggest otherwise would be both inappropriate and uncomfortable. Consequently, even in an 'enlightened' age allegedly without institutionalized racism, it is still difficult to find such representations in popular media. Given the context of the United States in 2007, it is worthwhile to ask, in light of current events, which other ways we (and our leaders) reject ideas and information that run counter to a particular worldview.

Presently, the United States is engaged in a war in which more than three thousand Americans have lost their lives, as well as tens of thousands of Iraqis. President Bush has offered no timetable for withdrawal, and his administration has not clearly articulated the war effort's remaining objectives. The president's premises for ordering the invasion of a sovereign nation were to root out weapons of mass destruction and to crush an alleged Iraqi link to al-Qaeda, both of which turned out to be nonexistent. Throughout the conflict, the Bush administration has refused to allow camera crews to photograph flag-draped coffins returning the bodies of fallen soldiers. The U.S. military has not undertaken any serious inquiry into the number of Iraqi civilian casualties, which may range from 30,000 to 100,000, according to independent estimates. Finally, the president has sung the praises of an Iraqi constitution that denies basic rights to women and establishes just the type of theocratic government that the United States sought to avoid.

According to the reality the Bush administration has constructed for itself and for the American people, invading Iraq was a necessary and just action that will ultimately result in a happy and positive outcome. We must "stay the course," repeats President Bush, because "great progress is being made," and the insurgency that is claiming dozens of lives each week only represents the "last throes" of rebel resistance. Evidence to the contrary is either ignored or discarded. Examples abound of instances when the Bush administration has rejected out of hand any voices that counter its preconceived notions of the situation in Iraq. Generals were fired or demoted for suggesting that a full-scale conflict in Iraq would require more troops and more money, both of which are predictions that have turned out to be true. The tragedy at the Abu Ghraib prison was written off as the random actions of a few rogue soldiers and not indicative of morally dubious orders emanating from the top of the chain of command. Finally, President Bush is declaring the Iraqi constitution a triumph for Arab democracy, even though many of its provisions are markedly undemocratic, and an entire section of Iraq's population (Sunni Muslims) refused to take part in the writing of it.

It seems Mr. Bush's "reality" concerning the Iraq war involves a relatively clean conflict in which death is an unfortunate but necessary byproduct that should not deter the nation from "staying the course." He champions the war dead for their sacrifice but will not appear at their funerals. He conveys his sympathy to the families who have lost loved ones but will not answer the fundamental question of what exactly they gave their lives for. He exhorts his constituents to "support the troops" while he himself plunged them into a deadly and entirely avoidable conflict and then shortchanged them on the resources necessary to fight it. Like those who consider the *Alabama Angels* a multicultural book respectful of black people, or who would never consider that heavenly bodies might have a bit more melanin in their skin, Mr. Bush seems willfully divorced from the reality of the world around him.

This disconnect is dangerous. Ignorance, whether it concerns race, politics, social welfare, or foreign policy, can have tangible consequences both for individuals and the world around them. For those who never question the whitewashed images of angels that are purveyed by popular media, the consequence is an internal reaffirmation of a centuries-old racial hierarchy that places whites at the top and African Americans far below at the bottom. For a leader who never acknowledges or examines ideas and evidence that cast doubt on his decisions, the consequence is often unnecessary suffering and pain. Lester's chapter reminds me of the perpetual need to parse the assumptions that underlay my views of the world around me and question whether by holding these assumptions (and the actions that stem from them) I am inadvertently oppressing or harming others around me. My only hope is that the leaders and policymakers, whose actions are much further-reaching than mine, are able to do the same.

TALKING OUT LOUD: IDEAS FOR DISCUSSION

1. To what extent do images of race around us have an impact on our self-perceptions and our perceptions of others racially?
2. How do language, visual, and narrative representations create and reinforce constructions of whiteness as an aesthetic and cultural ideal?
3. Consult a recent dictionary to determine the significance of connotations of *white* and connotations of *black*. Discuss your findings.
4. To what extent do the Bible and Christianity participate in creating and maintaining racial divisions socially, historically, and culturally?
5. How is a discussion of images of angels also a discussion of gendered and racial constructions?
6. To what extent is any children's text a potentially political text?

8

"DO YOU SEE WHAT I SEE? DO YOU HEAR WHAT I HEAR?"

Becoming Better Adults through Toni Morrison's The Big Box *and* The Book of Mean People

I'm not an expert mother, for example, as my children will tell you.

—Toni Morrison (Bonetti, 1983)

Nobel Prize in Literature author Toni Morrison (1993) is an advocate for children. Even as she writes about complicated black and white race relations, male and female relations, the intricate intersections of past and present in everyone's life, the culturally specific dynamics of slave mothering, the arbitrariness of race as a psychologically devastating social construct, she also presents for adult readers complex children's perspectives. Before coauthoring with her son Slade *The Big Box* (1999) and *The Book of Mean People* (2002), Morrison presented Claudia's child perspective on Pecola and Pecola's family's futile existence in her first novel *The Bluest Eye* (1970). So much of what we experience in that novel is based on the self-hatred of adults, on adults' failure or unwillingness to recognize the legitimacy and depth of children's innocence and wisdom in the adult world. One such instance in the novel is Claudia's account of Mr. Henry's arrival as a boarder in the McTeer home. Mrs. McTeer introduces Claudia and her younger sister Frieda as though they are family possessions or part of the physical frame of the house:

> We do not, cannot, know the meanings of all their [gossiping adults'] words, for we are nine and ten years old. So we watch their faces, their hands, their feet, and listen for truth in timbre. ... So when Mr. Henry arrived on a Saturday night, ... [h]e smiled a lot. ... Frieda and I were not introduced to him—merely pointed out. Like, here is the bathroom; the clothes closet is here; and these are my kids, Frieda and Claudia; watch out for this window; it don't open all the way. (16)

Even here, Morrison notes that what adults say and mean are not always clear to children. While there is no sense that adults do not "love" the children in the book—the notion of love is emphatically ambiguous throughout the novel in terms of the parent–child and adult–child relationships—children's perspectives are not always recognized and given legitimacy in the adult world of seemingly absolute authority.

Morrison underscores the fragility and vulnerability of adult authority in her Nobel acceptance speech (1993). Commenting on identity and self-identity within the structural framework of narrative process and storytelling, she tells the story of an old blind woman, a former slave, who forfeits her reputable wisdom about life and the world by making faulty assumptions about youngsters whom she thinks are trying to betray her. In a provocative narrative turn, the youngsters admit no intention to trick the wise woman by their question to her about the life or death of the alleged bird in their hand. Rather, they want to engage the elder in a dialogue; they want her to talk with them. When the old woman demonstrates her unwillingness to jeopardize "her peerless reputation," the "young people" admit their disappointment that they are not worth adult risks, not worth the honesty of admitting to adult vulnerabilities:

> Don't you remember being young when language was magic without meaning? When what you could say, could not mean? When the invisible was what imagination strove to see? When questions and demands for answers burned so brightly you trembled with fury at not knowing? ... You are an adult. The old one, the wise one. Stop thinking about saving your face. Think of our lives and tell us your particularized world. Make up a story. Narrative is radical, creating us at the very moment it is being created.

In the youngsters' declaration, Morrison portrays this old woman not as omniscient and wise but as an adult forced to reflect on how she views herself in relation to her community and how she views herself in relation to herself. Her esteemed and previously unchallenged reputation has brought her authority, and authority and reputation are manifestations of past narratives and of lived experience. Conversation, on the other hand, is life process, vulnerability, and possibilities. Their final plea to the old woman is an invitation for self-liberation rather than a ploy to mock her:

> We will not blame you if your reach exceeds your grasp; if love so ignites your words they go down in flames and nothing is left but their scald. ... For our sake and yours forget your name in the street; tell us what the world has been to you in the dark places and in the light. Don't tell us what to believe, what to fear. Show us belief's wide skirt and the stitch that unravels fear's caul. You, old woman, blessed with blindness, can speak the language that tells us what only language can: how to see without pictures.

To have vision, according to Morrison, is to accept that life comes with no absolutes, no single answers, no guarantees, and with myriad risks—realities that many in the adult world of authority are reluctant to admit. Acknowledging one's own vulnerabilities and inability to know all, to be all, and to see all is therefore, in Morrison's lesson, philosophically noble and real.

In many ways, these two aforementioned texts highlight the often-overlooked and dismissed perspectives of children when adults—teachers and parents, for example—are conditioned to believe that they know all and always know best. On this premise that adults can stand to learn much about themselves through children, Morrison offers *The Big Box* (1999) and *The Book of Mean People* (2002). Both picture books challenge adults to look honestly at what their relationships with young children tell them about themselves. While every adult has been a child, no child has been an adult. Fundamentally, should adults be as accountable to children for certain actions, decisions, and behaviors as children are expected to be to adults? Why should children be given limited "safe" choices in the adult world? Both books challenge adult readers to step outside themselves and their socially scripted roles as adults meant to control others. Both books challenge adults to listen to and to respect even children who seemingly occupy socially and legally powerless positions. Morrison's subversiveness comes in creating children's texts that are not tools for adult control over children's behavior but rather tools adults can use to better understand children's emotional positions and children's perspectives on and interpretations of adult behavior. A reviewer of *The Big Box* offers a perceptive observation appropriate to *The Book of Mean People* as well: It "encourage[s] everyone to stretch their minds and look at different sides of a story, especially a story that involves the ones who will create our tomorrow—our children" (Currie, 2000, 68). The freedom to step outside the boundaries of adult privilege and authority is Morrison's invitation to her adult readers.

FREEDOM TO BE

Based on her then nine-year-old son Slade's responses to a teacher's rather loaded comment that he "couldn't handle his freedom," *The Big Box* is a poetic meditation on the different meanings and manifestations of freedom for children and adults. Morrison admits the commercial riskiness of writing such a subversive text wherein adults who buy children's books might see themselves in a less-than-positive light:

> The story meant to provoke questions and reflections. When I first put this story together, I was told that it was unsaleable because: 1. Adults bought children's books, not children, and 2. No children's book that did not offer a reconciliation with the adult view was marketable. In short, it was disturbing precisely because it suggested a division, a conflict between a child's point of view and an adult's. That seemed to be a strong dismissal of children's intelligence. ("Toni Morrison Talks about *The Big Box*," 2003)

Indeed, critics have not embraced the book for the very reasons the book works for some other adult readers. Roger Sutton of *The Horn Book* finds that the book "relies on a heavy-handed irony" and conveys "a clichéd voice of childhood wisdom." He adds that "the lack of either thematic or narrative development makes the book tedious," and that "kids faced with reading this book might well be advised to take its advice and go out and play instead" (Sutton, 1999, 598). Another from *Publisher's Weekly* finds the story "mundane," "enigmatic," and ultimately lacking "the childlike perspective that so masterfully informs *The Bluest Eye*" ("Review of *The Big Box*," 1999, 95). Sutton boldly concludes that "Some authors should stick with their original genres." Perhaps a friend's comments in an e-mail discussion with me about the book best captures the book's deliberate tension between adult and child perspectives. My friend, who is also a parent, writes:

> The narrative makes sense to me … but I don't feel that I approve of it [because] it plays into the hands of a sort of Rousseauian, anti-adult attitude that I don't like. Fundamentally, this sort of attitude argues that children left alone are great but adults are narrow, bigoted, [and] unreasonable. That is why I call it Rousseauian. Since all adults were once children, then this only

makes sense if "[hu]mankind" in a state of nature is desirable, but civilized/disciplined "[hu]mankind" is unacceptable. ... Of course, I believe in freedom and fun, but I think these must be constrained. (e-mail message to author, 25 June 2003)

Interestingly, the rhetoric of this e-mail underscores a discourse of adult authority—"approve," "only makes sense," and "must be constrained"—as though there is a single absolute order operating between and within adulthood and childhood. Why is human behavior assessed more by some in terms of "approval" and "disapproval" than clarity and understanding from multiple perspectives? Surely, Morrison offers no attack on adults but rather challenges adults to self-assess their behaviors with the possibility of modifying their own limited thinking to become more wholly connected to children. Might this text lead adults to see themselves as fallible humans trying to make sense of the world and the complexities of life?

Similarly, a graduate student in a Toni Morrison seminar expresses disapproval at the book's representation of adults and adulthood:

> *The Big Box* seem[s] to be advocating a complete lack of discipline and suggest[s] that children, like animals, should be allowed to live by their instincts and run wild, doing whatever they want—scream like the sparrow, owl, or cow, or chew on trees when they need 'em just like the beaver. It seem[s] to me to ignore the fact that, unlike other animals, humanity has created a much more complex society that demands a bit more learning if you are to function even marginally against it. I don't advocate that everyone should fit the same mold, but there are certain things that children must *learn* beyond following whatever whim comes to mind. (e-mail message to author, 15 April 2003)

Clearly, the desire to order others' lives according to the design we think we use for our own is as much learned as instinctive. Rules can and do create an order, and this order helps us construct "civilization." At the same time, rules meant to orchestrate children's lives are often less about the children and their safety and well-being than about the ability and right to exercise adult authority. Surely the sentiment of the book is less that children are negative savages given solely to behaviors and actions and controlled solely by instinct than commentary on adult regulations which are often arbitrary, unclear, and unexplained to children expected to follow them. Neither is Morrison expressly suggesting that freedom on any level is without individual and collective agreement. With children, however, the arrangements being questioned in the text are imposed rather than discussed, unilaterally determined than mutually understood. Further, nothing in the text suggests that these children are breaking all rules and are totally out of control or uncontrollable. In fact, the children here may be expressing more self-control than the adults with the authority to determine for the children the consequences of the children's every action.

Actually, *The Big Box* challenges the very authority professed above in the name of "civilization," itself a relative construct operating on the basis of someone's definitions and perceptions of good and bad, better and worse, right and wrong, sensible and nonsensical, rational and irrational, moral and immoral. As perceptions of these ideals change, the ambiguous line of demarcation between childhood and adulthood remains clearly drawn for many. Hence, Morrison uses the book to demonstrate the difficulty many adults—parents, teachers, and neighbors—experience in "listen[ing] or hav[ing] conversations [with children] in which the parent [or adult] is vulnerable" (Peterson, 1999, 65). There is no reason to believe that this story is an indictment of all adults. In fact, Morrison acknowledges that there are certainly adults who encourage children's independent thinking and questioning, those who encourage children's safe imaginative exploration and those who do not buy their children with material gifts. She clarifies:

> Children have not changed, but adults have. Expectations are lower in some ways: Parents do not need the labor of their children as was once the case. While this is certainly not true of all families, certainly not true of working families with modest incomes. Increasingly, in the media and the discourse of parenting, one notices how irrelevant children have become. On the other hand, the expectations are higher than ever: Publicly approved "success" is intensely sought at earlier and earlier ages, and private achievement is devalued or taken for granted. More and more, children are regarded as "trophies," "Oscars" bestowed on the parents. ("Toni Morrison Talks about *The Big Box*," 2003)

By extension, children's orderly behavior based on adult instruction and prescription becomes a reward of sorts for those adults seeking the approval of other adult observers. Indeed, this text achieves its subversive end by disrupting adults' perceptions of order. Adult authority, to many adults, is often unwavering, absolute, and not subject to revision if adults are to be respected by other adults and ultimately respected and obeyed by children.

Interestingly, *The Big Box* narrative—first published in 1982 as a twenty-three-stanza, 195-line rhyming poem with primitive sketches in Letty Cottin Pogrebin's edited collection *Stories for Free Children*[2]—shows three children who are cast aside and "outside" into the box by the adult world because the children allegedly "can't handle their freedom." The gloominess of the book's tone is achieved through the controlled and monotonous rhetorical repetitions and refrains highlighting a child's perception of the adult world of rules and regulations that are pronounced and to be performed like military drills: without question, clarification, or qualification. According to Morrison, the narrative subversiveness is that hers is a "story of adults not listening to children and retreating into 'rules' that protect the adults—not the children" ("Toni Morrison Talks about *The Big Box*," 2003). According to adults' perceptions of adulthood, adults do not have to explain or justify their actions, especially to children. To better gauge children's understanding of rules and regulations, certainly some degree of explanation and reasoned justification is warranted. If, however, the rules are in place because adults can and do make rules, there is no need for adult self-reflection or revision, no need for children's understanding and investment in the decision making or the consequences of their own actions.

For many, Morrison opens Pandora's box by having children question adult authority, decisions, and attitudes. While these children are not being disrespectful, condescending, or impudent in their plaintive refrain—

> I know you are smart and I know that you think
> You are doing what is best for me.
> But if freedom is handled just your way
> Then it's not my freedom or free

—they exercise independent and intellectually sophisticated thinking as they move toward self-reliance, which is ironically an ideal that parents hope for in their grown children and something later considered a reward for their successful parenting. Importantly, these children have not done anything harmful or life-threatening to themselves or to others: Patty "had too much fun in school all day," "talked in the library and sang in class," "went four times to the toilet," "ran through the halls and wouldn't play with dolls," and "spoiled" the Pledge of Allegiance to the flag; Mickey "had too much fun in the streets all day," "wrote his name on the mailbox lid and sat on the super's Honda," "hollered in the hall, and played handball" where he apparently should not have; and Liza Sue "had too much fun in the fields all day," "let the chickens keep their eggs," "let squirrels into the fruit trees," "took the bit from the horse's mouth," and "fed honey to the bees." Such details prompt sympathetic readers to raise a flurry of questions to understand better the reasons for the children's banishment; hence, unthreatened adult readers act as stand-ins for the banished children. And, contrary to Emilie Coulter's negative assessment that the "thickly ironic book ... asks more questions than it answers," Morrison puts her children and adult readers into the circumstance of the children in the text as we try to make sense of these seemingly nonsensical adult decisions and actions: What are the children doing that constitutes fun? How are the adults and children defining fun differently? What does it mean to have "too much fun"? What are the dangers of having too much fun? When does having fun signal too much fun? Is Patty's fun causing her to mistreat others, to abuse herself, or to harm others? Is Patty's fun causing her to neglect her responsibilities and obligations? How does Patty "spoil" the Pledge of Allegiance? Does her decision not to participate in the recitation spoil it for others? How is Patty's running in the hall necessarily dangerous to others or to herself? How fast is Patty running? Is she running on a slippery floor? Is Patty actually using the toilet each time she goes? Is she smoking in the toilet? Is she stuffing paper towels down the commode or writing graffiti on the stall walls? Does she have an eyelash in her eye that is really bothering her? Is she going to the toilet to attend to personal hygiene matters? How loudly is Patty talking and singing in the library? Is Patty the only person talking and singing in the library? Has Mickey been told specifically not to write his name on his mailbox? Has Mickey been told why he should avoid sitting on others' property unless invited to do so? Has Liza Sue been instructed not to remove the horse's bit under any circumstances? Is Mickey bouncing the ball during classes or after or before school is in session?

Very rarely can adult authority be challenged without consequence to the child doing the questioning or challenging. Speaking to a specific detail of Liza Sue's action, my friend points out in her e-mail, "If you are a farmer and need those eggs to live, it's not just matter of preference." Yet, Liza Sue is not destroying the eggs, and certainly Liza, as a child, is not the major source of production on this family farm. The friend adds about community and "public good": "One should conform to being thoughtful of others in a group setting. People who live in groups must conform to rules that might not seem sensible [but] because it makes the life of the collective better." While this is a valid assessment, Morrison points out the double standard: Only adults can and do make rules for others based solely on their perceptions of what is good for the whole. Why and how have these children's relatively innocent and decidedly unmalicious actions "made the grown-ups nervous"? Are adults nervous that the children will hurt themselves or others, or destroy property, or reflect poorly on their own parenting practices? Without discussion or conversation with the children, the adults have the authority to put the children into a box. While the adults may think the children are guilty of not being able to "handle their freedom," the adults here seem to abuse their power for their own selfish ends. Morrison highlights her objective in presenting the parents and children as she does: "I had in mind what all parents think about—the difficulty of figuring out what is protection and what is suppression. What is freedom and what is license. An eternal and universal condition of parenting and of growing up. A very hard job" ("Toni Morrison Talks about *The Big Box*," 2003). Certainly, Morrison's position is sympathetic to adults who are subjected to these artificial and pervasive constructs of adulthood and childhood. If the children's actions threaten adult power, it is because the children's actions reveal that adult control is tenuous at best. Indeed, power in this adult–child relationship is a tacit agreement, not something that anyone can "own" permanently.

Emphatically, the three young children in *The Big Box* are not asking to exist in a world without rules or regulations. In fact, they follow rules adults have given them: Patty "folds her socks and eats her beets, changes her bed sheets, laces her shoes, washes her neck and cleans under her nails"; Mickey "combs his hair, doesn't do drugs, vacuums his rugs everyday, feeds the hamster and waters the plants, and hangs up his pants"; and Liza Sue has "worn her braces, given up peanut brittle, does her fractions and bottle feeds the baby lambs." Typically, these are not tasks many children willingly assume without adult prompting or direction. That the children are being chastised—relegated to an indefinite and adult-determined time out, much the same way the Christian God banishes Adam and Eve from the Garden of Eden also because of their independent thinking, curiosities, and ultimate disobedience— then reflects more on the nature of these adults and the extent to which they are controlled by their own limited views of what it means to be an adult. To impose rules and restrictions and then consequences for behavior without explanation or clarification to those affected by these rules represents unthinking and a lack of mutual respect and accountability on the part of the adults who here all insist that their adult love and approval come as contingencies. Hence, if adults agree on their assessments and interpretations of children's behavior, then the adults must be correct: "We all agree, your parents and we,/That you simply can't handle your freedom." Might the relationship between adults and children be profoundly enhanced if children and adults participate to the degree that is appropriate, in rule-making together? Notice also how the parents see the children's pleasure-seeking actions as a kind of sickness or disease for which they—as adult doctors and general persons of authority—can "try and find a cure." If "fun" is pleasure, the book champions fun and pleasure as a site that is most difficult for adults to regulate when children, even with the boundaries of adult restriction, create their own fun and pleasure. This principle then becomes the children's ultimate source of self-empowerment and self-reliance. Rhetorically important is the fact that parents might use this book and its loaded message about adult vulnerability to "find a cure" that liberates them from the shackles of weighty adulthood—the inclination to feel that they are always right about everything, that they always know everything about everything, that they always make the right decisions, that they always know what is best for others, and that they must define themselves through their perceived or real control of others. With such absolutes comes no room for individual growth and development, no room to experience the world as a wellspring of infinite possibilities for personal growth.

Implicitly, gender and race are also part of the boxed existence for both children and adults outside and within *The Big Box*. Within the narrative, adults find it problematic that Patty "wouldn't play with dolls." Patty's defiance counters social expectations of conformity, obedience, and passivity—traits for which girls are historically rewarded. Cross-culturally, girls continue to be less socially valued and arguably more socially prescribed than boys. For example, in Noida, India, girls are allegedly familial and are social liabilities in such patriarchal societies:

> In an overwhelming number of homes, girls are encouraged to cook rather than study and made to eat after the men. India is one of the few nations where a woman's life expectancy is lower than a man's, and the abortion of female fetuses is so common the government now bans doctors from revealing the gender of unborn babies. Parents favor sons because boys are seen as more useful and productive and because boys bring dowries rather than require their payment. Even when fathers express pride for their daughters, they say: "She is like a son to me." (Duff-Brown, 2003, A25)

Elisabeth Rosenthal's report on "baby trafficking," "China Area Is Rife with the Sale of Girl Babies" (2003), is not about the high value placed on girls in Yulin, China, but just the opposite: "'You can take medicine to end the pregnancy,' [a father of two daughters] said matter-of-factly. 'Otherwise you have the baby and if it's a female, you try to find another family who will take it, or you just put it up for sale'" (A21).

Early on, girls across the globe are subjected to the "pretty is as pretty does" societal teachings which connect their worth and self-worth to what they look like physically and how they behave in often restrictive ways—their talking, their walking, their appearance, their talents, their play interests, their intelligence, and their sexuality. While girls are allegedly made of "sugar and spice and everything nice," boys are made of "shells and snails and puppy dog tails." Equally restrictive are social rules that tell boys that real boys do not cry, real boys do not show vulnerability, and real boys do not play with dolls. Reports Janie McGruder in her piece, "The Nature of Boys: Moms Have to Buck the He-Man Culture to Raise Emotionally Healthy Sons" (2003):

> Whatever the role biology plays (and that role is by no means clear) in the way boys are characteristically different from girls in their emotional expression, these differences are amplified in the way culture supports emotional development in girls and discourages it for boys. ... Even the youngest boy learns quickly he must hide his feelings and silence his fears. (E1, E3)

Even within gender boxes, girls can be tomboys without the same social stigma that shrouds boys doing allegedly "girl things" and being called "sissies." Older unmarried adult males are bachelors; older unmarried females are old maids or spinsters. Interwoven in these rules for conduct and behavior are moralities and morals that are neither explained nor logical to those subjected to these rules. *The Big Box* points out the problem of adults not feeling the need to explain rules for the children subjected to them: "Now the rules are clear in everybody's mind/So there's no need to repeat them." These children are clearly not part of the "we" and "everybody" that makes all equally contributing members who are working toward the collective "public good." These often gender-specific rules of behavior manifest themselves in so many overt and subtle ways in all manner of literature, media, and popular culture, past and present—from music, movies, television, cartoons, books, and magazines to nursery rhymes and fairy tales. Adults have the power and authority to reward those who conform and punish those who do not conform to social prescriptions. Even though Mickey is relegated to the big box, as are the brown-skinned Liza Sue and Patty, he is part of white privilege that makes him more socially valuable than the two brown girls. More broadly speaking, as a white male child, he is also allegedly smarter, more likely to succeed, more physically attractive, and sees himself reflected in more positive ways in virtually every aspect of society. However, as a child in Morrison's world of adult privilege, adult omnipotence, adult omnipresence, and adult omniscience, he is as boxed and restricted as the girls.

Despite the restrictions imposed on them by the adult world, these three children are imaginatively and intellectually free within themselves, even inside the big box. The shackling of their bodies does not necessarily shackle their curious minds and their creative spirits. Refusing to allow the adult world to define for them freedom and what it means to be free, these three children liberate themselves through memory and possibility. No matter where they are physically, they can still imagine, hear, or remember the sounds of screaming porpoises, the sights of hopping bunnies, and the sights and sounds of beavers chewing trees. Morrison cheers them on as they will not be pacified or stifled by their imaginatively, spiritually, and emotionally neglectful parents bearing weekly gifts of "a jar of dirt," "a recording of a living sea gull," "picture of the sky and a butterfly under glass," "an aquarium thing with plastic fish," "dolls that are already named," or "a movie camera all set up with a film of a running brook." Susie Wilde, in her essay "Celebrity Coaching: Eight Tips for Stars Writing Children's Books" for *The Independent Weekly* (26 April 2000), clearly misses the point of *The Big Box* in her claim that, "At the story's conclusion, [the children] spring from this box without having taken any action and there's no reason behind why the release occurred. The only explanation is one of my Forbidden Four...*deus ex machina*." That the children demonstrate that they possess within themselves the resources to release them suggests on one level that the children really are not as boxed as the adults believe and expect them to be. That they are imaginative and question authority means that they are not boxed within themselves. Adding to the original poem and functioning as the final declaration of *The Big Box*—"Who says they can't handle their freedom?"—affords these children an agency the adult world seeks to deny them. Morrison thus questions the nature and quality of life and living for both adults and children who are slaves to routine and repetition with no acceptance of imagination and creative possibility.

When assessing the impact and purposes of *The Big Box*, many conclude that the serious mood and message of this book mean that it is more suited for adult readers than children. Ellen Fader, in her review for *School Library Journal*, insists: "This is a book that will have a hard time finding an audience: it looks like a picture book for younger children, yet the theme and images require some sophistication and a desire to explore life's boundaries" (1999, 227). Surely, the book is appropriate for both children and adult audiences. When rooms have "doors that only open one way," all readers are asked to recognize the complicated contradictions in human relationships. The visually detached and static quality of the illustrations and the darkness that prevail the text literally and figuratively underscore the irony of the alleged "prettiness" inside this big box or any other box that inherently restricts as it intends to protect and shield.

Those who assume that Morrison's message is too sophisticated for children's full comprehension fail to realize that children are well aware of contradiction and one-sidedness even if they are unable to articulate them fully and clearly, even when they are limited in the range of their public responses to such contradiction. Children also understand the importance of rules and fairness in their families, among their friends, in their schools, and in games that they play. Actually, their perceptions of rules and regulations may not be significantly different from those of adults. There is no reason to believe that elementary school children cannot determine when individuals—adults and children—will only see the world from one limited perspective. Endowing children with intellectual and psychological depth, Morrison encourages all readers to realize that they need not be intimidated in considering multiple ways of existing fully in and responding wholly to the world.

AN INVITATION TO BE KINDER AND GENTLER

In Tennessee Williams's play, *A Streetcar Named Desire* (1947), a troubled, deceitful, but ultimately sympathetic Blanche DuBois tells her spiteful beau Mitch that "deliberate cruelty to another human being is unforgivable." Expanding this theme about the rewards of kindness, Morrison's second picture book, *The Book of Mean People* (2002), celebrates a child's creativity in dealing with certain kinds of life challenges from a child's perspective. Also about a child's self-empowerment through creative expression, this book offers constructive advice on dealing with mean people—those people who are often deliberately cruel or unkind. Lessons of self-control and survival through one's own creative resources surely transcend adult/child age specificity.

Consisting of some thirty-three simple sentences with a Father-Mother-Dick-and-Jane rhythm and syntax, *The Book of Mean People* offers meanness as a temporary state of being based on unkind or harsh actions, words, tones of voice, or attitudes. The nature of meanness, according to Morrison, is such that even "good" people can be mean. The book's driving message is that "mean" people can also stop being mean. That adults are mean to children and to other adults and that children are mean to adults and other children make meanness a universal possibility for any and everyone across cultures, races, and genders. Even as newspaper headlines verify the existence of meanness in potentially every corner of our lives—"Girls Take Mean to a New Level" (Melendez, 2002, 1) and "Meanness Destroys Healthy Workplace" (McGuire, 2003, 8)—*The Book of Mean People* points fingers at mean acts by adults, teachers, and children.

Jokes, pranks and practical jokes, gossip, premeditated and hurtful criticisms, and badgering are some of the many manifestations of meanness from this little bunny's child perspective. While others' meanness is not something from which we can shield ourselves, we can rethink our meanness toward others and can draw on our own creative energies to combat the residual of our individual encounters with meanness. Even when another's actions and behaviors are not meant to be mean, Morrison shows that a receiver's feelings are not necessarily controlled by a person's intentions. Children can perceive as mean those actions they do not fully understand—for example, eating peas, sitting down and sitting up, writing evenly on the lines of the paper, and "wasting" time. For those hurt or angered by another's meanness, the book offers creative ways of dealing with those feelings so as not to become self-destructive or destructive to others. Although meanness is not universal, its potential to affect anyone and at any time is. Morrison's dedication of the book—"To brave kids everywhere (mean people, you know who you are)"— then signifies the universal potential of meanness and forces all readers at once into a moment of self-reflection and self-empowerment.

An equal opportunity emotional response to being mean to another or being the recipient of another's meanness makes everyone—male and female, rich and poor, black and white, young and old, tall and short, fat and thin—a potential perpetrator or recipient of a mean act, comment, gesture, attitude, or word. *The Book of Mean People* then lists ways in which babysitters, brothers, moms, teachers, parents, grandparents, and other children are mean to the little bunny. Sometimes, as the bunny details, mean people smile and frown; mean people contradict each other and themselves; mean people shout, yell, and scream; sometimes mean people whisper and gossip about others; sometimes mean people try to force children to eat foods they do not like. Mean people also expect a young child to fully understand the linguistic ambiguities—auditory and visual— not only of homographs but also of homonyms like *knight* and *night*, as when an older brother scolds during a chess game: "The knight can't go there," when in fact the child knows that "night" goes everywhere. Does eating green peas allegedly "because they are good for you" make you any less sick from eating them? How good are green peas for anyone's health? Is there a direct correlation between good health and eating green peas? How can children "hear" as they are being yelled at by loud booming-voiced and physically larger adults? Related to this point is a Scott and Borgman *Zits* cartoon (2003) that shows an obviously agitated parent yelling out demands about tidying a room to a teen child:

Parent: JEREMY! WILL YOU PLEASE GET YOUR SHOES OUT OF THE MIDDLE OF THE LIVING ROOM?
Jeremy: ALL RIGHT! ALL RIGHT! I HEARD YOU!
            (Jeremy walks away with head down.)
Jeremy: YOU KNOW, JUST BECAUSE SOMEONE DOESN'T RESPOND THE FIRST FEW DOZEN TIMES YOU TELL THEM TO DO SOMETHING DOESN'T MEAN THEY'RE NOT LISTENING! (E4)

When the adult yelling has escalated to this point, it is safe to say that all reason and reasoning are lost. Is this parent having a bad day and anything would trigger such an outburst, no matter the circumstance? Might this moment be an opportunity to discuss the parent's value of tidiness and a kind of order in the way that the child does not value or understand? Whatever the particulars, the yelling precludes at this moment any effort at conversation, dialogue, and mutual understanding. More often than not—and I know this from personal experience with my own teen children—my obsession/preoccupation with tidiness and my design for ordering our shared home environment is less about them as developing adults than about my illusion of controlling some aspect of my world. At the same time, as a family sharing a living space, we must all hear, acknowledge, and value each other's perspectives.

Unexplained or unclarified expectations about children's understanding further surface in inquiries raised in *The Book of Mean People* such as: How should a child understand as might an adult what it means to use time wisely when one construct of childhood is that it is not burdened with adult responsibilities and time constraints? Do adults always use their time wisely? What and who determines a wise use of time? Are there any variations on time used wisely? In much the same way that the children liberate themselves in *The Big Box*, this little bunny's resilient spirit is ultimately larger than those who unleash their meanness on it. The bunny realizes that big people who are mean become small, and that little people who are mean become smaller. That mean people belittle themselves and others reminds us all that no one is immune to being hurt by another, that being hurt makes us all feel small, no matter the age, gender, race, or size.

Importantly, an individual's creative responses to others' meanness become the focus of this book. That *The Book of Mean People* is self-reflective—its first page reads: "This is a book about mean people"—shows that writing, drawing, singing, dancing, or other creative expression in the face of meanness is the ultimate self-empowerment for this little ageless, raceless, genderless bunny that in the end triumphs with a resounding "I will smile anyway! How about that!" Such defiance through creative outlets helps prevent the meanness of others from seeping into our spirits and making us self-destructive or destructive to others. Such creative possibilities also help steer both children and adults alike from being consumed spiritually by the futility of cynicism and low self-esteem. Using an identity-less bunny rather than a human character reinforces the universality of the coexisting messages of innocence and meanness. Whether we are adults or children, we can perpetuate meanness. Whether adults or children, we can understand others' perceptions and perspectives in a way that can make our communications and interactions more significant, more productive, and more meaningful.

The same graduate student who did not like *The Big Box* also did not appreciate the child's perspective Morrison presents in *The Book of Mean People*:

> *The Book of Mean People* earned my dislike because it seemed to undermine parental authority/respect by labeling mother, grandmother, grandfather and siblings mean people for trying (possibly ineptly, but still trying) to teach a child how to *behave like an adult*. ... I will *never* let a child of mine read a book like that. (e-mail message to author, 15 April 2003; emphasis added)

Surely, a child's book on any serious subject should never stand alone without some degree of adult opportunity for discussion. This parent might well use this book as an opportunity to discuss with the child how and why this bunny perceives the various people and situations in the book as mean. Another part of the adult–child discussion might consider how others do not always intend to be mean. The book also raises these questions for adult readers: Are parents set on magically transforming children into adults through their prescriptions for children's behaviors? What does it mean to be an adult? What does it mean to be a child? To what extent are adults ever expected or asked to see the world through children's eyes? No matter what others' intentions are, hurt and feelings of belittlement from another's action, tone, gesture, or deed are real. The bunny is sharing a perspective. Who are we to challenge that perspective without adult efforts to understand it? Much kinder to this text than to *The Big Box,* critics agree with Morrison's publisher that "young readers know about meanness too and will feel satisfied by having their perspectives championed in *The Book of Mean People*" ("The Book of Mean People," rev., 2003). Again, this text reminds adult readers that we can be empowered by soliciting, listening to, and genuinely valuing children's perspectives. After all, is not adulthood, enlightenment, and maturity constructed around the ability to see, understand, and balance multiple perspectives in and of the world?

NOW WHAT?

Unfortunately, parenting does not come with a user's manual, a return policy, or warranty provisions. Real and immediate parenting moments cannot be revised or replayed. The challenges of "good parenting," then, are infinite and unpredictable and require of conscientious parents and adults continual introspection and self-reflection. Drawing parallels between writing and parenting, Morrison explains that the challenge of parenting is also the reward of parenting:

> [While I was writing and working on my first novel,] writing became a way of life. I felt good and excited and challenged. Once I got started, nothing—except parenthood—challenged me in that way. Parenthood challenges. As soon as you think you've got this age fixed, they [children] change, and it's the same sort of volatileness and change in writing. That I knew I would stay with—whether or not it was successful, or even then whether or not it was published. I was already committed. (Bonetti, 1983)

To admit uncertainty is to admit vulnerability, and to admit vulnerability is to admit humanness. As children grow and develop minds and spirits of their own, it becomes necessary for all adults to guide but not to dictate or to dictate without just cause. This is not to say that adults have no role in giving shape to youngsters' lives, but rather that adults recognize the pitfalls of insisting on absolute control in their guiding and directing. To allow children safe opportunities to discover themselves through their own experiences with and in the world is not bad parenting. Even as adults believe that we are protecting our children from the world and from themselves, Morrison challenges us to accept that adults' illusory control over children is less about children being controlled than about the adults trying to exercise adult control. To experience both *The Big Box* and *The Book of Mean People* is then an opportunity for all adults to reexamine their own motives when they involve conscious manipulation of others' independent and safe exploration and self-expression.

Because "childhood is a social construct," maintains Stephani Etheridge Woodson in her essay "Popular Culture and the Performance of Childhood" (2002), "adults regulate young people's identities and actions through … symbolic and embodied performances." The power to make rules, to regulate and restrict actions and behavior, to punish and to reward actions, and to create consequences for behavior ultimately come to define adulthood, the illusory opposite of childhood. If, as Susie Wilde contends, "the best children's books please both child and adult audiences, but this is incredibly difficult" ("Celebrity Coaching," 2), Morrison's books fit the bill. Their social and intellectual importance and relevance are not necessarily directly connected to their commercial and market appeal. A certain timelessness exists in *The Big Box* and *The Book of Mean People* as the alleged line between adult and child behavior and perspective is barely visible. Every adult was once a child, and every child will become an adult—at least chronologically. The gray libratory space that separates and defines these two positions is at the heart of Morrison's texts. Both books show the symbiotic existence of parent and child, of teacher and student, of adult neighbor and child neighbor, and substantiate Woodson's claim that "childhood, and a culture's or individual's conception of childhood, reveals reflexively what it means to be an adult but does not answer the question of how to be a child." (21)

Indeed, as an adult, as a parent, and as a scholar engaged with both of Morrison's texts, I am reminded that I have talked and written about *The Big Box* and *The Book of Mean People* as though they were authored solely by Morrison, when in fact mother Morrison insists that these stories are joint efforts with her son Slade. While it is clear that the adult influences the child, in actuality, the child equally influences the adult. Every adult parenting experience is fundamentally influenced by a child — a child's immediate presence, a child's very existence. Both of Morrison's texts then ask us adults to acknowledge the profound truth that we owe much of who we are as adults to children, ours or someone else's.

SECOND-GUESS PARENTING AND VISUALIZING YOURSELF THROUGH YOUR CHILD'S EYES
BY NATHAN STAMEY WINESETT

I am not familiar with either of these children's books by Toni Morrison except through the summaries and commentary of Lester's chapter. Nevertheless, the underlying themes of these books and the previous texts by Morrison, as discussed in the chapter, touch me through both my observations of others and through my own experiences. The application of these themes obviously varies greatly depending on the nature of the reader's own adult–child relationship.

I have often seen adults fail to give children adequate respect. This varies by degree, but all adults (and children's failure to respect other children for that matter) are guilty to some extent. Some adults routinely belittle their children, give them no respect, do not consider their feelings and viewpoints, and are otherwise very harsh toward them as in the adult behaviors and attitudes Morrison portrays. Yet, adults such as myself, who are respectful of children's thoughts and feelings, still experience moments that are somewhat akin to such behavior, albeit to a much lesser degree. This also happens in adult–adult relationships in which one adult feels or is perceived as superior to the other. Perhaps I see myself as an example of someone who has learned to become a better adult by visualizing life through the eyes of my two young children. This may explain my overall response to Morrison's texts: to adjust our adult relationships with children by perceiving from children's points of view; to be fair with them and respectful of them; to understand that children are autonomous; and to allow them greater freedom to interact with life physically and emotionally. Morrison urges us to keep the conflicting messages of freedom and the adult responsibility of raising children in the forefront of our minds as we interact with our children and others' children. But it is not an instruction to take literally or to provide unlimited physical and emotional freedom to our children.

I have a few recent stories that seem relevant to this point. I have two sons who are my pride and joy, my idols, and my best friends. Sam is one and a half, and Noah recently turned four. I focus first on Noah since he is older.

Since I work, Noah and Sam go to daycare. As I was driving them to school, we were singing Noah's favorite Johnny Cash song and otherwise having a great time doing the things we usually do during this weekday ritual. We walked in and did our standard things—dropped off Sam, hugs and kisses, some playful banter, and the like. Noah's class was outside, and he sprinted off toward them. On this particular day, I stuck around for a few moments and watched the youngsters from the window. Noah gave his friend Jackson a big, long hug. Then, he started talking to Jackson's brother, Jacob, and it was obvious that Noah was emphatically telling him some long narrative. They were having an in-depth discussion, and it occurred to me that I could not even imagine what they were talking about. Then, they both started hitting themselves on the head in a silly way. I turned to one of the teachers inside and commented, "He's his own man, huh?"

At some level, it was disconcerting not to know everything about Noah. He is my son, an extension of me, and there is a natural desire to guide him to be like me. Yet he is not. He is Noah, with his own experiences outside my control. At the same time, it was warming to see him growing up and developing his own personality and his own sense of himself. This experience of watching Noah is just one drop of water in an ocean full of similar experiences. Every day I see Noah do, say, or understand something that seems amazingly complex, sophisticated, and way beyond what I would have thought him capable just a moment before. Yet I never seem to grasp fully his capabilities, and I find myself often failing to give enough respect to those capabilities.

While there is a great deal of public discussion about the conflict between "freedom" and parenting, the real issue Morrison highlights in these books seems to be fairness. The world is a place of excessive stimuli, and each child, adult, animal, plant, and thing receives and provides stimuli. Absolute freedom cannot exist; the laws of physics and chemistry set nonwavering rules and regulations. Add to this the effect of constant interactions between living organisms. A child walking through the forest may be eaten by a mountain lion, brush up against poison ivy, or bump into another human. As you add up all the possible stimuli for all organisms, you make a society with rules and regulations for the sake of each other's survival. Sometimes these rules and regulations make sense and are fair. Sometimes, they are not. When they are not, adults are adversely affected. The same is true for children.

I know that discipline is important for a child's safety and allows adults and children to live peacefully with each other in our social world. A well-raised child should eventually do as told by a parent just because the parent said so. But, the child should do so because the child wants to please his or her parents, not out of fear. A child will only want to please his or her parents if the child respects those parents and feels that the parents respect her. To accomplish this, Morrison highlights, a parent cannot just instruct "because I said so," but needs to educate, explain, and discuss the reasons for certain rules and decisions. And, while it seems impossible because we always grossly underestimate a child's reasoning capabilities, the reasons must be explained such that the child perceives and understands.

With these guidelines I set for myself, I feel that Noah will develop the healthy ability to question and consider things for himself, confidently make his own conclusions and decisions, and develop a trust not only in his parents, but also in society.

My second story has to do with Noah's favorite color—pink. Purple is a close second, and both are pretty "feminine" colors according to society's rules. Who made these rules? Who assigned pink to girls? I cannot think of any sensible reason for this, except that I learned it somewhere on the way to adulthood and manhood. I have never made an issue of Noah liking pink. I have never been shy about others knowing that. I often joke about it. Yet I never talk jokingly about it in front of Noah because I do not want it to affect him negatively.

We went to REI, an outdoor store, which sells colored Nalgene water bottles. One bottle was bright fluorescent pink. Noah saw it and wanted it. I had no problem. I thought it was cool-looking too. We bought it. Then, we went to a sporting goods store because Noah was starting T-ball. I was very proud, and Noah was very excited. We had been practicing for several weeks with makeshift equipment. At the department store, I was picking out a bat, glove, and balls for Noah. Noah, with his pink water bottle in hand, spotted a bright pink batting helmet and asked if he could get it. I failed Society 101. I told him "no" and made up some excuse. Sadly enough, I was uncomfortable sending him out into the world with a pink batting helmet because of what others would think. I felt I was protecting him to some degree as well. Was it right? I do not know. If he insisted, then I would have probably let him have it, but I would have also probably joked about it to parents as a cover for my own insecurity. I still think it is cool that Noah loves pink. I guess I just have a limit on certain pink things. For some reason, the pink batting helmet was "too much," even though in my own childhood I had a favorite dress. It was even a flowered dress. I probably thought it was pretty. I wore it all over the house and never thought anything of it until I was older. I do not remember my parents ever making an issue of it, but I do not think I ever wore it outside the house either. I also am probably happy that I never wore it to school (presumably because my parents avoided it somehow) and was not mocked relentlessly. My parents saved me from bad social teaching at an early age: an unfair, non-sensical rule that could have ultimately impeded my parenting goal of developing a son who has the confidence to consider things and make conclusions for himself. I have subconsciously parented in the same way with the pink batting helmet.

And so it goes. We as caring parents feel the need to guide our children by what we perceive as fair and sensible rules, rules that also protect them from the unfair and nonsensical rules of society without damaging their long-term ability to think and act independently. The nonsensible rules related to race, class, age, weight, and sexuality are unending. Why is any stereotype (even positive or neutral ones) considered racist when used in connection with certain races? For example, Asians are smart; blacks can run fast and jump high or like fried chicken and watermelon. Just recently, hundreds of people were evacuated here to Utah from New Orleans. Based on videos and news reports, they are almost entirely black. There are very few blacks in Utah. No one would dare say, "Gee, I hope the black ladies bring some decent cooking here." (Note that Utah restaurants leave a little to be desired.) I would never say it because I know society would ostracize me, but, it did occur to me that just maybe some of them might open a decent Creole or southern-cooking restaurant. Now, why is it that such statements are banned by society, but other stereotypes are not? No one would think anything of the following: "Ooh, he's French. Maybe he'll have some good wine." Or, to a white person, "Oh, you're southern. Can you make grits and sweet tea?" You get the drift. To me, those who perceive the first statement above as racist have a racial problem. Why is there something negative about being black or Asian, because there is certainly nothing wrong with being smart, or eating fried chicken, or running fast? At worst, they are presumptuous stereotypes, but racist? It seems weird to me, but I comply because of society's rules. Defamatory stereotypes are another story, and parents must make every effort to save their children from these bad social teachings because they adversely affect the child: "Girls aren't as smart as boys." Defamatory stereotypes must be combated with respect to both the child and the child's perceptions of others.

So, do we teach our children these rules? The answer is that the adult must consider each issue and come to what he or she thinks is a sensible conclusion, balancing sensible and fair concepts with the facts of society. For me, pink REI bottle: yes; pink batting helmet: no. Defamatory stereotypes: no. Positive/neutral stereotypes: let the child have the freedom to decide.

I know I have not spoken much about "meanness" as discussed in the chapter, but it basically falls back to fairness and respect for a child's ability to understand. Noah hates brushing his teeth. Sometimes when he is being stubborn, I have to pin him down and forcibly brush them. He knows that he must do it so that he does not get cavities (at least theoretically, since he has never gotten one), just like he knows he needs to eat healthy foods to get big and strong. But he probably thinks I am mean when I forcibly brush his teeth and refuse to let him have a Popsicle. However, I hope he knows that it is because I love him and am watching out for him.

There is another issue in the chapter about meanness: the message that there should be empathy regarding perceived meanness. So perhaps *The Book of Mean People* helps a child to understand that a parent forcibly brushing the child's teeth is not so mean after all.

TALKING OUT LOUD: IDEAS FOR DISCUSSION

1. What defines and marks differences between adulthood and childhood?
2. What similarities exist between adulthood and childhood?
3. Is Toni Morrison's son and coauthor Slade "silenced" in our reading and talking about these books and these stories? How so?
4. To what extent is a parent and adult identity predicated on the existence of a child?
5. What kinds of decisions allow parents and children to share decision-making authority equally?
6. Based on Morrison's children's texts, how fragile or strong is the social and historical foundation of adulthood and adult authority?
7. What suggestions would you offer the parents and other adults in these two children's books about their relationships with youngsters?
8. What advice would you offer the children in these two children's books about their relationships with their parents and other adults?
9. To what extent is Morrison advocating or not advocating total childhood anarchy in these children's texts?

II
Dialoguing Reviews

9

REVIEWS OF ANNE SCHRAFF'S
LOST AND FOUND

REVIEWED BY JASMINE Z. LESTER

Anne Schraff's *Lost and Found* (2001) follows a teenage girl named Darcy as she tackles family and school conflicts. Due to her absent father, overworked mother, and bedridden grandmother, Darcy is forced to play the role of caretaker and parent to her younger sister. *Lost and Found* addresses issues of stereotypes and judging a book by its cover. Darcy undergoes a psychological transformation as she discovers that people are not always what they seem, and that prejudgments are usually incorrect.

Aside from these themes, Schraff attempts to intrigue the readers with a stalker/mystery plot. All and all, as a high school senior, I found this book to be boring and uneventful. It is probably more exciting from the point of view of a middle-school-aged child.

REVIEWED BY NEAL A. LESTER

The first installment in her *Bluford* (High School) *Series* of young adult novels, Anne Schraff's *Lost and Found* introduces the central character Darcy Wills, her family, and her circle of high school friends. With some degree of suspense and mystery, at least in the first section, the novel shows the kinds of family drama many young readers will surely recognize as familiar on some level. In a larger sense, the novel demonstrates how new hope and hopefulness can emerge from intense personal disillusion and disappointment.

Sixteen-year-old Darcy's responses to complicated life experiences constitute the focus of *Lost and Found*. We witness her paternalism toward her fourteen-year-old rebellious and confused sister, Jamee; her festering resentment and anger toward her father for abandoning the family and for his marital infidelities; and her responses to her sick grandmother's fast mental and physical deterioration as a result of a stroke. Throughout the novel, we also see Darcy's emotional and social growth as she opens herself to new and renewed friendships. For instance, resisting finally the uncomfortable influence of her snooty friend Brisana, Darcy moves from her lonely pedestal of public intellectual elitism and social snobbery to embrace and find comfort in difference. Her new friendships with Cooper and Tarah prove far more spiritually satisfying and honest than her unsatisfying relationship with the self-absorbed prima donna Brisana.

Darcy's admirable efforts to protect and parent her younger sister drive most of the plot in this novel. From Jamee's socializing with the wrong crowd to Jamee's dating an abusive and older boy who coerces her to steal for him to Jamee's lying to her mother and being blatantly honest with (though disrespectful to) their uppity Aunt Charlotte, and to Jamee's running away from home, Darcy presents herself as the model child and student. Unfortunately for Darcy, her reputation as an intellectually gifted student and her association with Brisana have left her alone and lonely, grossly in need of honest social and romantic companionship.

The novel introduces a number of issues relevant to both male and female teen readers: the magic of budding romance, the personal struggles of children with parents in the throes of serious marital conflict, the importance of social popularity to teens, and interestingly, male violence against females in teen boyfriend/girlfriend relationships. Although drugs and drive-by shootings are alluded to in the novel, bringing them into the story seems unnecessarily gratuitous and stereotypical in much the same way we might faultily associate Jamee's youthful rebellion with her listening to loud rap music, as though all rap music is the same. Surely, the author would not have us believe that rap leads to youth rebellion. As well, the presentation of the girls' mother, Mattie Mae Wills, seems problematic in terms of believability. That the mother, a single parent for the past five years, is struggling financially to support her two teen daughters and her own sick mother with no outside assistance of any sort is not farfetched; however, that she is so minimally aware of what is going on in her daughters' lives is hard to believe. As well, the mother's constant refrain that "she's tired" from working long and frequent hours unfairly thrusts Darcy into a kind of parental role. When Jamee disappears, it is Darcy, not their mother, who seems more committed to finding Jamee as quickly as possible. The mother says that she will return home to help with the search once she finds someone to cover her work shift. One might question the mother's life priorities—her job security or her lost daughter's safety. The novel offers no details that the mother made efforts to be temporarily relieved of her job responsibilities in light of this immediate family crisis. Ultimately, the story strives for contemporary relevance at the expense of constructing a tight and satisfying narrative.

10

REVIEWS OF ANNE SCHRAFF'S
A MATTER OF TRUST

REVIEWED BY JASMINE Z. LESTER

A Matter of Trust (2001) is about sixteen-year-old Darcy Wills and her issues: her boyfriend is losing interest in her; her sick grandmother needs the family's immediate attention and care; and her father returns after abandoning Darcy, her younger twelve-year-old sister Jamee, and their mother. Although Jamee seems to have forgiven their father for his actions, Darcy has a difficult time learning to trust him again and to harness and redirect her anger and resentment.

A Matter of Trust focuses on teenage insecurities and how to overcome them. It picks up where Schraff's *Lost and Found* leaves off, and traces of *Lost and Found*'s absent father theme are here. Nevertheless, the plot of this novel is a bit unclear. For example, there is no explanation of why and how such events as the park shooting fit Darcy's story. Also, some of the problems that should be resolved due to their importance in the story are not explained. For instance, the source of Darcy's grandmother's illness is never clear. We know that the grandmother had a stroke about a year ago but are not clear how the stroke has caused her to age so quickly and to waste away physically. The author does make it clear how Darcy's grandmother's health affects everyone in the family. Whether the grandmother might be better cared for in a nursing home is an important issue for the whole family.

Overall, the book is well written and easy to read. The situations hold the reader's attention and are ones to which teens can relate:

boyfriend/girlfriend problems and family conflicts like an absent parent and possible divorce. Since the main character is a girl—an illustration of Darcy is prominent on the book cover—this book would probably appeal more to teenage girls than boys. All in all, the story is about staying strong in times of hardship. I would probably recommend this book to middle schoolers and junior high schoolers because they may be able to relate more easily to some of the themes presented in the story.

REVIEWED BY NEAL A. LESTER

That real life has no happily-ever-after endings, but that one's attitude and perspective can add hope for possibilities, is one of the central messages of Anne Schraff's *A Matter of Trust*, from her *Bluford* (High School) *Series*. Chronicling some of the day-to-day experiences of sixteen-year-old Darcy Wills, this novel shows the emotional volatility of teen romance, teen friendships, romantic and sibling rivalries, and relationship betrayals. It also demonstrates emotional vulnerabilities of both youth and adulthood, showing that personal, social, and familial conflicts will not disappear with good intentions or a magic wand. As we witness Darcy's somewhat-misplaced maternal efforts to protect her romantic interest, Hakeem, from public embarrassment because of his stuttering, we follow her through a number of relationship conflicts that test her emotional maturity and her self-doubts. From her bitter dispute with her former best friend, Brisana, to her ongoing bickering with her younger sister; her anger and resentment toward her absent, then returning, father; her doubts about Hakeem's romantic interest in her; her impatience with her uppity Aunt Charlotte; and her confusion about and disillusion with the deteriorating psychological faculties of her live-in grandmother, Darcy is able to regain lost trust in those who have disappointed her and to find hope in the possibilities of tomorrow. Her various relationships map out the philosophical wisdoms sprinkled throughout the text as offered by both her new best friend Tarah and her grandmother before the grandmother's stroke and subsequent mental and physical decline. All of Darcy's experiences convince her that forgiveness, compassion, and hope can help everyone weather even the most bitter of life's storms.

With a straightforward uncomplicated plot, Anne Schraff offers an even-paced novel of interest certainly to early high school females. The rhythm of the language—the characters' and the narrator's—makes the various storylines engaging and real. Schraff captures well the workings of female cliques, of parental discord, of immediate personal responsibility in conflict with immediate personal desires, and of relationship healing. One potentially confusing part of the novel is the arbitrary drive-by shooting at the park during Darcy's friend's birthday party. While the event forces the high schoolers who witness the dangerous episode to reassess the value of life and relationships, it seems to lead the novel unnecessarily toward the dangerous waters of racial stereotyping: gang violence, single parent/mom households, and economic woes of a family life that is but a notch or two away from the ghetto. Still, that the novel ultimately asks readers to find a silver lining behind even the seemingly darkest clouds will surely connect with young readers across cultural, racial, and gender lines.

11

REVIEWS OF ANNE SCHRAFF'S
UNTIL WE MEET AGAIN

REVIEWED BY JASMINE Z. LESTER

Until We Meet Again (2001) focuses on a teenage girl, Darcy, and her ability to deal with major changes in her life. Not only must she endure changes in her family life that involve her father and her grandmother, but she also has to resolve issues in her love life. She loses one of the most important people in her life, and through the losses and the changes that she undergoes, Darcy is able to mature and learn valuable life lessons: she is able to look at death and life in a more positive light, appreciating that death does not have to be an end to fond memories. She also realizes that losses in life can feel like an emotional and spiritual death. Her losses make her stronger.

I recommend this book to middle-school children because, from the perspective of a high schooler, this book may not be as exciting or as complicated as the author intends and hopes.

REVIEWED BY NEAL A. LESTER

As a sequel to *A Matter of Trust,* Anne Schraff's *Until We Meet Again* challenges some of the idyllic notions of youth and focuses on the inevitability of change. In this installment of the *Bluford* (High School) *Series,* readers witness more complicated life experiences of sixteen-year-old Darcy Wills, who is forced to realize that part of the human condition is acknowledging one's own frailties and realizing that we can forgive ourselves for mistakes only when we can arrive at life lessons from those mistakes.

The novel opens quite positively for Darcy Wills and her family. Her absent father has returned home to unite with the family after a five-year abandonment, her father and mother have agreed to work on reconciling their marital conflicts, and the Wills family is moving from their run-down apartment to a new home. Amid the excitement of these developments, Darcy learns that her boyfriend, Hakeem, will be moving from California to Michigan because of his father's health problems and subsequent job loss. In dealing with the inevitability of Hakeem's departure, Darcy becomes selfish, expecting and almost demanding Hakeem's attentions when he is distracted by his own family matters. Darcy's confusion about how to respond to her own selfishness in light of Hakeem's family struggles makes her vulnerable to the dangerous allure of Brian, a magnetically attractive nineteen-year-old "bad boy." As Darcy gives in to her hormonal responses to Brian's overwhelming physical attractiveness and tries to substitute Brian's attention for the attention she feels she is no longer getting from Hakeem, she experiences feelings that force her to see herself in a different light. Keeping secrets from her parents and her best friend, Tarah, lying to her father, and ultimately falling prey to Brian's dangerous schemes to violate her innocence spiritually and physically reveal a Darcy that even she does not recognize. While Darcy tries to sort through her conflicting emotions about her commitment to Hakeem and her excited curiosity about Brian, her heart is broken when her ailing and feeble grandmother dies. Darcy is comforted only in the realization that her memories of the wise words of advice from her grandmother will always be guiding forces in her life. Significantly different from *A Matter of Trust*, in which other characters work to regain Darcy's trust after their mistakes, *Until We Meet Again* realistically shows Darcy's own need to regain others' trust after a series of bad choices and unfortunate occurrences.

An ominous and foreboding cloud hangs over the characters and follows the reader in this novel. Even though life seems good for the Wills family, the reality is that the grandmother is moving steadily closer to death. Darcy is also unhappy that Hakeem is moving, even though she realizes the move is a necessity. More important, though, and perhaps of most interest to teens reading this novel, is the dangerous mystery of Brian Smith and mounting sexual tensions between Darcy and Brian that dominate the second half of the book after Hakeem's departure. Schraff's clues to the reader about Brian's potential danger to Darcy can be traced through careful attention to his many calculated smiles, which Darcy reads as genuine, and in the frequent surprise visitations with an easily infatuated and confused girl. Given these details and the many subtle or aborted warnings about his past and present reprehensive behavior from Brian's sister and from Darcy's friend, it is not a surprise to the reader when Brian tries to exert his power over Darcy against her will.

Comparatively, this novel is by far more emotionally engaging than *A Matter of Trust*. Here, issues of sexuality (though not overt, graphic, or offensive), of self-disappointment and the reality of disappointing those who love us most, and of the value of true friendship will appeal to both male and female readers. For males, this novel speaks against the kind of unacceptable "bad boy" behavior on which many young and immature teen males pride themselves, especially as public performers. At the same time, this novel warns young teen girls about the dangers of some males who are selfish schemers and manipulators. The author has tackled a number of intricately complicated life issues for teens. Even the seemingly minor details of Liselle's unwed teen parenting, Darcy's father's violent beating of Brian for his ungentlemanly behavior with Darcy, and Brian's fathering out of wedlock a child he is not actively parenting can lead teens into important discussions of real-life experiences that they sometimes do not recognize in more "literary" narratives.

12

REVIEW OF ELIZA A. COMODROMOS'S
TEACHER'S GUIDE TO THE BLUFORD SERIES

REVIEWED BY NEAL A. LESTER

All good teachers continually seek new and different ways to enhance their classroom instruction, ways to make their teaching more exciting to them and to make learning more exciting for their students. Assuming that teachers are clear about what to teach and about the what, who, where, when, and why dimensions of those texts, others' suggestions of how to present texts and ideas within texts are almost always welcome. Particularly when texts deal with sophisticated, complicated, real-life issues such as race, class, gender, sexuality, and violence, for instance, veteran teachers might well turn to Eliza A. Comodromos's *Teacher's Guide to the Bluford Series* (2001).

Comodromos's *Guide* covers the first seven of the ten young adult novels that constitute the *Bluford* (High School) *Series*: Anne Schraff's five novels, *Lost and Found* (2001), *A Matter of Trust* (2001), *Secrets in the Shadows* (2001), *Someone to Love Me* (2001), and *Until We Meet Again* (2001); and Paul Langan's two novels, *The Bully* (2001) and *The Gun* (2002). A second *Guide* is forthcoming to cover Langan's three new books: *Blood Is Thicker* (2004), *Brothers in Arms* (2004), and *Summer of Secrets* (2004). The *Guide* is a valuable resource for secondary school educators integrating any or all of these texts into their middle and high school literature curriculum. Just as the novels themselves are accessible and easy to read, Comodromos's *Guide* is accessible and easy to use. Its four-part organization—"Introduction: To the Teacher,"

"Writing Skills Handouts," "Activities to Accompany Each Book," and "Answers to the Activities"—is sensible and clear.

Section I reminds teachers that the most important goal of reading these books—and by extension, any book—is to get students to read and to enjoy what they read. Even if they are not the strongest writers or the most skilled critical thinkers, students can realize the pleasure and excitement of reading. This section also encourages teachers to use ideas as directly presented or to choose and modify suggested activities and exercises as they see fit for their own personal instruction.

Section II provides substantial direction in getting students to focus on writing and critical thinking as natural and rewarding extensions of reading, not only with these books but also with any literature text. Beginning with exercises that give students practice in picking out main and supporting ideas in single paragraphs, the section ultimately guides students toward thinking and writing about ideas in the longer traditional five-paragraph essay. All of the components of "good writing" about ideas in any text are emphasized and explained through appropriate handouts and exercises—identifying topic sentences and pertinent supporting ideas, organizing ideas within and between paragraphs, providing transitions within and between ideas and paragraphs, writing introductions and conclusions, revising and rewriting, and proofreading. Certainly, this section on writing as process and product will serve any instructor in classes where students engage in essay writing across the curriculum.

The third section focuses specifically on the content of the seven young adult novels. Accompanying each novel are clear and concise plot summaries and basic character identifications, details that are fundamental to any student discussion and subsequent writing about the books. Each book comes with vocabulary-building and reading comprehension exercises, passage identifications, short and long essay assignments, and suggestions for small-group activities. The broad range and diversity of activities—writing letters to characters about issues or relationships in the books, writing reviews of the books, sending postcards as a character to another character, completing character or idea diagrams—are sure to move students beyond plot-centered thinking and writing and to engage them in deeper critical thinking and analysis.

Because even the most seasoned teachers forget minute textual details and answers to their own questions as they focus on the larger picture of presenting texts comprehensively, the fourth section of the *Guide* is a handy answers key to the short-answer and discussion questions.

The benefits of using this *Guide* are many. Including such varied activities will ensure meaningful thinking, talking, and writing about the ideas in these novels and other literature texts. The range of activities will encourage group idea exchanges and allow for individual student's creative expression, all working to encourage students to enjoy what they read.

One concern about the *Guide* for some instructors of advanced literature students might be the somewhat restrictive paradigm of the five-paragraph essay with its introduction, conclusion, and three supporting points of development. While this model offers a frame and security for beginning and timid writers, it may well hinder the creative energies of and unduly frustrate those young writers and thinkers who know that ideas need not be mechanically limited to this structure. For young writers, it may also create a false and inadequate sense of what constitutes a strongly argued and a well-developed essay.

It is interesting, though not surprising, that the *Guide* itself seems "sanitized" of the social issues presented in the novels. None of the discussions or writing activities deal with the issues of sexuality, violence, and race that make these novels interesting and relevant to young adult readers. For instance, even though the covers of all seven books present images of African American characters, there is nothing about race or culture in any of the activities. In fact, there seems an effort to erase race from the reference text, as indicated by the second line of the "Introduction: To the Teacher": "The novels focus on the lives of a group of urban high school students and their families" (1). While there is mention of the African American astronaut, Guion Bluford, for whom the high school in the novels and the book series itself is named, nothing clarifies that the characters in the novels are African American. Certainly, nothing about the success of reading or teaching these books is predicated on focusing only on the characters' ethnicity; however, instructors and students need not shy away from acknowledging and discussing what the novels present in terms of African American cultural influences in speech, language, and character names, for example. Cultural specificity need not lead to stereotyping or essentializing and can serve as an indication that honesty about difference and others' experiences can better help all readers understand what poet Maya Angelou has articulated about human difference: We are all more alike than we are unalike (Angelou, 1991, 5). Putting the books within age-appropriate social contexts need not be offensive to students or risky for teachers. Rather, honest discussions about the sometimes-sensitive issues of race, class, gender, sexuality, and violence would reinforce the relevance of these books to students' own real-life experiences.

13

REVIEW OF WALTER DEAN MYERS'S *THE BEAST*

REVIEWED BY JASMINE Z. LESTER

Walter Dean Myers's *The Beast* (2003) focuses on seventeen-year-old Anthony "Spoon" Witherspoon's transition from the streets of Harlem to an exclusive Connecticut boarding school. At first, it manifests in the sudden change of environment: the loss of the Harlem streets and the loss of familiar friends. Then it is seen in the change in Spoon, too. After spending months at the school, Spoon is looking forward to returning home to Harlem on his break. When he arrives, however, things are not the same. Everything has changed, from the friends he used to hang out with to his girlfriend, Gabi. He realizes his interest in her is dwindling as her once lively personality becomes tired and sad because her mother is sick. When he has a run-in with Chanelle, a girl from the prep school, over the break, he is almost sure his interest in Gabi is not what it used to be. Myers uses Spoon's relationship with Gabi to represent his feelings for his home in Harlem, where he would not have much of a chance of going to a good college. Chanelle, on the other hand, represents the school and the potential benefits it holds, such as the possibility of obtaining a scholarship to college. The book is centered on Spoon's actions that sometimes lead him closer to home and sometimes farther away. When he finds Gabi high on drugs in a house with other people who are high, he describes them as being prey for "the beast." The way Myers develops the beast, it is the force pulling Spoon away from the safety of his life.

Overall, *The Beast* is an okay book. It has small parts that may spark teenagers' interest and make them eager to read more such as the reasons that Gabi does drugs, but these events are not main events in the story. The book is slow moving and a little boring, but it does get the message across.

14

REVIEWS OF ANGELA JOHNSON'S
THE FIRST PART LAST

REVIEWED BY JASMINE Z. LESTER

Angela Johnson's *The First Part Last* (2003) is about how sixteen-year-old Bobby deals with the consequences of getting his girlfriend pregnant. Instead of giving the baby up for adoption when his girlfriend dies, he decides to keep it. The book focuses on Bobby's struggle and the help of his family and friends.

Johnson does a good job of portraying most of the hardships of being a teenage parent, such as still being young and having to take care of yourself as well as the baby, but she leaves out one critical detail. She does not mention how Bobby gets the money to buy the baby food and diapers. The author does, however, do a good job of showing the issues Bobby has concerning responsibility, such as when Bobby gets tired of having to take care of his baby and leaves it with the babysitter for too long. This shows that it is very hard for Bobby to deal with the responsibility.

I would recommend this book to teens, both boys and girls, because it shows them how hard it is to raise a baby at such a young age. Because many teenagers can relate to Bobby in that they perceive life the same way he does, the readers will know that if they do not act responsibly and stay away from sex before marriage, this could happen to them.

REVIEWED BY NEAL A. LESTER

Adolescents and teens are having sex. Adolescents and teens are thinking about having sex. Adolescents and teens have always had sex or thought about having sex. Adolescents and teens will always have sex or think about having sex. This is the fundamental premise on which award-winning young adult author Angela Johnson bases her novel, *The First Part Last*. Rather than lecture her intended twelve-and-older audience about birth control and the physical and emotional safety of abstinence, Johnson offers *The First Part Last* as a cautionary tale about aborted childhood innocence, which results from poor choices that affect not only the too-young-to-be-parents Nia and Bobby, but also their family and friends. The novel is then a litany of how past mistakes forever haunt these young characters' present dreams and future realities.

The novel's effective alternating "now/then" organizational pattern reinforces the theme that the present and past are inextricably connected because of choices that we make for ourselves, particularly bad choices made by youngsters who knowingly engage in risky behavior. Bobby and Nia are intelligent African American high schoolers who have unprotected sex, and Nia becomes pregnant. The story's format carries the reader back and forth between Bobby's life before, during, and after the pregnancy. He remembers his own childhood and acknowledges to himself that at age sixteen he is unprepared for his forced new identity and responsibility as a teen father: "I feel like I'm a baby with a baby most of the time. Just playing daddy until someone comes over and says, 'Hell, kid, time's up. No more of this daddy time for you, and anyway you've been busted'" (128). The truth, according to Johnson, is that parenting, especially as a teen, is serious business.

Telling the story from the perspective of the teen father affords an interesting lens through which to read gender and social constructions of "manhood." Too often, we read about the complex situation of young females forced to deal with unplanned pregnancies, while the young fathers are either absent or unavailable for any kind of support. To his credit, Bobby is not that kind of new father. From the moment he learns of Nia's pregnancy, he accepts his responsibility for his self-acknowledged "stupid" actions: "I'm going to be this baby's daddy now. ... I'm supposed to be her daddy and stay up all night if I have to. I'm supposed to suck it up and do all the right things if I can, even if I screw it up and have to do it over" (125–126). The novel then shows Bobby's personal struggles with Nia's emotional and physical health, with Nia's parents and their lack of trust in his decision making with their daughter, and his own parents' disappointment in his bad choices. After Nia dies following a complicated delivery, the daily tedium and enormous responsibility of young single parenting force Bobby to grow up overnight and convince him that his life as he once knew it will never again be the same. The reality of changing soiled diapers, cleaning up baby vomit, buying formula and diapers, juggling school and child care, forgoing opportunities to hang out with his buddies, and getting very little sleep around the clock intends to make youngsters think more seriously about giving in to their hormonal urges: "This little thing with the perfect face and hands doing nothing but counting on me. And me wanting nothing else but to run crying into my own mom's room and have her do the whole thing" (15).

Although Johnson's story is a valiant effort to bring us a perspective not often considered—that of a young single father fully embracing fatherhood—the story seems at odds with itself. One such instance occurs when Bobby visits Nia late into her pregnancy and they engage in sex. Their conversation before the encounter has little to do with the gravity of what has led them both to this pivotal moment in their lives—acting irresponsibly with their bodies and sexuality. While there is slight mention of their past carelessness—he says to her, "I figure we hadn't used too much common sense lately, or we wouldn't be pregnant" (49)—they nevertheless "head toward her [bed]room." Even though Nia cannot become pregnant again while she is pregnant, one expects there to be more substantive and cautionary dialogue acknowledging how their impulsive decisions to be sexually active just because the opportunity presents itself is a very serious matter. Instead, Bobby is only interested in whether having sex during her pregnancy will harm the fetus.

Second, while Johnson paints no cookie cutter tale of happily ever after—Nia's death is a contrived way to get her out of the initially intended legal adoption plan and to have the biological father exercise his right to keep the baby—the story leaves other narrative gaps that do not satisfy. Why does Bobby decide to leave New York and move to Ohio to start anew with his infant? How will he survive in Ohio with no job, no job prospects, and no apparent technical training beyond drawing pictures of his new daughter and illegally spray painting public properties? Although his divorced brother and nephews live in Ohio, why would he leave the New York support system of his parents, his daughter's grandparents, and his friends? How is raising an infant in rural Ohio any better than raising an infant in big city New York, especially when Bobby shares with us his love for the city—its smells, its sounds, its lights, and its people? Will he be able to finish his last two years of high school and adequately care for his infant daughter without some immediate financial assistance and other communal or familial support?

The novel consciously challenges us to consider different ways of viewing the world. For instance, gender role reversals are underscored.

Bobby's father is a more emotionally demonstrative nurturer than his mother; Bobby and his dad cry without concern for what others might think of their "manhood"; Bobby's buddies have no problems spending time and playing with Bobby's new child; and the cop who arrests Bobby for his spray painting is female, as is Nia's obstetrician.

It is also important that we recognize that Nia, Bobby, and their families are neither uneducated nor of low-income homes and lifestyles. Bobby's father owns a successful restaurant, and Bobby and his family frequently traveled abroad when he was growing up. Nia's parents have extensive and expensive art collections. Such details about their economics remind readers that unwanted pregnancies are not class, race, or ethnicity specific. Engaging in sexual activity can result in unplanned pregnancy, and any pregnancy changes on some level the lives of all those directly and indirectly connected with it.

As long as adolescents and teens are thinking about and having sex, this story needs to be read, told, and talked about. Because Nia and Bobby are sexually active, their lives will never again be the same. Nia and Bobby know about birth control, but they admit that they make bad choices. Remaining abstinent, then, is the only sure way to escape such life-altering results. The title of the novel, *The First Part Last*, works as warning, advice, and instruction to young readers. Do first things first, and do not put yourself in a situation in which you are forced to grow up before you have grown up. There is always time to become an adult but no opportunities to recapture stolen childhood.

This very accessible and easily read novel takes risks. Talking about the realities of sexuality and teen pregnancy is still a source of awkwardness and discomfort for some conservative adults, parents, and teachers. While the novel does not provide graphic details of sexuality or any specifics on how Nia becomes pregnant, it clearly addresses the fact that youngsters are not waiting until they are adults and married to become sexually active. It also responds to the fact that no matter how many parental and middle and high school health class lectures about abstinence, pregnancy, sexually transmitted diseases, and now AIDS, youngsters are engaging in risky sexual behaviors. To ignore this fact is to be an adult in denial about our sons' and daughters' real lives. The complications with Nia's pregnancy and the burdens of Bobby's single teen parenting might well open the eyes of many young, curious, and confused readers.

15

REVIEWS OF KELLY McWILLIAMS'S *DOORMAT*

REVIEWED BY JASMINE Z. LESTER

Kelly McWilliams's novel *Doormat* (2004) is an entertaining narrative that follows a young girl through a tough time in her life. The story is told by fourteen-year-old Jamie Charleston and gives readers an insider's look at teenage angst. Jamie believes that she is a person who lets people walk all over her, and she constantly thinks of herself as a doormat.

Doormat is full of typical teenage drama: school friends, crushes, and so on. The novel gives the reader a refreshing taste of teenage life, and thanks to Jaime's witty and clever narration, there is rarely a dull moment. In a nutshell, *Doormat* is a tale of self-discovery. Jaime makes the transformation from a doormat to a person she is happy being. She is still the same person, just improved and stronger. *Doormat* is an empowering novel about finding inner strength.

REVIEWED BY NEAL A. LESTER

I am the father of two teens—a fourteen-year-old boy and a seventeen-year-old girl—so I want to listen to and understand what teens have to say about their lives and their experiences. I have never, however, read a novel written by a teen about teen life, so I was not quite sure what to expect in fifteen-year-old Kelly McWilliams's debut novel *Doormat*. What I get in this novel is some insight into and responses to growing social concerns about teen pregnancy, particularly from the perspective of a female teen observer whose best friend finds herself in this dilemma. The novel maps its way through rather commonplace teen concerns: social performances or "drama" (the word itself is perhaps overused by the author) among girl groups—the popular, the unpopular, and the geeks; communication or the lack thereof between parents and teens; and the giddiness of teen crushes. It also reminds us that teens are having sex and that pregnancy can and does result from this risky behavior. The first line is indeed pregnant with narrative possibilities: "My best friend thinks she's pregnant."

While the novel is framed around best friend Melissa's decision of whether to abort or have her baby, the drama of the novel is really narrator Jaime's efforts to convince readers that she moves from doormat to non-doormat status through her interactions with Melissa. We are to believe that by the novel's end Jamie is an independent thinker, able to put her needs ahead of the others'. What is not clear is how Jaime became a doormat in the first place. We never really understand why and how Jaime and Melissa are friends. Jaime says that they have always been friends. Is Jaime a doormat to everyone around her? The examples of Jaime's doormat status seem to be the actions of anyone willing to help out a friend in need. At the novel's end, we are not sure if Jaime and Melissa will ever be friends again because their lives have changed so drastically. Yes, many narrative gaps are left open, not necessarily to ponder in this novel, but that might be more fully developed. For example, why are most of the males in the novel literally or figuratively absent or irresponsible? I suppose this move highlights that the pregnant female has to deal alone with any decision about her body. The gaps in the story line do not necessarily add up to complex narrative ambiguities.

Short and conversational, this book is a quick-and-easy read. Certainly, preadolescent teen girls will find this novel of some appeal. While it is not a preachy novel telling readers to do one thing or another, its message is that teen mothers can survive pregnancy. The novel makes clear, though, that this survival is largely based on a support system of some sort. Melissa has Jaime to babysit, and Melissa's parents are helping care for Melissa and their new grandchild. There is also an educational component implied for young teen girls: the address for the Planned Parenthood website presented at the end of the book. Readers do not know what happens in Melissa's closed-door visit at Planned Parenthood but are sure to see this as an option for dealing with this life-changing dilemma. Indeed, the novel reminds us that pregnancy need not ruin a teen girl's life. It nevertheless encourages, through implication, teens' responsible actions. Jaime, although pretty self-absorbed (as might be any teen at her age and development level) becomes the alternative teen model, with concrete dreams of becoming a playwright by the novel's end. In contrast, Melissa, as a young unwed teen mother, will necessarily have to revise her dreams of becoming a fashion model—at least for the moment—because of her risky behavior and life choices. The book is an ambitious first novel. It is an opportunity to hear from a voice often absent amid adult decisions, prescriptions, and expectations. Between obsessive teen instant messaging, hanging out at the mall with friends, and music swapping, any opportunity for an adult parent, sister, brother, uncle, aunt, or neighbor to hear what teens think and do must be welcomed and listened to carefully.

16

RESPONSE TO "DIALOGUING REVIEWS"

*Parents, It's 10:00—Do You Know What
Your Children Are Reading?*

James Blasingame, Jr.

As editor of the Books for Adolescents pages of the International Reading Association's (IRA) *Journal of Adolescent and Adult Literacy*, I am always looking for good reviewers, people to read and write reviews of the latest and most popular novels written for young adults. I have tried undergraduate English majors, doctoral students majoring in education, experienced middle and high school English teachers, and even university professors. The reviews that are most popular with the IRA publications directors, however, and the ones that I find the most revealing about the genre and its readers, are the paired reviews done by parents and their children. In these paired reviews, one parent and one child read the same book and write reviews separately. They may look at each other's reviews and discuss their content before finalizing their drafts. They may even comment on their partner's ideas in their own reviews, but they do not devalue or invalidate judgments the other person has made in his or her review. Interestingly, these parent–child reviews are generally similar in their appraisal of a book's value, although the specific elements that appeal to them may differ. Often, each reviewer arrives at similar conclusions about plot development or characterization. And often, the parents are impressed with what the young reviewers have to say and learns as much about the workings of their offspring's mind as they do about the book. Both are important:

knowing what young people are reading and understanding how this literature fits into their worlds.

When Neal Lester and his then fifteen-year-old daughter, Jasmine, first agreed to review some books from Townsend Press called the *Bluford Series*, I wondered how far apart their views on this series would be. The *Bluford Series* is set at fictitious Guion Bluford High School, named for the first African American in space. Dr. Lester is a professor specializing in African American literary and cultural studies. Surely, I feared, he would find this young adult literature sadly lacking from a scholarly point of view, perhaps urging Jasmine toward more sophisticated reading, something with less emphasis on action, conflict, and social events (in other words: high school life). Surely he would eschew the popular reading of today, expressing frustration with what kids see in popular young adult fiction.

Nothing could have been farther from the truth. To date, as he continues to review young adult literature, Dr. Lester has never backed off from challenging an author's flawed plot development or weak characterization, and he will never let a gratuitous drive-by shooting pass as anything less than a cheap appeal to stereotype. He has embraced the young adult genre for what it is and more. He has recognized it as a meeting place where he and his daughter can talk about ideas and values as they manifest themselves in literature, as well as what this co-reviewing lets them learn about each other. I suspect they may one day do the same thing with more sophisticated literature (what a wonderful lifelong relationship constant), but for now, young adult literature is the venue, and hurray for Dr. Lester for not pooh-poohing it.

THE CASE FOR READING AND DISCUSSING WHAT TEENS ARE READING

Back in the Ozzie and Harriet days of the late 1950s and early 1960s, local television stations often ran a silent public service message when the national networks broke for station identification: "Parents, It's 10:00—Do You Know Where Your Children Are?" The intent was to heighten parental awareness of the comings and goings of children, a subtle reminder that the world children experienced in "modern" times was not exactly the same as the world their parents remembered from their own childhoods in the 1930s and 1940s. Times had changed, and parenting strategies needed to change, too. As changes continued from the Cold War era into the future, who could have predicted the sources of information and entertainment kids would have access to now, such as the Internet, cell phones, and virtual reality video games?

The thrills of homemade soapbox derby cars have been replaced by *Grand Theft Auto III,* and the school dances with the Beatles played on 45-rpm vinyl records have been replaced by midnight raves and by downloading Eminem and Mary J. Blige onto iPods.

PARENTS, IT'S 10:00—DO YOU KNOW WHAT YOUR CHILDREN ARE READING?

As times have changed, the young adult novel has changed as well, offering new reading experiences unlike that of generations past. *Hotrod, The Black Stallion*, and *Nancy Drew* gave way to *The Outsiders, The Chocolate War*, and *Mr. and Mrs. Bo Jo Jones,* but even these landmark novels of the late 1960s and early 1970s are very G-rated compared to *Rainbow Party* (2005) or *Little Chicago* (2002), novels dealing with oral sex parties for fifteen- and sixteen-year-olds and sexual abuse with little or no need for inferring any specifics. And, books are easy to obtain—a lot easier than cigarettes, drugs, or alcohol, as a matter of fact. The world of young adult literature is a lucrative one for publishers, and the further innovation of Amazon.com, BarnesandNoble.com, and eBay make any book cheap and available to any young person, anywhere. Books, unlike movies, do not receive R or PG-13 ratings, and young readers need not show proof-of-age ID to buy or to read them. Should we be encouraging this kind of reading—not the "classics" found in school literature anthologies but popular literature written for teenagers, about teenagers, centered on the kinds of problems and concerns teenagers deal with—possibly even in, gasp, paperback form? Absolutely! Popular literature written specifically for a young adult audience may seem literarily inferior to the classics of American, British, or world literature at first glance, but those classic works are not the most developmentally appropriate reading for teens. Teens will read and grow from reading those works when they have reached the appropriate age when those works begin to appeal to them and are relevant to an adult life. In the meantime, kids want and need to read about characters with whom they can identify, characters in whom they see themselves or their peers. They need to read about characters that face the same issues that they or their peers face or fear facing.

Good young adult literature does exactly this. As retired high school English teacher and highly successful young adult author Mel Glen explains, "A major key for good young adult literature is one word—identification... . When a reader can say, 'Hey, I feel what that character is going through,' a tangible connection has been made between printed word and human recipient" (interview, 9 November 2004).

When young readers begin to see themselves, their peers, and their problems in their reading, a whole new world opens up for them. As another icon in young adult literature, highly decorated and highly censored author and family therapist Chris Crutcher says, "Stories can help teenagers look at their feelings or come to emotional resolution, from a safe distance. ... I have never met a depressed person, or an anxious person, or a fearful person who was not encouraged by the knowledge that others feel the same way they do. 'I am not alone' is powerful medicine" (Crutcher, 1992, 39).

Not only authors but also experts on adolescent psychology agree that adolescence is a tough time. According to the Academy of Child and Adolescent Psychiatry (2001), a lot is going on at this age, including "worries about being normal" and "development of ideals and selection of role models." Venerated pioneer in adolescent psychology Erik Erickson described adolescence as a time when young people face a constant tension between "ego identity" and "role confusion," in which they try to find themselves and to balance an independent sense of self with a role in and responsibility to society. Erickson suggested that healthy teenage years include experimentation with different roles and identities as teens attempt to figure out who they are and how they fit into the overall scheme of things.

How much better would it be if the very first time our young people were confronted with some of the most serious issues of life—sexual experience, violence, substance addiction, and the many forms that human abuse can take, for example—it did not happen in real life but instead happened in their reading so that they would have a chance to process it, to think about what choices they would make if they had time to think rather than be forced to live with a split-second decision? Let them read about the world first even though the books may present some difficult situations; it is better than first meeting those situations by living them. "The ideal way to meet the tough books of childhood," says two-time Newbery winner Katherine Paterson, "is before you need them" (Ondanaka). Obviously, all adults would agree that when kids are at that point in their lives of figuring out the transition from childhood to adulthood, the experimental possibilities for reading their way along are much safer and more fruitful.

A GUIDING THEORY OF READING

We are talking not only about reading for satisfaction and enjoyment, but also about reading for meaning and for improvement of reading skills, including critical literacy. Educational professionals, especially reading specialists, espouse a theory of reading development that fits perfectly here: reader response theory. Reader response, with origins that are traceable to Louise Rosenblatt's *Literature as Exploration* (1938), emphasizes the reader's interaction with the book, the meaning, and the understanding that he or she arrives at by comparing lived experience with what the reader perceives the author to be saying. Reader response deemphasizes telling a reader what a literary work means and instead facilitates readers to arrive at their own meanings. Another guiding figure in the evolution of reader response theory, Robert Probst, makes this point:

> If we accept the idea that literature ought to be significant, that readers have to assimilate it and work with it, that transforming it into knowledge is more significant than memorizing the definitions of technical terms, then we need to find some ways of bringing readers and text together, and of forcing upon readers the responsibility for making meaning of text. (1988, 38)

And, as noted language arts scholar Arthur Applebee concludes in his 2003 study of nearly 1,000 young readers in their quest for literacy, it is the interaction with ideas through rigorous discussion and writing activities that leads to higher order literacy (Applebee, et al., 2003). Applebee's team took a hard look at the reading and writing learning experiences of 974 students in 64 middle and high school English classrooms in nineteen schools in five states, trying to determine which experiences were most likely to lead to what they called "complex literacy tasks":

> The approaches that contributed most to student performance on the complex literacy tasks that we administered were those that used discussion to develop comprehensive understanding, encouraging exploration and multiple perspectives rather than focusing on correct interpretations and predetermined conclusions. (722)

So, we see that the experts on reading hold that young people need to read books that they can interact with successfully, they need to express their own thoughts and feelings about these books, and they need to engage in interactive discussion with other people about their reading.

IT IS THE RIGHT THING TO DO, SO LET US HEAR FROM PEOPLE WHO READ!

Unfortunately, some very vocal and aggressive folks, although seldom actually reading more than just a few passages from widely read young adult novels, are seeking their wholesale removal from schools and libraries across the country and a return to the classics and the lecture and note-taking method of years gone by. Many so-called conservative religious groups across the country are actively seeking the removal of award-winning young adult novels from school and public libraries, books recognized as the very best by the American Library Association, the National Book Foundation, IRA, National Council of Teachers of English, the *New York Times*, and others. They primarily claim objection to profane language and sexual situations, although they often are unaware of the context or purpose for including these things in fiction.

In the face of these ill-informed attempts at hijacking teenage reading, it is imperative then that parents, scholars, and champions of "adult" literature read (in books' entirety) what young people are reading, discuss them with those young readers, and have conversations about these books out in the open. Adults cannot often be present to guide their children through the most difficult experiences thrust on them in real life, but responsibly literate adults can participate in the reading lives of their children to great avail.

AND SO A PROFESSOR OF LITERATURE CAME TO READ TEEN FICTION

Certainly, as Dr. Lester reads the novel and his daughter Jasmine's thoughts about it, he comes to understand much about his daughter's world and has the opportunity to share some thoughts of his own—thoughts informed by his own adult experience, his skill as an adult reader, and most importantly, his love for his daughter and concern for her healthy adolescence. Jasmine, for her part, can express her thoughts and feelings about the novel as framed by the sensibilities she is developing as a young adult, making her viewpoint on life quite evident. The *Doormat* (McWilliams, 2004) review provides a wonderful illustration of how this interaction can take place.

From Jasmine's perspective, *Doormat* provides a plausible and accurate portrayal of the problems of teen pregnancy. Kelly McWilliams, the author, creates a main character whose "witty and clever narration" creates "an empowering novel about finding inner strength" (183). Jasmine also praises the novel for providing "an insider's look at teenage angst" and "a refreshing taste of teenage life" (183). The latter comment may very well be in reference to the portrayal of teenage life in the media and adult literature, a portrayal that is often demeaning and condescending. Both Nancie Atwell, author of *In the Middle* (1987), the quintessential work on reading and writing workshops for teenagers, and Chris Crutcher (1992) warn against this attitude, emphasizing that the world kids face has real and serious problems, but that regardless of magnitude, these problems are very real to the young people experiencing them. Apparently, *Doormat* does not portray teenage life disrespectfully.

Jasmine read the novel for fun and personal involvement, bringing to bear on her analysis of it the natural intersection of her experience with the book and her experience with life. Dr. Lester, on the other hand, is bringing to bear on his analysis of this novel the intersection of his skills as a university professor of literature and his desire as a "father of two teens—a fourteen-year-old boy and a seventeen-year-old girl—… to listen to and understand what teens have to say about their lives and their experiences" (183).

And, what understanding did he gain? "What I got in this novel is some insight into and responses to growing social concerns about teen pregnancy, particularly from the perspective of a female teen observer whose best friend finds herself in this dilemma" (183). Lester's review highlights some points that Jasmine might not have noticed on a first reading, like the fact that "most of the males in the novel [are] literally or figuratively absent or irresponsible" (184), a fact he supposes may "highlight that the pregnant female has to deal alone with any decision about her body" (184). Dr. Lester also points out a balance in the book, which "is not a preachy novel telling readers to do one thing rather than another, [but rather] its message is that teen mothers can survive pregnancy," although it may involve the need to "revise" life's dreams (184–185).

The most striking and insightful thoughts expressed by Dr. Lester are not, however, in his thoughts about the meaning of the novel. While his analysis is insightful and makes for good conversation in juxtaposition with Jasmine's analysis, it is actually what he says in this final paragraph that is most instructive to all stakeholders in the nurturing and education of young people. He praises the book as:

> an opportunity to hear from a voice often absent amid adult decisions, prescriptions, and expectations. Between obsessive teen instant messaging, hanging out at the mall with friends, and music swapping, any opportunity for an adult parent, sister, brother, uncle, aunt, or neighbor to hear what teens think and do must be welcomed and listened to carefully. (185)

As Dr. Lester espouses, any opportunity to learn about what teens are thinking and doing is priceless, especially when that teen is your own son or daughter. Although a stereotypical father–daughter relationship between a college literature professor and his teenager would most likely include harangues about "pulp nonsense about boyfriends and hairdos for the prom" and "old geezer literature that no one can understand without a Ph.D. about stuff that happened 500 years ago," this was hardly the case. Dr. Lester's respect for the problems and experiences of this age group and his realistic expectations for the literary sophistication of the text make it possible for him to enter his daughter's world through her literature and to accompany her around in it for a while through the exchange of thoughts and ideas about the story. *Doormat* is a book that both readers award merit, but another book might have been fatally flawed in message or method, and as daughter plunged through the pages, her father would have accompanied her, not to tell her what to think but to ask what she was thinking and to share his thoughts and feelings as well, reader to reader.

Dr. Lester and Jasmine, now a high school senior, continue to review young adult novels for *Journal of Adolescent and Adult Literacy*, promoting a sort of family connection through books that would seem to prize and praise a shared moment of literacy in a way that no expensive prep school, tutors, or home schooling could ever accomplish.

TALKING OUT LOUD: IDEAS FOR DISCUSSION

1. To what extent are categories of young adult and adult literature arbitrary?
2. To what extent might a parent's perspective on the world have an impact on a child's? How might that influence be manifested in this kind of shared review exercise?
3. What determines a book's subject appropriateness for young adult audiences and adult audiences?
4. What distinguishes a literary classic from a popular classic? Might there be intersecting indicators?
5. How might adults and youngsters see the issue of literary censorship differently?
6. What kinds of young adult literature subjects would most likely appeal to male audiences, to female audiences, and to audiences of both males and females?
7. What makes a literary text "a classic"?
8. How are new literary texts added to the "classics" list? In other words, how do new and cutting edge works become "classics"?
9. How important are race and gender in these young adult texts?

III
Extending Discourses

17

UNLOCKING THE BEAUTY OF HAIR
A Review of Joyce Carol Thomas's Crowning Glory

Doth not even nature itself teach you, that if a man have long hair, it is
a shame unto him? But if a woman have long hair, it is a glory to her.

—1 Corinthians 11:14–15

For any female child of African descent old enough to notice and
care about her own hairstyles and hair texture, the Pantene commercial ideal of Barbie/Rapunzel's bone-straight, limp, loose, long, and
flowing hair can render her frustrated and self-conscious. If she has
been anywhere near adult conversations and news reports of recent
assaults on Afrocentric hairstyles, from dreadlocks to cornrows and
twists—"Dallas Police Place Two on Leave for Dreadlocks" (May
2001); "Rastafarian Children in Louisiana Ok'd to Wear Dreadlocks
in School" (October 2000); "Hair Bias in Promos Irks Black Students"
(December 2001); and "My [Twists] Hairstyle Is No Longer Professional" (August 2002)—she and those adults can well appreciate Joyce
Carol Thomas's children's book, *Crowning Glory* (2002), as another
contribution to the growing gallery of children's texts celebrating
the rich creativity and cultural exhalation of African American hair.
Thomas—a poet, novelist, short fiction writer, and playwright—is also
the prolific and award-winning children's book author of *A Gathering
of Flowers: Stories about Being Young in America* (1992); *Brown Honey
in Broomwheat Tea* (1993); *Gingerbread Days: Poems* (1995); *I Have
Heard of a Land* (1998); *Cherish Me* (1998); *Marked by Fire* (1999); *You
Are My Perfect Baby* (1999); *The Bowlegged Rooster and Other Tales*

that Signify (2000); *Blacker the Berry: Poems* (2000); *Hush Songs: African American Lullabies* (2000); *A Mother's Heart, A Daughter's Love: Poems for Us to Share* (2001); *The Angel's Lullaby* (2001); *Joy* (2001); and *House of Light: A Novel* (2001).

This new book finds a comfortable place among other children's texts primarily about African American girls and issues of beauty—among them Camille Yarbrough's *Cornrows* (1979); Alexis De Veaux's *An Enchanted Hair Tale* (1987), about a little boy with dreadlocks; Nikki Grimes's *Wild, Wild Hair* (1997); Carolivia Herron's nationally controversial *Nappy Hair* (1997); Natasha A. Tarpley's *I Love My Hair!* (1998); bell hooks's *Happy to Be Nappy* (1999); and Alile Sharon Larkin's cartoon *Dreadlocks and the Three Bears* (1991).

Thomas's *Crowning Glory* is a series of connected poems about the aesthetic and spiritual beauty of African American hair. While Yarbrough and Tarpley incorporate poetry within their narratives and Herron recreates the sermon and the call-and-response formats of traditional Southern black churches, Thomas's collection of fourteen poems ascribes cosmic proportions to perceptions of African hair. Individually and collectively, the poems offer profiles of African American girls, women, sisterhood, family, and community. Cataloguing an array of hairstyles and hair textures of African American mothers, daughters, grandmas, great-grandmas, aunts, and female cousins, the poems challenge the still-popular perception that long, straight, and silky is the beautiful hair ideal.

Thomas organizes *Crowning Glory* loosely around female-centered intergenerational and familial hair experiences from youth to old age. Based on her personal life growing up with a hairdresser mother and raising a daughter and seven granddaughters, the text takes adult women back to their roots, to those earliest moments of mother–daughter bonding through hair rituals of "First Braids" and sitting still in the chair as one's hair is being hot pressed in "Wavy." At the same time, it teaches young great-granddaughters how great-grandma "winds the thread/ through the hair on her head/to make the hair strong ... nothing's better/to wrap and keep loose ends together" ("Great-Grandma's Way"). Announcing a kind of "call" in the opening poem's little-girl-voiced question, "Is [my hair] my crowning glory?" ("Tenderness"), each subsequent poem in the collection "responds" with a resounding "yes, indeed!"

The collection is very much a how-to cultural primer, and also documents the sheer artistry of African hair, hairstyles, and hair adornments. From sitting between mother's knees as hair is being combed ("First Braids"); sitting in the kitchen chair having one's hair pressed straight ("Wavy"); learning about great-grandma's method of saving her loose ends ("Great-Grandma's Way"); observing a cousin's hair transform itself from twists into dreadlocks ("Locks"); sitting in the shampoo chair at the local beauty shop ("At Glory's Beauty Shop"); and letting cornrowed hair splish splash in beach water ("Swimming Hair"), Thomas raises the seemingly mundane to the level of high art. Those who perform these tasks are sculptors ("Mama's Glory"), designers ("Wearing Art"), weavers ("Great-Grandma's Way"), and decorators ("Adorned"). Hair in loops and curls and with "ribbons and combs/ feathers and beads/bands and bows/shells and nets/flowers and hairpins/rainbow barrettes" ("Adorned") or covered with brilliant scarves and wraps ("Wearing Art") or the parade of decorative hats to suit any and all occasions ("Glad Hats") speaks as well to the artistry of their creators.

Thomas further demonstrates how hair care and such hair adornment rituals are at the very foundation of community and cultural self-affirmation. While *Crowning Glory* includes details about hats used to "shade us from the sun" and "for walking in the rain," Maya Angelou, in her Foreword to Michael Cunningham and Craig Marberry's *Crowns: Portraits of Black Women in Church Hats* (2000), explains the high-art ritual of church hat wearing among African American women, a familial and cultural ritual to which young African American girls are introduced at a very young age:

> She dresses in the finest Sunday church clothes she owns, layers her face with Fashion Fare cosmetics, and sprays herself with a wonderful perfume, and then she puts on THE HAT, and it is The Hat. She leaves home and joins the company of her mothers and aunties and sisters and nieces and daughters at church whose actions had been identical to hers that morning. They too had waited longingly for the gift of Sunday morning. Now they stroll up and down the aisles of the church, stars of splendor, beauty beyond measure. Black ladies in hats. (2–3)

Thomas's illustrator Brenda Joysmith's warm pastel blues, greens, pinks, browns, yellows, and purples accentuate a softness and a tenderness that bespeak spiritual nurturing in each poem throughout the book. Clustered females smiling, playing, frolicking, wrapping, threading, twisting, covering, laughing, smiling, running, pretending, listening, waiting, touching, and adorning underscore the text as one of African American females enjoying life and celebrating themselves and each other.

Through the vehicle of poetry, such cultural celebrations of African hair and hair rituals individually and communally take on cosmic proportions, especially evidenced in the language that punctuates the text and accentuates a spirituality even in the mundane: "crowning glory"; "my crown"; "a gift"; "dream"; "glory be"; "halo of a crown"; "glory on earth"; and "blessed." There is no doubt that Thomas experiences, witnesses, and testifies to these culturally affirming rituals as "a shimmering mirror of [African American] women's souls" ("Author's Note"). As such, the poems and the collection constitute a gift of "Tenderness" from one culture keeper and celebrant to another—those just stumbling into the complex identity politics of hair as well as those veterans with life lessons to share and stories to pass on. With humor—Grandma borrows somebody else's hair when she cannot get to the beauty shop ("Grandma's Helper")—and due reverence—"hair/ a gift/wrapped/ribboned/curled/tied" ("Crowning Glory"), Thomas's book is another important testimonial of African American female self-acceptance. For old and young alike, it is a bold proclamation that all hair is "good hair," communicating this message to young African American girls and acknowledging Jacklyn Monk's sentiments in "How to Get Good Hair" (1995):

> It wasn't so long ago that "good hair" meant only one thing for Black women: long, shiny, and straight. If you were lucky enough to have it, you either got it from your mama and daddy or got yourself to the beauty shop each week for a patent-leather press and curl. Otherwise, you suffered the social indignity of hair that was somehow considered too kinky, too wild, too nappy around the edges, or maybe, as others exclaimed with a snap of the fingers, too short.
>
> Well, no more. We sisters are finally emancipated from the oppression of the Anglo aesthetic. And now, as they say in the 'hood, "it's all good." Straight, nappy, or curly; braids, locks, or a 'fro—we have more words for "good hair" than Eskimos have for the snow! (57)

Adult women who have had their feelings about their hair as political symbol expressed in the poetry of Dudley Randall's "On Getting a Natural, For Gwendolyn Brooks" (1973); Natasha Tarpley's "Haircut" (1991); Gwendolyn Brooks's "To Those of My Sisters Who Kept Their Naturals (Never to Look a Hot Comb in the Teeth)" (1983); Gloria Wade Gayles's "Cracked" (1991); Naomi Long Madgett's "Black Woman" (1972); Sara Martin's "Mean Tight Mama" (1922); Carolyn M. Rodgers's "For Sistuhs Wearin' Straight Hair"(1969); and Isis Jones's "Nappy Hair" (1998)—to name a few—can now pass along this new gift of cultural self-acceptance to future generations of young African American girls and in a voice that such young ones can recognize and understand. As a companion to *Crowns* and now *Crowning Glory*, *Queens: Portraits of Black Women and their Fabulous Hair* (2005) is a photograph and testimonial book that further accentuates a kind of "marvelous trinity of black women, hair, and beauty salons" (from book jacket). Thomas's short four- to thirteen-line poems in *Crowning Glory*, with their rhythmic language and accompanying brilliant pastel paintings, afford young readers a lesson in racial and gender identity politics wrapped in a caressingly honest simplicity.

18

NAPPY HAPPY
A *Review of bell hooks's* Happy to Be Nappy

African American cultural critic and feminist theorist bell hooks's first children's book, *Happy to Be Nappy* (1999), is the political calm after the two-year storm of controversy that accompanied African American author, scholar, and educator Carolivia Herron's *Nappy Hair* (1997).[1] Clearly not the socially and politically controversial text that Herron intentionally or unintentionally creates and defends as a positive message about the personal and communal acceptance of black folks' hair—particularly little girls' hair—*Happy to Be Nappy* comes from a veteran participant in this discourse about the gender and racial politics of hair. Dedicated to her nieces Katrese and Sarah, whom hooks identifies as "the sweetest of the sweet," the book achieves its race- and gender-positive message by unilaterally challenging and replacing negative images and attitudes about black people's hair—its textures, its lengths, its grades, its shapes—with unquestioningly celebratory ones that define, self-empower, and unite.

Happy to Be Nappy follows a trail of children's books about African Americans and their hair. For instance, one of the earliest celebratory treatments of black children's hair comes in Camille Yarbrough's *Cornrows* (1979), a book that uses the ritual and occasion of African American hair braiding as a lesson in African history and storytelling. The inside cover describes the book's focus: "Mama's and Great-Grammaw's gentle fingers weave the design and their lulling voices weave the tale as they braid their children's hair into the striking cornrow patterns of Africa." In Alexis De Veaux's *An Enchanted Hair Tale* (1987), young Sudan initially dislikes his dreadlocks because his friends and neighbors mock him, saying that it's "ugly, unsightly, and uncombed," and insisting that because of his dreadlocks, "He's strange. He's queer. He's different." When Sudan discovers a group of traveling circus performers with dreadlocks like his, he is convinced that his hair is wonderfully magical and enchanting. Tololwa M. Mollel's *The Princess Who Lost Her Hair: An Akamba Legend* (1993) is a parable that attacks vanity and selfishness associated with a girl's long hair, hair that is initially taken away and then restored. Nikki Grimes's *Wild, Wild Hair* (1997), an early reader, shows the Monday morning ritual of a young girl's hair braiding. Because "Tisa Walker's hair was long and thick and wild," the morning combing ritual between Tisa and her mother becomes for the family a game of hide-and-seek as they each try to find Tisa to avoid being late for school. In the end, Tisa's hair is braided royally and adultlike.

Carolivia Herron's *Nappy Hair* (1997) details in a call-and-response format of black southern churches a family's playfulness with a little brown girl's "nappy, fuzzy, screwed up, squeezed up, knotted up, tangled up, twisted up hair,"[2] hair that cannot and need not be tamed by harsh chemicals, a hot comb, or public perception. Although there were parental objections to Herron's use of the loaded term *nappy* and to the fact that the white, allegedly culturally uninformed third-grade teacher "performed" the text in the black vernacular with her African American and Hispanic students, the book is one of celebration and cultural affirmation. Addressing her intentions in the book on the *Today* show (2 December 1998), just a week or so after the controversy made national news, Herron clarifies: "I was just celebrating my hair and my little character's hair, my Brenda's hair. I was not trying to write a political book at all, although, I do, of course, know that the word 'nappy' is loaded for many people. I'm a '60s person [and] ... thought we went through the '60s and ... dealt with this hair problem and that we loved our hair. I guess I was living in another world" (transcript, 34).

Finally, Natasha A. Tarpley's *I Love My Hair!* (1998) is a kind of fictionalized autobiography celebrating family and storytelling. In her "Author's Note," Tarpley explains:

> This is how I fell in love with my hair. When I was a little girl, my mother would often comb my hair in the evening before I went to bed. I would make myself comfortable between her knees as she rubbed sweet-smelling oil along the line of my scalp where she parted my hair. Then she would start to comb.
>
> Sometimes she would tell me stories to distract me from the pain of stubborn tangles. But what I enjoyed most about those evenings was being so close to my mother—the texture and sound

of my hair sliding through her fingers, the different hairstyles she would create, the smell of the hair oil mixing with the lingering scent of her perfume. I loved the way we laughed and talked about the day's events, just the two of us.... When I sat between Mom's knees, I was at peace with my hair, at home again with myself.

In notes compiled by Rebecca Platzner at the "New World (Dis)Orders: Globalization, Culture and Identity" conference, sponsored by the Comparative Literature Department at Rutgers University in February of 1999, bell hooks weighed in on what she perceived as the media bias fueling the academic and cultural debate around *Nappy Hair*:

> bell hooks saw the controversy surrounding *Nappy Hair* as a "dangerous cultural narrative," in which the players were the "shadow figure" of the "educated Harvard black woman" who is given legitimacy by her Harvard ties and the "Playboy bunny white woman teacher" (photographed seductively in hotel bedrooms by the press) who was "bringing truth to the natives." "And who are the natives? The parents, demonized by the press." Why, hooks asked, hadn't she read any articles in which the parents were given a voice? She felt that the real problem was that "poor, black, working class parents actually felt that they could make an intervention, and they were stomped on." The story was presented as if "Liberal white brings food to the natives, and the natives didn't have the sense to eat." "The tension started with the parents jumping out of their class to make a critique." "How," she asked, "do we divest ourselves of our white supremacy enough to hear the critique?" (1)

The contribution of hooks to this dialogue on racial and gender politics of hair is an affirmation and self-acceptance of little black girls and by extension black women and their hair. Without the political binaries that can disrupt and confuse communal and individual identities in terms of artificial and polarized Eurocentric ideals and Afrocentric ideals related to hair, *Happy to Be Nappy* is total affirmation—of cultural uniqueness, cultural ritual, and cultural identity.

The book's affirming and even defiant tone is imaged on the cover with its vibrant and warm pastel colors (oranges, light blues, browns, greens, and yellows)—colors often associated with cheerfulness and playfulness, precisely the energy derived from experiencing and reading hooks's book. The drawings are playful, the language is simple and whimsical, and the incidental rhyming punctuating certain ideas and drawings—sweetest/nieces, crown/round, play/away—reinforce the plethora of positive adjectives sprinkled throughout to describe the hair types, textures, styles, shapes, and sizes: adjectives that can also characterize the attitude of self-acceptance presented throughout the text: happy, nappy, sweet, clean, soft, smooth, patted down (as in grounded and sure), tight (as in uptight and out of sight), close (as in unified and unifying), hopeful, joy(ful), short and strong, girl happy. The words themselves create a mood poem, and the drawings dance, as does the strand of hair that, as my then ten-year-old daughter and seven-year-old son pointed out to me, is imaged in the words cursively written on the pages. The unfanciful, almost rudimentary penmanship underscores the book's message of little black girls' fundamental self-acceptance, devoid of adult confusion about beauty politics and female identity.

The forthrightly political implications come in the book's deliberate denial of racist stereotypes associated with black people's hair: that it is dirty and stinky because of the hygiene grooming techniques exactly the opposite of hair grooming for whites. For instance, few black females and males are able to wash and dry their hair and head straight to the outside world—the white way—without oiling the scalp to avoid scalp dryness. Indeed, one sign of dirty hair for whites is that it is oily. Contrastingly, oiliness for blacks helps alleviate scalp flaking and itchiness. Here, hooks recognizes the racist myths of whites who know so little about black people's hair and respond to it simultaneously with curiosity[3] and repulsion. African American sociologist, comedian, and former talk show host Bertyce Berry offers a personal testimonial:

> One day in a grocery store, a young [white] girl looked at my dreadlocked hair and loudly exclaimed, "Mommy, that black lady has funny hair." The mother, clearly embarrassed, and for some reason frightened, quickly hugged the child and said, "Yes, it is fancy." Not wanting to deny the child the opportunity to learn, I walked over and said, "No, she said 'funny.'" I offered the child the opportunity to touch my hair and she [the child] burst out into tears. I quickly grabbed her mother's hand and placed it on my hair. The mother, now slightly less frightened, was amazed by the feel. "It's beautiful. How different," she said. The child now asked if she could touch it also. She did and a transformation occurred. She no longer found my hair strange, but asked her mother if she could make her hair like mine. (1992, E8)

Berry's account is all too familiar to African Americans with new white college and grad school roommates or acquaintances. In this regard,

Happy to Be Nappy is also directed toward white audiences, who are almost always amazed that there is such complexity associated with black people's hair. For those blacks subjected to white scrutiny of their hair—having it fondled and patted to see if it is as coarse as steel wool or sandpaper, or sniffed to see if its scent is unpleasant—hooks merely asserts without adornment: "Girlpie hair smells clean and sweet/is soft like cotton, flower petal billowy soft,/full of frizz and fuzz."

Importantly, the book's whimsical feel and sound are balanced by the inclusion of important cultural rituals associated with hair. For instance, at least five of the thirty-two pages present ritual hair combing, brushing, and styling in process. Mothers and daughters and sisters and aunts and neighbors have used this time of hair preparation as familial and communal bonding. Although hooks has talked on other occasions about hair straightening as a time for female bonding with other women—a time full of rituals from gossip to storytelling—she recreates in this children's text these same rituals of safety, security, and intimacy:[4]

> On Saturday mornings we would gather in the kitchen to get our hair fixed, that is[,] straightened. Smells of burning grease and hair, mingled with the scent of our freshly washed bodies, with collard greens cooking on the stove, with fried fish. ... In those days, this process of straightening black women's hair with a hot comb ... was not connected in my mind with the effort to look white, to live out the standards of beauty set by white supremacy. It was connected solely with rites of initiation into womanhood. To arrive at that point where one's hair could be straightened was to move from being perceived as a child (whose hair could be neatly combed and braided) to being almost a woman. It was this moment of transition my [five] sisters and I longed for. (hooks, 1992, 291)

While hooks makes no mention of hair straightening or relaxing in *Happy to Be Nappy*, she at the same time places no value on whether a child's hair is straightened chemically or unstraightened. Rather, hooks's emphasis is steadfastly on how the child feels about her hair no matter what has been done to it stylistically. Female bonding occurs in the everyday rituals of hair preparation, presumably between a mother and daughter; hooks adds:

> Hair pressing was a ritual of black women's culture—of intimacy. It was an exclusive moment when black women (even those who did not know one another well) might meet at a home or in the

beauty parlor to talk with one another, to listen to talk. … It was a world where the images constructed as barriers between one's self and the world were briefly let go, before they were made again. It was a moment of creativity, a moment of change. (291)[5]

Not coincidentally, the two-page spread in *Happy to Be Nappy* of the four little girls having their hair combed by four women creates the image of a "beauty salon"—even if it is the family kitchen—similar to what hooks's childhood revelry describes.

The fanciful text neutralizes potentially loaded political words associated with blacks' hair—naps and kinks—and their negative associations by not polarizing the somewhat arbitrarily defined Eurocentric and Afrocentric ideals suggested in Carolivia Herron's *Nappy Hair* (1997): "Ain't going to be nothing they come up with going to straighten this chile's hair. … I'm talking about straightening combs. … I'm talking about relaxers and processes. … Ain't nothing going to straighten up the naps on this chile's head" (Herron). In her book, hooks demonstrates that public discussions of hair among black folks need not be politically divisive. Hence, her contribution to these hair tales is hope, celebration, and joy, both personally and communally.

Aside from Chris Raschka's effective rudimentary crayon drawings with watercolor strokes, the text reiterates community, especially among black women, by presenting about fourteen variously brown-shaded "girlpie"[6] heads sprinkled throughout the text. While one of the girlpies stands defiantly smiling on the cover of the book with both hands on her hips and a wide smile on her face—the young child clearly is not angry, confused, or being womanish—she is joined at the story's end by the other thirteen girlpies in an eternal circle of personal and communal defiance. Their symbolic bond recalls Little Sally Walker and her sister friends who "put their hands on their hips and let their backbones slip, as they shake it to the east and shake it to the west, steadily shaking it to the ones that they love the best." The young girls' creative hair styles, textures, lengths, and shapes—along with their individual facial expressions but different skin colorings—render *Happy to Be Nappy* a performance of black "girlpie happiness" in their celebrated nappiness. hooks's intent is *Heart and Soul* Editor-in-Chief Stephanie Stokes Oliver's dream regarding African American female identity:

Surely we are coming into more positive thinking about our hair as we embrace the many varieties of natural hairstyles—and we find less damaging ways to "relax" it. But we should never relax our effort to keep it healthy and to *instill in our children positive feelings about their hair, whether it's straight, naturally curly, or*

tightly coiled. Celebrate [black hair's] versatility and resilience. …
Give thanks for the beautiful, unique, and wondrous textures of
hair that we African Americans have been blessed with. (1995,
55; emphasis added)

To the childhood tune of "If you happy and you know it, clap your
hands," hooks's *Happy to Be Nappy* might well add the following verse
as African American mothers and daughters, sisters and aunts, female
cousins, and female neighbors join hands singing:

If you happy to be nappy, clap your hands—
If you happy to be nappy, clap your hands.
If you happy to be nappy, any hairstyle's really snappy,
If you happy to be nappy, clap your hands.

19

"SHAKE IT TO THE ONE THAT YOU LOVE THE BEST"
A Review of Juba This & Juba That

If you can talk, you can sing. If you can walk, you can dance.

—African Proverb

African American psychologists Drs. Darlene Powell Hopson and Derek S. Hopson have appeared on *Geraldo* a number of times as experts on African American identity issues, and the husband–wife pair has also authored important books on the complex dynamics of African American experiences, addressed primarily to an African American readership: *Different and Wonderful: Raising Black Children in a Race-Conscious Society* (1991); *Raising the Rainbow Generation: Teaching Your Children to be Successful in a Multicultural Society* (1993); and *Friends, Lovers and Soul Mates* (1994). Their publication, *Juba This & Juba That: 100 African-American Games for Children* (Fireside, 1996), created with Thomas Calvin, is a potpourri of activities that entertain and teach children. *Juba This & Juba That*, while it is a parent's or sitter's quick-and-easy resource to quiet children's frequent cries of boredom, ultimately reveals the power of folklore rituals to link past and present, to unite generations and different cultures, to sustain cultural ties within families and communities, and to demonstrate the universality of child play. And while the games and activities are sources of entertainment, Hopson, Hopson, and Calvin have created a text that also teaches parents and adults of any culture about African and African

American experiences, musical forms, communal structures, religious ceremonies, crafts, myths and legends, and language.

The book is divided into five sections: "Outdoor Games" (includes thirty-nine examples), "Indoor Games" (includes seventeen examples), "Board Games" (includes nine examples), "Craft-Making Activities" (includes ten examples), and "Musical Games" (includes twelve examples). A final section is devoted to abbreviating the history and practice of the African American holiday Kwanzaa. This section also includes children's activities associated with the celebration of this holiday. Each of the five major sections, as well as each of the alphabetically arranged activities, is briefly introduced to contextualize the activities tribally or regionally. Each entry then offers the following details: number of players needed, age-appropriate range, equipment needed, brief statement concerning the origin of the game/activity, and simple instructions regarding "how to play," some with rudimentary drawings for clarification. For the most part, the games are simple to carry out and involve minimal adult supervision once instructions have been given. Another important element with this selection of games and activities is that equipment is minimal and inexpensive, ranging from common household items such as metal bowls, brooms, cardboard, rope, and balls, to organic items like beans, nuts, branches, leaves, corncobs, and grass.

The first section, "Outdoor Games," includes those based largely on the fact that Africa's generally mild climate lends itself to the creation of many activities designed to accommodate children who spend lots of time playing outdoors. Grounded in the African proverb that "it takes a whole village to raise a child," the activities celebrate community and communal rituals. According to the authors, "The combination of open space, climate, and a large number of youngsters led to developing games that included a lot of physical activity for as many as three dozen players" (15). Games in this section range from those for three to more than twenty players. They teach leadership and cooperation skills and engage youngsters in lots of physical activity, from running ("Hawk and Hen") and jumping ("Jumping the Beanbag") to scooting along the ground as a snake ("Banyoka").

For those inclement weather days when youngsters have allegedly exhausted their own creative resources for self-entertainment, the second section, "Indoor Games," includes those "suitable for living rooms, basements, and small courtyards." These games may require no adult supervision only in that furniture and breakables need to be cleared from the general playing areas. Among some of the more interesting games in this section are "Here Comes Martin," a game "taught in schools and at playgrounds in connection with Martin Luther King

Day" (68), and "Numbers," a game that allows children six years and under to practice speedy number groupings (78). In the first game saluting Martin Luther King, Jr., six to ten players, ranging in age from about three or four to eight, learn the following chant:

> Here comes Martin Luther King
> Marching 'round our great big ring!
> He needs someone who will share
> Follow him and show you care.

As the children are in a circle holding hands, one child is selected as King. King circles the chanting children. The object of the game is clarified: "At the word 'care,' King taps a child and runs around the circle to escape being tapped back. If King is able to take the place of the tapped child, then that youngster becomes King" (68). Such a game can do much to teach children about the civil rights leader's leadership, particularly his efforts to obtain equal opportunities for everyone through nonviolent activities such as marches. It might also be used to comment on the fact that young children were instrumental in advancing the civil rights cause through marching and singing. Finally, one might reiterate the value of communal singing in this civil rights protest. In this activity that requires no equipment, students are taught through doing rather than through being told.

"Numbers," a game that can incorporate from ten to fifteen players ranging in age from three to six, allows young ones to practice sets and groupings in a timed setting. "Attributed to the Ovimbunde tribe who live in what is now Zaire" (76), this game requires no equipment. It involves selecting a leader or caller who organizes the children into a large circle as they march around the room. When the caller yells out a number, the children divide themselves into groups based on the number called. They continue to march, more numbers are called out, and the fun comes in the youngsters' quick efforts to count as they are being counted. As the authors point out, "There is no winner, but youngsters enjoy seeing how quickly they can divide into the called number" (76). A suggested teaching dimension of this activity is to have an adult call out the numbers in the Ovimbunde language: "talu" (five), "qualla" (four), "tatu" (three), "vali" (two), and "mosi" (one). The players then have to listen carefully, translate from another language, and move quickly.

The third section, "Board Games," is described as containing "strategy activities" that were and are extremely important in African cultures. The authors offer fairly extensive commentary on the role of board games in African religious ceremonies, adding that many of these games "were played by kings and queens and other levels of royalty"

(82). They also recommend Louise Crane's *African Games of Strategy* as another source of further commentary on and examples of these board games. These games involve making the actual game board and pieces, another important exercise in following instructions. Adult supervision is often necessary with these activities.

The fourth section of *Juba This & Juba That*, "Craft-Making Activities," can be used generally with older children able to safely use scissors, glue, paint, needles, and thread. Here, youngsters, with adult supervision, can create and reproduce African dolls ("Akuaba" ["Ashanti Doll"]); masks ("Ceremonial Mask," "Poro Mask"); hats ("Kufi"); shields ("Shields"); and necklaces ("Corn Necklace"). "Musical Games," the fifth section of activities, celebrates the wedding of song and dance in African and African American rituals. While "the scenarios and movements are basic ones, and the lyrics are not complicated" (120), these games demonstrate the importance of rhythm and improvisation in such cultural rituals. These games can be used to discuss or supplement discussions of African and African American poetry traditions from rhyming to call-and-response. Two of the more common games presented are "Juba This and Juba That," a nineteenth-century song that involves lots of clapping and can involve, as explained by singers Sweet Honey in the Rock's tune "Juba," from their audiocassette *All for Freedom* (1989); transforming the body into an African drum as the chant is being performed. "Little Sally Walker" (132–133) was, according to critic Lawrence W. Levine in *Black Culture and Black Consciousness: Afro-American Folk Thought from Slavery to Freedom* (1977), a significantly different song. The following version of "Little Sally Water" was performed by little white children:

> Little Sally Water,
> Sitting in a saucer,
> Weeping and crying for some one to love her.
> Rise, Sally, rise,
> Wipe your eyes;
> Turn to the east,
> Turn to the west,
> Turn to the one that you love the best. (198)

In the African American revision of this song, Sally is not simply turning toward a loved one; she is "shaking" more aggressively. As Sally puts her "hands on her hips and lets her backbone slip," it is clear that Sally will survive this moment of loneliness through dance and communal connection. In fact, it is this same kind of independence that African American feminist poet-playwright Ntozake Shange communicates through her use of this children's play song in one of the structurally important opening moments of her Broadway-acclaimed *for colored girls who have considered suicide/ when the rainbow is enuf* (1976).

The final section of *Juba This & Juba That* is devoted to the African American holiday Kwanzaa, established by Dr. Maulana Karenga in 1966, not as a religious holiday but as a celebration of African Americans' philosophical connections with African origins. "Celebrated by more than 18 million black peoples all over the world," according to Shirley J. Pitts in "Kwanzaa Holiday Celebration" (*Child Times of Alabama* December 1993–January 1994), "This is a time to reaffirm [African] culture, history, traditions and plan ... for the future" (10). Not only are the seven principles of Kwanzaa defined in *Juba This & Juba That* (141), but also the daily focus and activity of the seven-day celebration beginning 26 December through 1 January are outlined (144–145). This section involves activities designed to create the items used during this celebration. For example, one such activity details the making of a "kinara," the display of the seven candles (147). Another involves making the big cup from which everyone drinks during this celebration ("Kikombe Cha Umoja," 149). The section and the book end with a "Candle Game" (152–153), a card game created by the young players that teaches the Kwanzaa principles through focus on the candle colors and the candle order.

Juba This & Juba That is an important book for several reasons. First, it illustrates and celebrates the diversity of African and African American cultures via children's play rituals. Through its many examples of rituals and games from all over the African continent (Nigeria, Ghana, Kenya, Zaire, Zambia, Guinea, the Congo [now Zaire], the Ivory Coast, Angola, Zimbabwe, Uganda, Malawi, and Ethiopia), it dispels the myth that there is a single monolithic African culture. Second, it serves as a reference guide for parents, teachers, and caregivers in search of activities to supplement explorations of and presentations on African and African American cultures. While the games and activities entertain and teach—they teach as they entertain and entertain as they teach— they also provide physical exercise and encourage individual and group teamwork and decision making. Plus, the book further preserves and passes along these rituals. And although the authors are quick to point out that all of the activities are not necessarily connected with African origins—included are several variations on tic-tac-toe ("Achi"); hopscotch ("Tsetsetse"); tag ("Beware the Antelope," "Fox," "Big Snake"); hide-and-seek ("Cock-A-Loo," "Sikileko" ["Whistle for Me"]); tug-of-war ("Tug of War"); bean and beanbag tossing ("Bean Hole Toss," "Haba Gaba"); follow-the-leader ("Banyoka"); and jacks ("Kudoda")—

they clarify that such rituals are popular in African communities and have invariably taken on recognizably African textures, rhythms, and language ("Chinene Nye?" ["What Is Big?"]). Another African American consciousness-raising text and a nice companion to Cheryl Warren Mattox's book (with audiocassette) *Shake It to the One that You Love the Best: Play Songs and Lullabies from Black Musical Traditions* (1989), *Juba This & Juba That* can be used in classroom settings and during vacation travel, family reunions, birthday parties, and play dates, as well as times at the beach ("Ambutan," "Bathing Game," "Ataklui Dada"); it promises something for every child from preschool to middle school. Through the authors' careful attention to balancing masculine/feminine pronoun references to children described in the playing of the game, it importantly and effectively works against gender stereotyping certain games or activities as "boy games" or "girl games," a lesson too early learned by children and too often perpetuated by adults.

20

RESPONSE TO "EXTENDING DISCOURSES"

Elizabeth McNeil

(RE)FIGURING OUR CULTURE

Reading Neal Lester's children's literature book reviews, I am reminded of the long history of image and narrative construction that has supported hierarchies of socioeconomic difference. In the imperial age (the Age of Discovery, Enlightenment, Reason, Science), images and literature produced by science helped Europeans to weigh their worth. In the scientific rendition of the Great Chain of Being, the European male was the hierarchical norm, chosen by nature, according to European (overwhelmingly male) scientific authorities, with European women and children and the "races" of newly "discovered" "savages" from around the globe in descending layers underneath. To support this fantasy of superiority, Western scientists produced drawings and wax anatomical models that, not surprisingly, located the European male as the perfect specimen of humanity. Exploitation of imperfect and even questionably human persons could thus proceed from a tidy taxonomic and moral base of natural, divinely ordained selection.[1]

Other persuasive imagery during the colonial slavery and postslavery period included newspaper caricatures that, along with naturalists' drawings,[2] became iconic misrepresentations of the personhood of Africans, African Americans, and other non-whites.[3] Numerous other common events and everyday visual aspects of European and U.S. culture also served to remind viewers of the social and human order. While the popularity (and size) of carnival "freak" shows grew in nineteenth-century Europe and the United States,[4] World's Fairs/Expositions also began to appear, the first in London in 1851. Purportedly in contrast to the exploitation of the audience by carnival showmen, the World's Fairs exhibitions were constructed under the pretext of international scientific "education" for the largely white masses.[5] Constructed villages of Africans (who were actually from a variety of nations), along with a lucrative souvenir trade in half-nude photographs, especially of African girls and women, created an ongoing, highly objectified idea of "blackness"/Africanness in the dominant European/Euro-American imagination. In U.S. homes, black lawn jockeys and Aunt Jemima pancake syrup bottles likewise portrayed (and continue to portray today) a smiling black serving class whose individual personality and therefore humanity has been made invisible.[6]

As Lester emphatically points out in his critique of the illustrations in Mary Barwick's *Alabama Angels* (1989) and *Alabama Angels in Anywhere, L.A.* (1991), such vivid imagistic objectification lingers in contemporary children's literature as well, and along with delimiting images has come figurative language with its similar power to create and control European and U.S. thinking regarding race and power. Such imagery and language have been patterned into our daily lives. Lester's book reviews suggest the imagistic and figurative power that children's literature inherently has to shape the young minds that will one day construct U.S. culture and the body politic.

In his reviews, Lester appreciates children's texts that offer positive, celebratory images, self-affirming diction, and a degree of complexity that reflects lived experience. The intimate colloquialisms in bell hooks's *Happy to Be Nappy* (1999) (e.g., "girlpie" as an endearment for the loved little protagonist) and the spiritually elevating stance of the poems collected in Joyce Carol Thomas's *Crowning Glory* (2002) celebrate mother–daughter bonding over daily hair rituals. In Chapter 17 of this collection, Lester notes that the texts send a positive message to children about their "wild," "nappy," "frizzy" hair that counters the Anglo/Eurocentric ideal of "long, straight, and silky" hair as "the beautiful hair ideal" (198). Particularly via his detailed appreciation of hooks's representation of African American life in *Happy to Be Nappy*, Lester is also implicitly reminding us of the deeper figurative obfuscating that centuries of negative images and narrative have wrought. Positive, culturally intimate children's texts have the power to supplant simplistic stereotypical views with a complex perspective bespeaking rich experience on the levels of both personal and cultural continuum.

On the other hand, notes Lester, stereotypical images and diction like those found in Barwick's *Alabama Angels* series nostalgically place

African Americans in their "natural"/historical place as servants/objects gently facilitating white comfort and happiness. Adding to generations of dehumanizing misrepresentations by whites, images and narratives like Barwick's are psychically damaging for black children and are, of course, as Lester points out, dangerous for white children, too. When supplied with figurative, deeply historically and socioculturally textualized notions of racial superiority, white American children grow up to perpetuate destructive stereotypes that fuel race-based hierarchies of sociopolitical opportunity and power in every aspect of the society. In as much as the United States is controlling the world today, such abuses are felt globally as well.

Many U.S. readers today can readily see that texts offering caricature, such as Barwick's, are actually negative and can damage young psyches. Some U.S. readers may not as readily notice that texts that do not seek specific authority from imagery and details of lived African American experience may be pandering to European middle-class norms and, as such, are continuing the five-hundred-year campaign to eradicate African American power and presence in the U.S. cultural imagination. In literature, ignoring aspects of African American culture that are "different" from Europe/European America has traditionally disenfranchised black children who have naturally sought themselves in narrative and image in public libraries, bookstores, and school texts. Until rather recently, these American children have not seen themselves as visible agents in the grand U.S./European narrative.

This corruption of our shared story has reduced access for all readers of U.S. texts to ways of knowing and being that continue to persist, shape, and enrich American culture. The perspective that produced nostalgic racist Americana in Barwick's images and notions of a kindly African American class/race who live to serve whites is combated by publications like those of hooks, Thomas, and Darlene Powell Hopson and Derek S. Hopson (*Juba This & Juba That: 100 African-American Games for Children*, 1996). These texts are excellent teaching tools for audiences of all ethnic heritages because they serve to detail and celebrate everyday personal experience and familial and communal rituals in African American life.

The conscientious efforts of parents, teachers, artists, theorists, and critics who are interested in supporting and educating children regarding the complexity of American (and global) human experience should mean that we produce and engage texts that appreciate human beings rather than (sentimentally) caricature segments of the population to continue historical privileges of power. Through a consciously constructed, fair-minded, accurate, and multiculturally rich body of children's and adult literature that demonstrates critical thinking about history, identity politics, and ethical relationships with others and the environment, teachers today can combat lingering racist images and ideologies, supplanting inaccurate and damaging representations with realistic notions of personhood and an appreciation of both delightful and culturally difficult and complex aspects of "difference."

TALKING OUT LOUD: IDEAS FOR DISCUSSION

1. What popular African American characters today (in books, film, and TV) are caricatures (i.e., stereotypical in some way) and thus do not represent lived experience?
2. What popular African American characters today (in books, film, and TV) are more complex?
3. How do the complex African American characters demonstrate aspects of lived experience (e.g., through characterization, illustration/animation, dialogue, plot)?
4. In the various aspects of your everyday life, what is the value for you of reading or watching these more complex African American characters?
5. If you were to be represented as a character in a book, film, or TV show, what personal characteristics, specific actions, and interactions with others would you want to be included in your character? Why?
6. Bring in and discuss other stereotypical images of African Americans in children's books.
7. Discuss the history and controversy of Helen Bannerman's profoundly popular children's book *Little Black Sambo* (1899). To what extent are narrative and imagery problematic or non-problematic?

AFTERWORD

Khafilah McCurdy

Literature gives us images with which to think.

—Virginia Hamilton, 1986

A good number of departments of literature and humanities still dismiss books written for children as unworthy of serious scholarly examination. More specifically, literature by African American authors and illustrators is often egregiously overlooked. A perfunctory glance at the history of children's literature reveals that portrayals of black experiences in children's literature are riddled with omissions and stereotypes. In addition, book awards and library summer recommended reading lists provide a great deal of insight into the minimalist value placed on African American children's literature. Moreover, institutions in their various forms—parents' groups, school systems, library associations, organizations such as the National Reading Council, the National Council of Teachers of English, the International Reading Association, and publishers—are all major forces shaping the livelihood, accessibility, and availability of this children's literature. Much of what is written in and about children's literature seeks to examine specific issues such as multiculturalism, historical aspects of children's literature, or specific genres. Children's literature is, with few omissions, entirely absent from the acknowledged canon of great literature.

With the publication of this collection, Neal Lester seeks to revise and challenge the conceptual categories that structure critical understanding of children's literature and more specifically African American children's literature. Courses in children's literature are typically intended as preparatory training for pre-service teachers and librarians. These courses generally reflect topical issues, history of children's literature, or multiculturalism. The contributors to this collection seek to challenge that ideology by going beyond history, beyond genre-specific topics, and beyond multiculturalism. An in-depth critical discussion of such issues as racism, gender, and identity politics is at the center of this book.

The issue of heterosexism in fairy tales and nursery rhymes is especially noteworthy. This collection challenges readers to rethink the messages and images represented in specific books that are deemed childhood "classics" — Mother Goose, Goldilocks and the Three Bears, Cinderella, and Sleeping Beauty, for instance. A comparative study of these classics juxtaposes alternative versions of these narratives to disrupt the status quo and to challenge the conventional paradigms of gender identity. The issues raised in this book invite us to reassess gender, sexuality, and other tenets that shape our identities. Indeed, these analyses provide readers with multiple and diverse approaches to gender and identity issues for both males and females. Lester further posits that as adults, we need to reconsider what we elect to read to our children at bedtime. He also asks that we think about the subtle and overt messages we are promoting as professors of children's literature in pre-service teacher education programs where these texts are regarded and held up as models for early literacy acquisition, both alphabetical and cultural.

Other chapters address such concerns as literacy and the politics of hair. One seeks to validate the importance of "creating spaces" where both parent and child can transcend (il)literacy by using African American children's literature as a tool to engage both in giving meaning to multiple literate practices and inherently giving voice to those marginalized not by selfish neglect but rather by historical and political circumstance. This book recalls the importance of validating cultural experiences and creating spaces where "black parental identity and authority" is holistically represented and transformed.

The chapters that address the politics of hair demonstrate that despite the social and political strides and accomplishments of the 1960s Black-is-Beautiful movement, African American children continue to be assaulted with messages through the media, magazines, and communities that "light skin," "light eyes," and "good hair" are the qualities most desired, rewarded, and sought after in American culture. Although there are those who question the appropriateness of these images and their value, there is still consensus among members of society that certain images are more celebrated and valuable than others. These chapters provide a brief historical analysis and reflect the current debates in an attempt to contest the very nature of perceptions of beauty.

The sections "Dialoguing Reviews" and "Extending Discourses" are pertinent because they highlight what teens identify as interesting and enriching reading as well as how adolescents either identify or don't with the characters in the books they are reading. These reviews and commentaries reveal how adolescents come to understand critically their world as well as make transitions from adolescence to young adulthood. These reviews and commentaries also provide guidance for teachers and librarians searching for literature that addresses contemporary adolescent concerns. In addition, their scope and purpose call attention to the many challenges teens face, such as low self-esteem, sex curiosities and risks, negated cultural heritage, and human frailties; in essence, the life circumstances offered in adolescent literature can help teens cope with a changing world.

This collection creates a space in which teachers, librarians, and professors can begin to study race, gender, and identity politics within the context of children's literature. This is indeed a lofty and admirable goal, given the fact that topics such as these are often sensitive and not well understood or even talked about in an academic setting. Neal Lester and these contributors successfully map a literary landscape with the nuances in African American children's literature by expanding and discussing complex issues related to identity politics and constructions. This book serves as a lens through which to better understand how race, gender, and politics structure who we are, how we see ourselves, and how we interact with and respond to the world.

NOTES

CHAPTER 1

1. Our seventeen-year-old daughter explains her disturbingly real brush with homophobia in children:

> This summer at choir camp, I was assigned ten- and eleven-year-old buddies to befriend and to help with their study of music theory. The buddies and I asked each other questions and got to know each other, and finally, the all-important question arose from them: "Jasmine, do you have a boyfriend?" My response was a simple "no." I didn't plan to take it any further until one of the older kids decided to be a smart-aleck and say, "Yes, she has a boyfriend. His name is Steve." And then the little kids asked me about Steve, to which I could only reply, "No, I don't have a boyfriend; I have a girlfriend."
>
> They didn't quite understand that by "girlfriend," I meant in a romantic sense, not just a friendship sense, and I didn't expect them to. I feel they should understand. Children of a young age should understand and be exposed to diversity. It's never too soon to teach kids to tolerate difference. Unfortunately, the rest of the world disagrees with me. Society brainwashes children to believe that it is only acceptable to be heterosexual. Movies, television, and literature continue to hammer this heterosexist bias into the impressionable minds of children. Never once is a child exposed to the idea that it is entirely possible to fall in love with a member of the same sex.
>
> This ignorance transforms into bigotry, and bigotry in a child is one of the most disgusting things I have ever witnessed.
>
> At choir camp, I was walking to the cafeteria with one of the little kids when she said: "I have a friend who's a nasty bisexual. She's gross."
>
> "What makes her gross?" I asked.
>
> "Because," the girl says, laughing as if I'd asked a silly question, "People who like the same gender as them are gross."
>
> Then she asks if one of our choir directors is married because she suspects he's gay.

"So what if he is?" I asked.

"I hope he's not. I'd hate him if he was," she responded.

"Why?"

"Because I think it's just weird."

"Well, I think people in Africa who stretch their lips with plates are weird, but I don't hate them for it," I retorted.

She's 10 years old. She obviously wasn't following the logic of my argument, nor did I expect her to. The sad part is that intolerance is programmed into children at such a young age, making it difficult for them to let go of that intolerance as teenagers and adults. It's also sad that there are actually teenagers and adults who think just as this ten-year-old does. What's the world coming to?

CHAPTER 2

1. Langston Hughes, "Mother to Son," *Selected Poems of Langston Hughes* (New York: Vintage, 1974), 187. This poem is selected and recited by Precious Jones, Sapphire's illiterate teenage African American female in *PUSH* (1996), as one of her pre-GED adult illiteracy course assignments and is dedicated to her infant son Abdul (112–113).

2. Eve Bunting's *The Wednesday Surprise* (1989) presents an elderly and presumably white grandmother learning to read as a "gift" to her adult son on the occasion of his birthday. The story postures as a warm, fuzzy, middle-class, white family moment celebrated when an elderly grandmother and her seven-year-old granddaughter, Anna, give the adult son a gift: The grandmother learns to read from the granddaughter's instruction. Although the message encouraging everyone to value reading is undeniably important—"It's much smarter if you learn to read when you're young. ... The chance may pass along with the years"—the story is full of unanswered questions that might explain rather than boldly proclaim, without explanation or clear illustration, the advantages of literacy. As in other children's books examined in this exercise, illiteracy is synonymous with an individual's lack of self-esteem and poor self-image and is tainted with presumed immorality. As the narrative moves rather fumblingly, it leaves more narratively unsatisfying questions than answers and explanations: How does the grandmother choose the books from which the granddaughter will teach her? How has the family responded to the grandmother's illiteracy up to the point of this story? What is the grandmother's life like as a nonreader? Why has the grandmother resisted her son's insistence that "she must learn to read"? Why does the son insist that his mother become literate? ("'You were always telling me to go to classes, classes, classes,' Grandma says to Dad.") To what extent does the relationship between this mother and son suffer *because* she is a nonreader? To what extent has the grand-

mother's illiteracy affected the son's literacy? What are the specific circumstances of the grandmother's illiteracy? To what extent does a seven-year-old read well enough to teach anyone how to read? How long has the granddaughter been teaching the grandmother? Why has no adult in the family bothered to teach grandma to read? Why and how is grandma's reading "the best gift ever" for her son? While Bunting supports the notion that everyone should learn to read when young, her book never explains through the grandmother's experiences why and how reading is important on many levels. Once grandmother "performs" her literacy—"this wonderful thing"—before the family at her son's birthday party, how does literacy change her life or the family's? Mom will continue to have her office job, Dad will continue to work as a truck driver, and Sam will continue his sports practice. Once grandmother learns to read, will she and Anna continue to read during their weekly Wednesday night sittings?

Dick King-Smith's *The School Mouse* (1997) deals with the issue of nonreading parents in the racially and culturally neutral world of mice: young, literate Flora "saves" her illiterate parents from eating poison. A level four reader and chapter book, it is the story of a mouse, Flora, desperately making herself literate: "By day she educated herself, and in the evenings she taught her class" of other mice. While the story champions literacy in the very act of the mouse's saving her mouse parents from eating "poison" because she has learned to read—"Thank goodness I have learned to read ... or else I might well have sampled these attractive-looking blue pellets" (28)—the journey toward literacy is both dangerous and lonely for Flora. She meets with hostility and resentment from the mouse family, who initially have no interest in learning to read. Flora's literacy quest begins as and leads to arrogance and alienation from her other mice. She says: "I am not an ordinary school mouse. I'm sure I'm not. I'm sure I can learn all sorts of things that no mouse has ever learned before, if only I study hard enough, and then I shall be an extraordinary school mouse" (16). Flora has accepted the culturally biased assumption that literacy elevates individuals from the masses, and that such elevation is socially valued by all. Despite her mouse family's initial resistance to Flora's "too high an opinion of herself" (15), Flora recognizes her literacy acquisition as part of her self-esteem: "I *am* lucky. I don't suppose there's another mouse on the face of the earth that knows as much as I do already. But I can't talk much about my lessons to the others because they wouldn't understand. ... They're all uneducated. And why? Because there's no one to teach them" (King-Smith, 1997, 104). Literacy isolates the questing mouse; she is lonely until she meets another literate male mouse, and they live happily ever after. As do other children's texts, this one misleadingly idolizes literacy through Flora's action and proclamation that "the first and most important thing, for mice and humans, is to learn to read. Once you can do that, there is no limit to what you can get into your heads" (108). Certainly there is more to life and human worth and self-worth that extends beyond an ability to read and write.

3. Even though the "readerly" narrative is a model of rhetorical flourish at its best and reads as a demonstration of "mastering the master" through mastering or at least imitating the master's language, other rhetorical strategies by Douglass—emotional flourishes, metafictive moments, and rhythmic patterns—render the *Narrative* its distinctly sermonic/ "speakerly" textures and its clear connections with orality and African American folk storytelling. Robert G. O'Meally, in his 1978 essay, "Frederick Douglass's 1845 *Narrative*: The Text Was Meant to Be Preached," comments on the oral preacherly dimensions of Douglass's text:

> The *Narrative* does more than touch upon questions often pondered by black preachers. Its very form and substance are directly influenced by the Afro-American preacher and his vehicle for ritual expression, the sermon. In this sense, Douglass' *Narrative* of 1845 *is* a sermon, and, specifically, it is a black sermon. This is a text meant to be read and pondered; it is also a Clarion call to spiritual affirmation and action: This is a text meant to be preached. ... But Douglass, who grew up hearing sermons on the plantation and who heard and delivered them throughout his life, produced, in this greatest account of his life, a text shaped by the form and the processes of speaking characteristic of the black sermon. This is a mighty text meant, of course, to be read. But it is also a text meant to be mightily preached. (192–193, 210)

4. For example, my then 79-year-old grandfather, with whom I spoke about his own illiteracy when I was mulling over ideas for this project, does not read and write, and to my knowledge, this reality has never been an issue of family concern or discussion. It was an understood and rarely spoken of fact and clearly evident when, for instance, other family members read Father's Day and birthday cards to him. The whole tenor of my conversation with him was one of apology from him for this inability to read. He had a third-grade education when his parents died, and he was forced to leave school to help work for the livelihood of his five siblings. My grandfather and his older brother—who became a minister—were the only two who had minimal reading and writing skills. Others managed to continue studies along the way. With my doctorate in English—a sign of my alleged mastery of alphabetical literacy—I felt awkward, embarrassed, and invasive talking about something the family had never broached in such a manner. My conversation with my grandfather about his illiteracy was a lesson for me in his personal history and circumstances, a lesson of which I had no previous knowledge.

In circulating early drafts of this chapter, a couple of African American friends, responding with familiarity to these details of my illiterate grandfather, were compelled to share illiteracy details in their own families. Both e-mail accounts show how adult family members' illiteracy had an impact on their own educational values. One, an adult literacy volunteer teacher, writes:

> The men on my mom's side of the family are illiterate. They were not encouraged to do well in school like the women were. So they didn't. None of my uncles could read or write past elementary school level. Survival came from what they learned on the streets and from others doing their reading and writing for them. My dad, who was a math whiz, dropped out of school in the third grade to roam around and do nothing. In his fifties, he joined a literacy organization to learn how to read and write. We are proud of his accomplishments. It was never a secret in my family. When my brothers slack, they try to use the excuse that [since] dad made it without an education, why can't they? He sets them straight.
>
> One of my students (female) also quit in the third grade to help feed the family. She never really had the opportunity or drive to go back until recently. She is now eighty years old. (e-mail message to author, 19 January 2000)

Another writes of the circumstances of her parents' illiteracy:

> My mother died at the age of forty; she did not get her GED until she was thirty-seven. She was a very smart woman and it was fun when she went to school because we sometimes got to help her with her homework to an extent. My stepfather never graduated from grade school as I can recall; however, he traveled the world in the army. It was not until I was a grown woman that I found out how extremely good his math skills were, something I suffer with. The point is that neither Mom nor Dad ever helped us with our homework. There was no doubt that we would go to school and were expected to graduate, but there was never any reading to help us or helping with math so that we could move to the next level. Other than school books and the Bible, we had no books around our house. There was no money for them and of course we never went to a library. I do, however, remember them telling stories when the weather caused the lights to go out. That was fun! As you can tell, I sometimes have very mixed feelings about education and its benefits. So many non-formally educated folk have become millionaires. (e-mail message to author, 2 February 2000)

5. Barbara Kantrowitz and Anne Underwood, "Dyslexia and the New Science of Reading," *Newsweek*, 22 November 1999: 72. In their investigation of this disorder that affects about 20 percent of children, Kan-

trowitz and Underwood point out that this inability to decode sounds, essential to reading, results from mixed brain signals; in this case, "reading disorders are most likely the result of what is, in effect, faulty wiring in the brain—not laziness, stupidity, or a poor home environment" (74). They also cite instances of individuals who are successful despite these childhood reading and learning challenges: "Indeed, famous and successful dyslexics include Tom Cruise, artist Robert Rauschenberg and Olympian Dan O'Brien" (74). Although the article obviously does not champion nonreading, it emphasizes that nonreaders can succeed, further evidenced in the example of John Corcoran: "By sixth grade John Corcoran, a severe dyslexic, still couldn't spell 'cat' and could tell MEN from WOMEN on restroom doors only because one was longer. Still illiterate as an adult, he taught social studies in high school—by using movies for lessons, inviting guest speakers and having students grade papers. At forty-eight, he registered for a public library literacy program. ... Now sixty, he published *The Teacher Who Couldn't Read* in 1994" (78). Corcoran's book details his life of deception and riskiness as he successfully moved up the career ladder through elementary and high school, college, and ultimately to his own classroom as a teacher unable to read words on a page. Learning how to read was to him like "being set free from almost five decades of bondage." Notice the analogy made here between illiteracy as a form of enslavement and Frederick Douglass's alleged liberation from slavery through his ability to read and write.

Although not a children's text, Sapphire's controversial novel *PUSH* (1996) is the disturbingly graphic account of an adolescent African American girl's tortured journey to realized selfhood through literacy. The novel demonstrates the complex circumstances—emotional, psychological, social, and physical—that interfere with Claireece Precious Jones's efforts to become literate. Because of many complicated circumstances and situations revealed in the novel, Precious is sixteen and unable to read and write. In fact, she confesses in her narrative that except for pages with pictures, "the pages look all the same" (48). Importantly, literacy is less Precious's "savior" from her traumatic life of paternal and maternal abuse and incest and two subsequent pregnancies, AIDS, and social neglect, than her teacher, Blue Rain, whose approach to helping Precious realize her own self-worth despite her past and present circumstances is through reading and writing. The narrative shows Precious's spiritual blooming after enrolling in a pre-GED adult literacy class for beginning writers. In addition to mastering alphabetic literacy, Precious gains a community of fellow students who respect and care for her as never before. The novel ends with Precious reading to her infant son and committing herself to making his life better than hers. Interestingly, some details of Precious's circumstances echo a situation shared in one of the e-mails from an adult literacy tutor friend who, after reading a draft of this chapter, shared an experience that she had with one of her students:

> I had a student once who quit school in the ninth grade. She thought she was stupid because she never did well. It was not until just before we began our lessons that she found out that she was dyslexic. When I started working with her, her kids would make fun of her. When she started improving, they started helping her with her homework. When she was on her way, she got a job in her child's school as an office aide. Before, she was on welfare, just passing the time doing much of nothing. I would say she had very low self-esteem. In the two years we worked together, I saw her grow as a person. (e-mail message to author, 19 January 2000)

6. Historically, the intraracism that exists within African American communities and households associates light skin with power, authority, and success. Dark-skinned African Americans were presumed to be, were treated as, and perceived themselves as less socially advantaged. Such dynamics emerge from the history of American slavery that rewarded on many levels African Americans closest to masters' white ideal in skin color or hair texture. Masters' children with slaves often were treated as privileged and socially gifted. See Kathy Russell, Midge Wilson, and Ronald Hall, *The Color Complex: The Politics of Skin Color among African Americans* (New York: Anchor Books, 1993).

7. Nikki Giovanni's autobiographical poem, "Nikki-Rosa" (1998), is an adult's perspective on childhood memories often misrepresented or misinterpreted when others impose their values onto another's realities or experiences. Despite her family's material lack and problems with a father who drank too much and too often, Giovanni is not necessarily in psychological and emotional denial when she insists that her childhood "was quite a happy one":

> childhood remembrances are always a drag
> if you're Black
> ... and if you become famous or something
> they never talk about how happy you were to have your mother
> all to yourself and
> how good the water felt when you got your bath from one of those
> big tubs that folk in chicago barbecue in
> ... and though you're poor it isn't poverty that
> concerns you
> ... I really hope no white person ever has cause
> to write about me because they never understand that Black love

is Black wealth and they'll probably talk about my hard childhood and never understand that all the while I was quite happy. (295)

8. This instance of illiteracy is explored briefly in Harper Lee's *To Kill a Mockingbird* (1960) when the young white narrator Scout attends her black maid Calpurnia's church and wonders why the congregation is not reading from the hymnals as they sing. Coupled with the economic issue of the black church not having sufficient funds to buy enough hymnals for its members is the fact that most of the congregation is illiterate. Calpurnia's literacy came from the whites whose house she keeps, and she has passed that "gift" of literacy on to her son Zeebo, who lines hymns—announces the words of hymns for the congregation in a call-and-imitation response format. Notice the conversation between Scout and Calpurnia about this literacy performance:

> "How're we gonna sing it [hymn] if there ain't any hymn-books?"
> Calpurnia smiled. "Hush baby," she whispered, "you'll see in a minute."
> Zeebo cleared his throat and read in a voice like the rumble of distant artillery. ...
> Miraculously on pitch, a hundred voices sang out Zeebo's words. (121)

It never occurs to Scout that folks who cannot read as she and others around her can function quite efficiently. Scout's naïveté highlights again the assumptions of privilege attached to literacy. The reality of illiteracy in her church congregation offers Calpurnia the opportunity to explain literacy as something that potentially separates rather than unites her with other blacks socially:

> Jem [Scout's older brother] said it looked like they [illiterate congregation] could save the collection money for a year and get some hymn books.
> Calpurnia laughed. "Wouldn't do any good," she said. "They can't read."
> "Can't read?" I asked. "All those folks?"
> "That's right," Calpurnia nodded. "Can't but about four folks in First Purchase [church] read. ... I'm one of 'em." (124)

Class and race are here connected with literacy. In this moment, Lee shows that illiteracy does not mean individuals are unable to function or that they suffer from low self-esteem because they are unable to read and write. At the same time, the literacy and Calpurnia's attachment to her white family further separate her from the "regular" lot of blacks in Maycomb County.

Not only are illiterate church members able to function in literate circumstances, but there are even illiterate preachers who manage effectively as well. My maternal grandfather's older brother is an illiterate preacher and has been all of my life. For those who do not know that he is illiterate, he "performs" literacy quite effectively. He has heard biblical scriptures so often that he has memorized them, giving audiences a sense of his spiritual commitment. He knows familiar songs and the Word of God so well that he does not have to read them word for word. Since there are so many translations and modifications of the Bible for various audiences, his recitations might easily be taken as a modernized revision of scriptural texts. He does open the Bible to some text as he recites. Those who know him well know how he skillfully manages to avoid situations calling for spontaneous reading on his part. Since a number of illiterate black preachers in my childhood were not formally trained in seminaries or other theology schools, they managed quite effectively to preach soul-stirring sermons and to negotiate masterfully their leadership, authority, and credibility.

Literacy as privilege and a means of separating blacks from the illiterate masses is evidenced in Harriet Jacobs's slave narrative *Incidents in the Life of a Slave Girl, Written by Herself* (1987). Notice the emphasis as in Frederick Douglass's title when both authors clarify that their narratives were "written by [themselves]." Literacy marks their liberation from slavery. Jacobs, who allegedly taught herself to read, is more self-confident, arrogant even, because she is literate, unlike the other slaves around her: "I was invited to attend [slaves' churches] *because* I could read" (emphasis added, 45). There is no sense that Jacobs/Brent has any other connection, spiritual or communal, with those who share her lot beyond her ability to read to them. She even comments on her ability to pass on news information because others depended on her reading abilities: "They knew that I could read; and I was often asked if I had seen anything in the newspapers about white folks over in the big north, who were trying to get their freedom for them" (45). While literacy puts Jacobs/Brent on equal ground with the white populace, it separates her from her fellow lots of slaves. This middle-class preoccupation with literacy surfaces again when Jacobs/Brent is reunited with her nine-year-old daughter Ellen after seven years of being in bondage. Although Jacobs/Brent is concerned about Ellen's unkempt appearance, she is most bothered by her daughter's inability to read: "When she [Ellen, the daughter] was placed with Mrs. Hobbs, the agreement was that she should be sent to school. She had been there two years, and was now nine years old, and she scarcely knew her letters. There was no excuse for this, for there were good public schools in Brooklyn, to which she could have been sent without expense" (166). At the same time, Brent/Jacobs's concern for her daughter's literacy might seem any literate parent's desire that her child receive an education that will aid that child in living a "better" life than the parent.

9. Story reading and storytelling need not be as dichotomized culturally as this narrative presents. Reading stories is certainly not any more important than good storytelling. For instance, Angela Johnson's *Tell Me a Story, Mama* (New York: Orchard Books, 1989) is an African American children's book that celebrates a storytelling tradition. When a young daughter requests that her mother tell her a story as the child is being tucked into bed, the young preschool girl clarifies which story she wants her mother to tell by ultimately telling the story to the mother as the mother has told her many times over. The narrative re-creates the mother's childhood story through the daughter's retelling. Whether the mother is literate does not influence this equally important parent–child ritual. Two other children's texts importantly present talking and storytelling as a source of communal celebration: Deborah M. Newton Chocolate's retelling of the Ashanti legend, *Talk, Talk* (Mahwah, NJ: Troll, 1993) and Angela Shelf Medearis's *Too Much Talk: A West African Folktale* (Cambridge: Candlewick Press, 1995).

10. According to a 1987 report, *The Subtle Danger: Reflections on the Literacy Abilities of America's Young Adults*, published by the Educational Testing Service (Princeton, NJ), "on the average, African Americans perform 20% behind whites on literacy tests and Hispanics perform halfway between the two." "The Typical Adult Non-Reader," http://indian-river.fl.us/living/services/als/typical.html (26 January 2000), 1.

11. Not only slaves were punished if caught learning to read and write; whites who assisted in slave learning were subject to legal consequences. Describing feminist abolitionist Lydia Maria Child's crusade against slave illiteracy in Child's *An Appeal in Favor of Americans Called Africans* (1833), Cecelia McCall, in her undated essay "A Historical Quest for Literacy," recounts the deliberate obstacles to slave learning:

> [Lydia Maria Child] reports that various laws were enacted to maintain illiteracy. For instance, South Carolina was the first state to order that any person caught instructing a slave be fined one hundred pounds. Virginia declared that schools established to teach either slave or free Black people should be disbanded and each pupil lashed twenty times. Anyone caught teaching slaves in Georgia was imprisoned for ten days and given thirty-nine lashes. By 1837, all states in the slaveocracy had enacted similar laws. ... In the free North, ... Ohio, for instance, refused to educate "colored" children at the public expense or allow them to attend schools with white children. (4)

After slavery ended, literacy continued to be a weapon of white supremacy used against black social and political participation: "Literacy or other tests as a condition for voting were suspended by the Voting Rights Act in 1965 initially only in those states in which Congress found there had been pervasive discrimination against blacks in registration and in which literacy tests had been specifically designed to disfranchise racial minorities. Later, the ban on literacy and other tests was made nationwide and permanent by amendments to the Voting Rights Act in 1970 and 1975. The Supreme Court held the nationwide ban constitutional after concluding that literacy tests had reduced voter participation in a discriminatory manner throughout the country and not merely in those states originally covered by the Act" Laughlin McDonald, "Minority Vote Dilution: The Fourteenth Amendment and the Voting Rights Act," http://www.aclu.org/aclu-e/course3_mcdonald3.html, (4 January 1980) 3.

12. Recall that Frederick Douglass (1845), even after being free from slavery and "armed" with literacy, is unable to secure a job as a calker because whites will not work with him: "I went in pursuit of a job of calking; but such was the strength of prejudice against color, among the white calkers, that they refused to work with me, and of course I could get no employment" (714). The myth of Frederick Douglass's liberation from slavery and racism is perpetuated even in historical texts for elementary students. As if literacy exempts Frederick Douglass from racial discrimination, Karen H. Dusek's 1989 essay, "Frederick Douglass, Abolitionist Writer," boldly asserts: "When Frederick Douglass was a boy, he wanted more than anything else to be free. Believing that he would never be truly free without an education, he learned to read and write. His ability to read and write soon proved to be his most powerful weapon in his lifelong fight against slavery and prejudice" (21). Neither Douglass's narrative nor this essay on him speaks of literacy—the ability to read and write—as a way of personal liberation imaginatively. Rather, liberation is ideally connected to overcoming social circumstance.

13. John Corcoran (1994), chronicling his life as an illiterate parent and high school teacher, offers a similar experience with the fairy tales he pretends to read to his young daughter. Because of the pictures and his familiarity with the fairy tales orally, Corcoran confidently embellishes the stories of the Three Little Bears and Cinderella but is at a total loss when his young daughter requests a story with which he is unfamiliar. He recounts the pain of that experience:

> The big Golden Books and their wonderful pictures would stimulate my imagination to weave some crazy yarns. When I told the Three Bears, Cinderella, or another well-known fairy story, they were embellished with all the drama of Orson Welles or Alfred Hitchcock. Sometimes I could hear Kathy [Corcoran's wife] laughing in the kitchen at my tall tales. I had a lot of practice at storytelling.
>
> Colleen had a surprise for me that night. "Read this Daddy," she said, snuggling closer to me. She held out a new book, one with

smaller pictures and more words. Her blue eyes were bright with anticipation.

... I looked at the first page, hoping there would be a clue. ...

I couldn't decipher one word in this preschool children's book.

How I wanted to be able to read, to help her [daughter] during those valuable growing-up years before school. Parents who can't read, can't teach their children to read. My heart was wrenched, knowing that I could not give her what I didn't have. (4–5)

CHAPTER 3

1. The idea for this chapter came during conversations with then undergraduate student Arleen Knowles, who was taking my African American children's literature class. Since the conception and writing of this chapter, Randall Kennedy's book *Nigger: The Strange Career of a Troublesome Word* (New York: Pantheon, 2002) has garnered much public attention as a biography of one of the most politically and socially charged words in the English language. Aside from presenting in an annotated bibliography format the many controversies surrounding the word *nigger* in American literature, popular culture, sports, politics, history, and jurisprudence, the book does little to address how American society might close the racial divide created and maintained by the sometimes absolute, sometimes ambiguous, and sometimes ambivalent uses of and responses to this single word.

2. When I recently presented an abbreviated version of this chapter at a conference, I was intrigued by an audience member's notion that to discuss such hurtful experiences once they have occurred painfully reminds parents of their own emotional vulnerabilities and their ultimate helplessness in protecting their children from social ills or others' bigotry.

3. I recognize that the human body can physically heal in ways that are indeed easier than recovery from spiritual, emotional, or psychological injuries. As well, I do not mean to imply that physical attacks do not and cannot damage a person's psyche. Nonvisible wounds can also result from being physically victimized with or without damaging words. Nevertheless, in the context of this discussion, I reiterate, as does Karina Bland in her essay on parental verbal child abuse: "The injuries from verbal abuse don't show on the outside, the way a beating does. ... Words hurt kids on the inside." See Bland's essay, "Hurtful Words Abuse, Too: Kids' Self-Image Easily Harmed by Careless Remarks," *Arizona Republic*, 12 April 1998: A8.

4. Other venues have addressed derogatory naming of blacks by whites, but no name seems to carry the all-encompassing American furor of the word *nigger*. For instance, the satirical sixties musical *Hair: The Ameri-*

can Tribal Love-Rock Musical (Rado and Ragni, 1968) includes the song "Colored Spade" that recites a litany of racist and dehumanizing names African Americans have endured both past and present:

> I am a colored spade a nigra a black nigger
> A jungle bunny jigaboo a coon a pickaninny mau mau an
> Uncle Tom Aunt Jemima Little Black Sambo
> Cotton pickin' swamp guinea junk man shoe shine boy
> Elevator operator table cleaner at Horn and Hardarts
> Slave voodoo zombie Ubangi-lipped
> Flat-nosed tap dancer resident of Harlem (22–23)

Garland Jeffreys's title song from his album *Don't Call Me Buckwheat* (New York: Black and White Alike, 1991) adds to this list of derogatory labels:

> This is a song about words
> The power of words
> Don't call me buckwheat
> Don't call me eight ball
> Don't call me jig jig jig jig …
> Watch that word
> Don't call me Sambo
> 'Cause it hurts
> And that ain't nice
> And it sticks like white on rice.

He further adds the names "nig nig nig nig," "coonskin," and "spook spook spook spook."

5. Although I acknowledge the ongoing censorship debates surrounding the use of the word *nigger* in such texts for older readers as Mark Twain's *The Adventures of Huckleberry Finn* and William Faulkner's "A Rose for Emily," I purposely avoid commenting on that angle because it has already received significant critical and social attention. Furthermore, by the time youngsters become experienced readers and more independent thinkers, it is highly likely that they will have already been introduced to the word. Nevertheless, the unexpected presence of the word and its accompanying stereotype took my wife aback as she was reading Hugh Lofting's classic *The Voyages of Doctor Dolittle* to our then nine-year-old son. She posed our parental concerns in an e-mail to an educator's listserve. In chapter 5 of the 1951 edition, Polynesia, the parrot, states to Dr. Dolittle, "You know what those niggers are—that ignorant!" My wife questioned whether such racist comments have been edited from more recent printings. Excising the offensive word does not compromise the integrity of the story but may protect an unsuspecting child from an encounter with a racist sentiment that, occurring casually in a beloved

children's "classic," lends the slur authenticity and cultural legitimacy. Such editing, however, also presents a slippery slope that is not so easily navigated.

Respondents to the listserve recognized the problematic in this situation and offered that this occurrence might create an opportunity to teach about racist comments and stereotypes, again assuming that an adult is available to do so. Subsequent editions of the novel series, my wife discovered, include introductions explaining the novel's "historical" political incorrectness. And, in one edition, the line about *niggers* is deleted.

CHAPTER 4

1. See Candy Mills's "A HAIR-y Situation," *Interrace Magazine*, June 1992: 23, about a biracial (African American and white) female child's experiences with her hair from the perspective of the child. Dori Sanders's novel *Clover* (1990) also includes details concerning the hair issue from a ten-year-old black girl's perspective. The black girl, through the death of her black father, "inherits" a white stepmother. Hair becomes a central focus of this black–white, stepmother–stepdaughter relationship.

   Caroline Bond Day's *A Study of Some Negro-White Families in the United States* (1932) examines the hair textures of black–white biracial offspring. Using photographic and statistical data, this study explores the varying degrees "of curvature in head hair … , from the extremely curved condition found in most Negroes to the straight hair form found in many Whites. In this study six degrees of curvature, or types of hair form, are recognized: straight, low waves, deep waves, curly, frizzy, and wooly" (12–17).

2. Even the term *relaxing* suggests that one's hair is tight and kinky and needs to be loosened or straightened. *Kinky* carries with it obvious negative associations of deviation from an established standard or norm.

3. The very process of making African Americans' hair straight is potentially dangerous. Home relaxer kits come with bold warnings about chemicals in the relaxer that can, if not properly applied, cause skin and scalp burns and irritation, hair breakage and loss, and eye injury. The person applying the relaxer is encouraged not only to wear gloves, but also to heed other warnings, including not wetting, shampooing, brushing, or scratching the scalp for two to three days prior to using the relaxer, not applying the relaxer directly to the scalp, and not pulling hair forcibly during the relaxation process. Those with relaxed hair are also warned that hair with relaxer chemicals is flammable. Recall Michael Jackson's chemically treated hair catching fire in the 1980s Jheri curl heyday when he was too close to stage lights. Jheri and California curls gave African Americans bouncy, wet and

often drippy, loose curls with added length. Once hair was chemically curled, daily maintenance involved using greasy activators and moisturizers.

Even straightening with a stove-heated hot comb has left many a young girl with ear, forehead, or scalp burns in a hairdresser's efforts to get at the roots and the "kitchen," the nape of the neck. Paulette M. Caldwell, in an excellently detailed 1991 essay on the centrality of head hair as an interactive sexist and racist reality for black women in court litigations, offers further possible side effects and dangers of continued chemical hair straightening:

> Many of us [black women] risk losing [hair] permanently after years of chemical straighteners; [or risk] the entry of chemical toxins into our bloodstream through our scalps [that may] damage our unborn or breastfeeding children. (369)

While Jacklyn Mock, in "How to Get Good Hair," alleges that women's relaxed hair "spells sophistication" and allows "busy sisters ... hair ... manageability and endless range of styling options," she cautions that "relaxed hair ... does lose some of its protein and moisture in the process, leaving it more fragile than natural hair. If your hair is relaxed, keep in mind that it needs an extra dose of tender loving care to avoid breakage and control dryness and split ends" (58).

4. Veronica Chambers, in "Dreading It" (1999), details others' responses to her dreadlocking:

> I have occasionally thought that I carry all of my personality around on my head. ... I sometimes walk into a cocktail party and let my hair do the talking for me. I stroll through the room, silently, and watch my hair tell white lies. In literary circles, my hair brands me as "interesting, adventurous." In black middle class [circles], my hair brands me as "rebellious" or "Afrocentric." In predominantly white circles, my hair doubles my level of exotica. My hair says, "Unlike the black woman who reads you the evening news, I'm not even trying to blend in." Hair surely becomes a source of others' interpretations of one's politics, one's social agenda, one's personality, one's profession, even one's (un)professionalism. (178)

5. Getting a "touchup" or "retouching" is not chemically relaxing the entire head of hair again but rather applying chemicals to the new growth. There is even a relaxer product called Smooth Edges that can "smooth new growth around the hairline" when the greater part of the hair is already treated. "Just Do the Edges" comes as a tube applicator and is used when "you just have to smooth out the edges."

6. For extensive treatments of Western perceptions and symbolisms of hair, see Wendy Cooper's *Hair: Sex, Society, Symbolism* (1971), and the chapter "The Hair Project: A Hair-Raising Story of Socialization," in Frigga Haug's *Female Sexualization: A Collective Work of Memory* (1999). Neither text considers the race dynamics and hair, however.

7. Interestingly, except in the story's title, Goldilocks's hair of the classic "Goldilocks and the Three Bears" is not described in most versions. Cultural and social politics have created the "definitive" images. For instance, no specific hair details are offered in the following random sampling: Tim and Jenny Wood's *Goldilocks and the Three Bears* (1991); the Little Golden Books edition of *The Three Bears*; and Carol Burnett's *Goldilocks and The Three Bears* (1990). Only Dom DeLuise's 1992 version, *Goldilocks*, describes the character's hair:

> Once upon a time, in a forest far away, lived a beautiful girl with the most gorgeous blond hair you ever saw. It was very long, very shiny, and very curly. I mean it really got your attention. … Goldilocks had such beautiful hair, people were always complimenting her on how wonderful she looked and pretty soon she began to think so, too. (1–3)

8. Francesco Mastalia and Alfonse Pagano's tabletop picture book *Dreads* (1999) is a global journey documenting adult individuals' personal, spiritual, political, historical, and cultural reasons for locking their hair. Introduced by veteran dreadlocker and author Alice Walker, the book reiterates a centrality of head hair to identity. Of the many testimonials accompanying the black and white hair portraits, Jacqueline "Setra" Collins's comments are especially relevant to this investigation:

> Blonde hair, pale skin, blue eyes:
> Without them, one was considered ugly. Such attitudes prevailed in my mother's time, in her mother's time. They still exist today, but it stops here with my generation, with me.
> It's only recently that Black beauty has gained any recognition.
> Dreadlocks express my faith in myself and my culture. They are the pathway to a natural and spiritual life. (135)

Echoing the message in De Veaux's text, Davine Del Valle sees her dreadlocks as the natural extensions of her self: "My dreadlocks have as much to do with my biology as my ethnicity. It's genetic: This is how my hair is, and locks free me from the losing fight to tame the life out of it" (140).

9. In many ways, this book's glorification of "long, long hair" echoes lyrics from the Broadway rock musical *Hair* (Rado and Ragni, 1968), wherein the title score lauds: "Give me a head with hair—long, beautiful hair. Shining, gleaming, steaming, flaxen, waxen / Give me down to there hair, shoulder-length or longer" (64–72).

In keeping with this ideal of long hair and white females, Mattel's Barbie doll is hailed as "America's favorite doll." A 1991 *Parade Magazine* advertisement for the 1959 Barbie Bride-to-Be (Danbury Mint) describes Barbie as America's ultimate icon of female beauty: "For over 30 years, Barbie has reigned supreme as America's fairy tale princess. She is every little girl's dream of the woman she hopes to one day become—beautiful, glamorous" (9). As a response to this long hair beauty ideal, African American poet-playwright Ntozake Shange, in her choreopoem *spell #7* (1979), introduces a white girl character fantasy that centers around the hair flinging obsession. In the skit, "Being a White Girl for a Day," the character explains:

> today i'm gonna be a white girl
> i'll retroactively wake myself up
> an low & behold
> a white girl in my bed
> but first i'll have to call a white girl i know to have some more accurate information
> what's the first thing white girls think in the morning
> do they get up being glad they aint niggahs
> do they remember mama
> or worry about getting to work
> do they work? Do they play isadora & wrap themselves in sheets
> & go tip toeing to the kitchen to make maxwell house coffee
> oh i know
> the first thing a white girl does in the morning is fling her hair. (47)

Shange stereotypes white females, signifying on images prevalent in magazines and commercials with white girls flinging their hair. The hair flinging is something that shows up even when least expected. My children and I are always amusingly distracted whenever we watch Disney's *Pocahontas* and see the title character's long, flowing hair waving flaglike throughout the movie even when there are no other signs of blowing breezes.

10. See Neal A. Lester, "Nappy Happy: A Review of bell hooks's *Happy to Be Nappy*" (1999).

11. Herron's award-winning children's book drew national attention in November 1998 when a white teacher in Brooklyn, New York, read the book as a celebration of cultural diversity to her black and Latino third-grade students. Although the students loved the book and the teacher's allowing their participation in the book's call-and-response performance, some African American parents accused the white teacher of racial and cultural insensitivity. The teacher was threatened with violence and eventually left that teaching assignment for another. If anything, the controversy over the book highlights the cultural ignorance

of many non–African Americans about this loaded intraracial politici-
zation of hair. It also reintroduced in the social and political arena the
complicated notion of who has the right to "perform" black texts. The
white teacher's reading of the book was further complicated by the fact
that the book uses black vernacular, and the teacher's whiteface reading
was too close to blackface minstrels mocking blacks primarily through
exaggerated and artificial language. Still another reason for the controversy is the fact that many African Americans have not found a political,
historical, personal, and social space where "nappy" is devoid of negative
cultural self-perceptions.

12. This is not to suggest that males do not straighten or relax their hair as well.
My own experience with lye relaxing parallels Malcolm X's. While black
men—importantly, not boys—may choose to straighten their hair, the target audience for relaxing products is black women and their daughters.

13. Some children's relaxer kits are now equipped with voice instruction
cassettes, presumably to reiterate the warnings about "unprofessional"
usage to avoid injury or to serve those who are unable to read and understand clearly that the product must be used safely to prevent physical
harm. This is also an acknowledgement that not everyone who uses this
lye-based chemical product is literate and able to read in print the multiple warnings associated with the process.

14. Common words and phrases for the ideal hair found in adult and children's relaxer ads include the following: "soft and silky and manageable";
"style, body and shine"; "worry-free combing and styling"; "soft, silky
and free"; "soft, easy to manage, with glorious sheen and great body";
"soft, healthy and beautiful"; "wonderfully moisturized, soft, full and
glossy"; "visibly softer, smoother, shinier, healthier … so beautiful";
"smooth and soft so that you'll always be able to get a comb through it";
"great body, glorious sheen, softness and manageability." Finally, Gold
Medal Hair Products, in Freeport, New York, offers in its early 1990s cat-
alog, an herbal product that avoids relaxing with chemicals altogether:

> Herbal Tame-Natural Hair Relaxer is just what Afro hair has
> always needed. It is a mild, herbal relaxer that gradually and natu-
> rally releases kink without chemicals. It is so beneficial, your hair
> becomes stronger, straighter, smoother, silkier, easier to manage.
> For the first time since you were a baby, your hair will be healthy,
> growing strong, and shining, without frizz.

While alleged softness, healthiness, silkiness, manageability, and shini-
ness are also the desired ends of hair products for white women generally, these results for whites are achieved through rinses, conditioners,
or shampoos that do not equal chemical treatments through relaxers.
These characteristics also presume that Afro hair is not healthy, strong,
shiny, manageable, or soft organically.

15. Marcia Ann Gillespie, in "Mirror Mirror" (*Essence,* January 1993), says that Eurocentric ideals potentially surface even when African Americans choose more Afrocentric hairstyles:

> Despite all the talk about the ways in which the American beauty standard automatically negates all who are not European, we get sucked in even when we think we're standing pure. We afrocentrize by wearing dreadlocks, twists, cornrows, but still there's the desire to have shake-your-head hair that moves and flips and flies. So we end up buying hair by the pound in order to achieve the desired effect while being ethnically correct. ... Programmed to want hair on the pillow, to become fixed on having long hair, lots of hair to flick and shake in weaves, braids and instant Afro-Asian dreads. Bushels and bales of hair to meet the ever-increasing demand are shorn from the heads of wrenchingly poor Asian women. Sold American—a perfect study of exploitation all around. (74)

CHAPTER 5

1. Nikki Grimes's elementary school reader *Wild, Wild Hair* (New York: Scholastic, 1997) could be considered a companion to Carolivia Herron's *Nappy Hair* (1997). Grimes's is the story of an African American girl probably between the ages of five and seven whose "hair was long and thick and wild" and "full of knots." *Wild, Wild Hair* uses humor to talk about Tisa Walker's efforts to escape her Monday morning schoolday combing ritual. The book presents Tisa's efforts to escape getting her hair combed and braided as a game of hide-and-seek for all of Tisa's family members. While Tisa's hair might be considered "nappy," the words *nappy* and *kinky* are strategically euphemized as wild and knotty. Interestingly, while Tisa's hair is eventually braided in an African style, it is still long and cascades heavily down her back.

2. Used by whites to refer to black people's hair, the term *nappy* is always condescendingly negative. However, among African Americans, according to economist Julianne Malveaux, in "Just a Nappy-Headed Sister with the PC Blues" (*Black Issues in Higher Education*, 24 December 1998), *nappy* has multiple meanings: "a term of endearment," as in "Come on over here with yo' nappy-headed self"; "a term of derision," as in "Who that nappy-headed sista think she is?"; "a symbol of seduction," as in "Let me run my fingers through that nappy, red stuff"; "and a token of rejection," as in "She doesn't even have that much hair—can you hear the finger snap?—and it's nappy" (30).

3. Although not a children's book, Alile Sharon Larkin's children's storytelling-with-collage-art video *Dreadlocks and the Three Bears* (Inter Image Video, 1991) recasts the traditional blond, straight-haired Goldilocks as a "cinnamon brown child [Nimi] with lots of pretty African

curls on her pretty little cinnamon brown head." Nimi's nickname in her family and her Caribbean village derives from her hair texture and style: She has "curly-curly-kinky-curly-nappy-curly hair." Her "curly curly-kinky-curly-nappy curly twists and locks of hair called dreadlocks [are] so *divine* that everyone just called her Dreadlocks" (emphasis added). Dreadlocks must be an adolescent/teenager since she cooks delicious cheese grits for the bear family at the story's end.

4. Twenty-ninth Popular Culture Association and Twenty-first American Culture Association Annual Conference, San Diego, CA (31 March to 3 April 1999). The session was on the controversy over Carolivia Herron's *Nappy Hair*.

CHAPTER 7

1. After many years of trying to locate angels of color on Christmas cards, our family received its first in 1992. It is a print/card of eleven brown, unclothed infant angels; the original pastel is by Brenda Joysmith (1982). This print/card and another of a nativity scene with brown characters (original watercolor by Robert Steele, 1991) come from Frederick Douglass Designs (P. O. Box 3303, Berkeley, CA 94703). *The Frederick Douglass Designs' Christmas, All Occasion, and Print Catalogue* (1992) includes another Christmas card with a young brown angel sitting among clouds and holding a dove in his lap. Black ceramic Christmas cherubs with "ethnic" features are advertised in *Ebony E Style/Spiegel Magazine* (Holiday 1993), 25.

2. Georgia-Pacific's Angel Soft toilet tissue commercials evidence this near lack of angels of color. Of two commercials that aired over a two-day period (17 and 18 May 1993) on two Birmingham, Alabama, television stations, only one of the commercials has a black infant in it. The first Angel Soft spot presents about five diaper-clad, pink-winged white babies cooing and floating among clouds and with pink-winged packages of Angel Soft tissue. Of the five infants, one may be Asian. The longer of the two commercials presents about ten babies costumed and doing the same as in the previous one. In this commercial, one of the ten infants is an African American girl. Interestingly, this infant appears near the end of the commercial for a split second and is never in a prominent position on the screen. Rather, she is off to the right and shares the viewed area with two other white angel babies. Georgia-Pacific is based in Dallas, Texas. Another later Angel Soft tissue commercial features the black infant baby center screen. While this apparent "revision" is important, it does not explain why the other infants include eight whites and one Asian. In addition, when Georgia-Pacific was asked to share printed advertisement visuals of their Angel Soft tissue product, it distributed a poster (17 × 24 inches) of two white infant angels pictured with three packages of tissue.

The tissue packages have drawings of white infant angels. When asked specifically if Georgia-Pacific had printed advertisements with angels of color, a smaller poster (8.5 × 11 inches) with a brown infant angel pictured next to a package with its white angel drawing was forwarded.

The rock group R.E.M. features a black male angel with blond hair in their hit music video "Losing My Religion" (*Out of Time*, Warner Brothers Records, 1991). This image of an angel and other progressive ideologies and symbols have replaced outdated and false traditional ones of white male angels and a white Christ hanging on a cross. That a black angel is featured challenges complicated layers of myths associated with Western religious thought. The blond hair adds still another dimension of an ideal under attack.

3. Such questions are examined culturally and historically in William Moseley's *What Color Was Jesus?* (Chicago: African American Images, 1987).

4. To name a few, these include Sophy Burnham, *A Book of Angels: Reflections on Angels Past and Present, and True Stories of How They Touch Our Lives* (New York: Ballentine Books, 1990); Eileen Freeman, *Touched by Angels* (New York: Warner Books, 1993); Billy Graham, *Angels: God's Secret Agents* (Waco, TX: World Books, 1991); Tony Kushner's award-winning plays *Angels in America: Millennium Approaches* (1993) and *Angel Dance* (Marshall, MN: Crossing Press, 1990); and Gordon Legge, "Angels Enjoy Popularity as God's 'Messengers'" and "Angel Lore Is Soaring as Public Responds," *Birmingham News*, 15 January 1993: H1–H2. Accompanying Legge's articles is a drawing by *Birmingham News* staff illustrator Wanda Rutherford of a white female angel peering over a white female.

5. Until being introduced to Frederick Douglass Designs, I had not found illustrated biblical/scriptural texts with non-white angels. All of the mainstream books of Bible stories present white angels.

6. Visual artist Alison Saar presents a dapper black male angel in her mixed media fresco "Uptown Bound" (1988), and a black Gabriel blows his horn in James Leonard's "Wind Machine with Gabriel, Eleanor Roosevelt, and Louis Armstrong" (1984).

7. Essex Hemphill, *Ceremonies: Prose and Poetry*. Black angels appear to the accompaniment of Hemphill's reading of this poem in British filmmaker Isaac Julien's *Looking for Langston* (1989), an artistic exploration of Langston Hughes's homosexuality.

8. In his short story "Angel Levine," in *The Magic Barrel* (New York: Avon/Bard, 1980), Jewish author Bernard Malamud presents a Jewish male, Manischevitz, who has to contend with a doubly contradictory image of a black Jewish angel: "A black Jew and angel to boot—very hard to believe" (46). In an initial meeting between the angel named Alexander Levine and Manischevitz, Manischevitz asks: "So if God sends to me an angel why a black? Why not a white that there are so many of them?" (45).

While the image of an old black Jewish angel is intriguing, Malamud's black characters speak in stereotypical exaggerated black dialect and are in the story's background doing little more than dancing, laughing, and partying; invoking familiar images of American minstrelsy.

9. A 1940s Merry Melodies cartoon spoof of Broadway classics "Have You Any Castles?" includes black angels singing with large and exaggerated lips and playing instruments. As cartoons, their connection to blackface minstrels is clear.

10. A sampling of children's books about angels offers evidence of the general lack of angels of color. *Hark, The Littlest Angel* (New York: John Day, 1965), written and illustrated by Mircea Vasiliu, tells of a mischievous, untidy, clumsy but ultimately ingenious little white angel who, in search of earthly fun and games, leaves his cloud home above a large busy city. With unpolished halo, spotted robe, and unkempt hair, the littlest angel is thought to be an earthling costumed as an angel. Of the thirteen youths costumed as angels for an upcoming Christmas pageant encountered by this angel, only two are close to being non-white, suggested with the illustrator's very subtle pencil shadings of their faces and hands and their darker, denser hair. Peter Collington's *The Angel and The Soldier Boy* (New York: Knopf, 1987), a picture book without words, is the story of a white mother who reads a bedtime story, "Treasure Ahoy," to her blond white daughter. As the little girl sleeps, two toy figurines—a white soldier boy and a white female angel—come to life to rescue the little girl's stolen piggy bank money from the pirates who have escaped from her book. The soldier is captured by the pirates, and the angel rescues him; together, the soldier and the angel restore order to the sleeping girl's room. (This story has been adapted to video.) Posy Simmonds's *Lulu and the Flying Babies* (New York: Knopf, 1988) involves a disgruntled little white girl, Lulu, who, visiting a museum with her father and baby brother, witnesses the coming to life of white infant angels in paintings and from statues. Lulu calls these little angels "flying babies." Singer/author Debby Boone, in her book *The Snow Angel* (Eugene, OR: Harvest House, 1991), illustrated by her husband, Gabriel Ferrer, presents a little red-haired white girl, Rose, who creates a snow angel with her body and witnesses the angel's coming to life. While the angel is about the same size, height, and age as Rose, this angel, interestingly, has shoulder-length yellow/blond straight hair and a tilted halo. The angel, Rose, and Rose's grandfather restore the busy adults' faith in fantasy and childhood innocence. There are no black people in this fictitious city. One wonders why Rose's angel is blond with long hair since Rose is not and since the angel otherwise might be a kind of a mirror image of Rose. Of the approximately fifteen angels in Ann Pilling's *Before I Go to Sleep: Bible Stories, Poems, and Prayers for Children* (New York: Crown, 1990), illustrated by Kady MacDonald Denton, none of the angels are non-white. These examples reveal that nothing in the various

texts specifically dictates the skin color of these angels. Instead, that they are almost always white seems a result of an author's limited creative possibilities, or of social and cultural expectation.

11. Charles Tazewell's *The Littlest Angel* (Nashville: Ideals Children's Books, 1991), illustrated by Paul Micich, presents a racially integrated heaven with brown and white angels. Although the book is about the adventures of a four-year-old white male angel, Tazewell's heavenly choir has two brown angels—one an adult female and another a teen male. Tazewell even has a black elderly man as the heavenly gatekeeper.

CHAPTER 8

1. Toni Morrison (with Slade Morrison), *The Big Box*, illustrations by Giselle Potter (New York: Jump at the Sun/Hyperion Books for Children, 1999). Toni Morrison (with Slade Morrison) *The Book of Mean People*, illustrations by Pascal Lemaitre (New York: Hyperion Books for Children, 2002). Subsequent citations in the chapter come from these editions. Although this exercise is limited to Morrison's first two children's books, her repertoire of children's texts includes the following: *Who's Got Game? The Ant or the Grasshopper?* (Simon and Schuster, 2003), *Who's Got Game? The Lion or the Mouse?* (Simon and Schuster, 2003), *Remember: The Journey to School Integration* (Houghton-Mifflin, 2004) and *Who's Got Game? Poppy or the Snake?* (Scribner, 2004).

2. Toni Morrison, "The Big Box," in Letty Cottin Pogrebin, ed., *Stories for Free Children* (San Francisco: Ms. Foundation for Education and Communication, 1982), 47–48. The book version updates the references to popular culture from some twenty years ago, changing, for instance, Patty getting a "hi-fi stereo set" instead of a "Japanese stereo set"; receiving "Nikes and a Spice Girl shirt" instead of "pumas and Farrah Fawcett shirt"; Mickey's parents visiting "after their comedy show" instead of "after the Merv Griffin show"; Mickey getting a "store-bought cake" instead of a "Bakermaster's cake" and "an autographed basketball" instead of "a poster of Jethro Tull"; and Mickey not "doing drugs" instead of not "smoking hash."

CHAPTER 18

1. Recall the November 1998 controversy over Herron's *Nappy Hair* (1997) when a white third-grade teacher in Brooklyn, New York, read the book to her students as part of a multicultural celebration. While the students allegedly loved hearing the book read in its folkloric call-and-response, improvisational format, and even dramatized movements with the responses to the teacher's calls, some African American parents were outraged when they found student-requested Xeroxed copies of pages from the book in their children's book bags. Xeroxing rendered the pho-

tographs of African Americans caricaturishly dark. These parents were equally offended by the black vernacular language used in the text as well as the very use of the word *nappy*, assumed to have a racist and negative connotation, especially read aloud by a white teacher to black and Latino students. Concerns of racism reached national news, and the teacher and the author were threatened with violence by angry parents.

2. Perhaps hooks offers a direct response to Herron's text as hooks uses variations on Herron's words: frizz and fuzz, tight and close, combing, brushing, twisting, plaiting and lying flat, kinks gone, and tight naps. Interestingly, this text is adapted as an HBO hip hop animation, and is read by Mary J. Blige: *Happy to Be Nappy and Other Stories of Me* (Home Box Office, 2004).

3. I was attending a multicultural children's book fair a few years ago and was seated on a bench examining my purchases when a little white boy, perhaps three or four years old, who was climbing on the bench already, came over unexpectedly and started playing with my then six-inch dreadlocks. He flipped them up and down without saying a word as his mother looked on mortified. She apologized for the son, and I explained that there was no need for an apology. Meanwhile, I have a white female colleague in my predominantly white English department who always questions me about dreadlocks—why I decided to grow them, how they grow, how they are cleaned, what "dreadlocking" means etymologically. I see parallels in white curiosity between the adult and the child, curiosity that I had not witnessed in twenty years when my first college roommate, a white male, wanted to pat my hair as "cultural exploration," and he discovered that it really doesn't feel like steel wool.

4. Alice Walker shows in her story "Olive Oil" (1992) the sensuality and sexuality also associated with this ritual of hair care and grooming, a ritual foreign to many whites on many levels. Walker explains first how Orelia discovers the shame of using vaseline to rid her skin of its dryness:

> She remembered being a little black girl with skinny, knock-kneed ashy legs, and how every morning her mother had reminded her to rub them with Vaseline. Vaseline was cheap and very effective. Unfortunately Orelia almost always put on too much or forgot to wipe off the excess and so everything she wore and everything on which she sat retained a slight film of grease. This greasiness about herself and her playmates (most as ashy as she) eventually sickened her, especially when television and movies made clear that oiliness of any sort automatically put one beyond the social pale. The best white people were never oily, for instance, and she knew they put down readily poor whites and black people who were. (364)

The mundane ritual of oiling her husband's scalp is heightened to the level of sensuality and eroticism, however, as John sits between her legs as his wife massages and fondles his scalp:

> Orelia carefully covered John's shoulders with a towel and soon she was scratching huge flakes (embarrassingly many and large, to John) off his scalp and explaining how dandruff, especially among black people, was caused not only by a lack of moisture but by a lack of oil. "We're drier than most people," she said, "at least in America we are. ..."
>
> As careful as a surgeon she divided his hair into dozens of segments and poured small amounts of oil between them. Then, using her fingers and especially her thumbs, she massaged his scalp vigorously, humming a little tune as she did.
>
> After she'd thoroughly oiled and massaged his scalp ... , she amused herself by making tiny corkscrew curls, "baby dreads," she called them, all over his head. She explained that tomorrow he could wash out any excess (though surprisingly the oil seemed to have soaked in instantly and there didn't seem to be any), leaving his scalp comfortable and his hair shiny. ...
>
> It was wonderful to John, sitting between Orelia's knees, feeling her hands on his head, listening to her hum softly and talk to him, an intimacy he'd longed for all his life. But one he had assumed would never be for him. His sisters, with their unruly locks, had enjoyed the haven between his mother's knees and between each other's knees, and between his aunts' cushiony knees, as they fiddled with each other's hair, but he, a boy, had been excluded. He imagined himself as a small child and how much he must have wanted to get between somebody's knees; he imagined the first few times being cajoled and then being pushed away. He knew that if we went far enough back in his memories he would come upon his childhood self weeping and uncomprehending over this.
>
> But now. Look.
>
> John knew there was a full moon, he could feel it in the extra sensitivity of his body, and the fire made a gentle droning sound in the stove; the leaping of the flames threw heat shadows across his face. He felt warm and cozy and accepted into an ancient women's ritual that seemed to work just fine for him. It turned him on and gave him an idea. (365–366)

5. Hair grooming has also been a time for teaching lessons when the younger child combs or scratches the head of an elder, particularly an elder woman. Such a moment occurs in Spike Lee's movie *Do the Right Thing* (1989) when Jade "parts, greases, and combs" Mother Sister's hair on the apartment stoop and listens to Mother Sister's comments on the ways of the world.

Additionally, a limited edition decorative collector plate, "A History Lesson," shows a young African American girl of about four or five combing her grandmother or great-grandmother's hair. The advertisement for this Black Heritage Collection series item by Aaron "Skip" Smith reads:

> A History Lesson: It was the early days, when a child was taught with feeling and spoken words of wisdom which came from the Elder of the Family. Even before thoughts of reading and writing entered their minds, this learning process set the foundation of Life. A phenomenal occurrence took place. "The Comb" acted as "Knowledge Conductor." The scratching and combing motion drew from every core, traveling through the fingers onward, into the memory banks of the child from Eldest female to the youngest. Indeed a unique and indelible history lesson! (*Parade Magazine*, 8 September 1996, 17)

6. The term *girlpie* is used by hooks as a term of endearment to describe little black girls, a word similar to perhaps more common words like "sweetie pie" and "cutie pie."

CHAPTER 20

1. See Londa Schiebinger, chapter 7, "More than Skin Deep: The Scientific Search for Sexual Difference," in *The Mind Has No Sex? Women in the Origins of Modern Science* (Cambridge, MA: Harvard University Press, 1987): "The European male was always on top of the hierarchy, and black/African women and men always at the bottom, but the European woman was more perfect than white men in one regard: her pelvis was larger to accommodate the superior skull size of the male European infant" (209).

2. See Jennifer L. Morgan, "'Some Could Suckle over Their Shoulder': Male Travelers, Female Bodies, and the Gendering of Racial Ideology, 1500–1770," in *Skin Deep and Spirit Strong: The Black Female Body in American Culture*, ed. Kimberly Wallace-Sanders (Ann Arbor: University of Michigan Press, 2002), 37–64. Morgan includes a range of drawings that show the interrelated concepts of gender and race during the "discovery" and colonial period.

3. Among the most widely reported on, caricatured, and sentimentalized in the early nineteenth century was the "Hottentot Venus," Sarah Baartman, a young Khoikhoi woman from the Cape of Good Hope, South Africa. Baartman was displayed in England and then France from 1810 until her death in 1815. The most famous French scientist of the period, Georges Cuvier, made a cast of her body before dissecting it. Baartman's body cast, skeleton, and preserved brain and genitalia were displayed in the Parisian Musée de l'Homme for 160 years more, then put into storage. In 2002, after nearly a decade of efforts by politicians such as Nelson Mandela, her remains were finally repatriated and appropriately buried

in South Africa. See Lucille Davie, "Sarah Baartman: At Rest at Last," *South Africa*, 12 August 2002 and 12 December 2005, http://www.south-africa.info/ess_info/sa_glance/history/saartjie.htm. See also Suzan-Lori Parks's controversial drama *Venus* (New York: Theatre Communications Group, 1990) and Barbara Chase-Riboud's novel *Hottentot Venus* (New York: Doubleday, 2003).

4. See Leslie Fiedler, *Freaks: Myths and Images of the Secret Self* (New York: Simon and Schuster, 1978).

5. See Deborah Willis and Carla Williams's segment on "World's Fairs and Expositions" in *The Black Female Body: A Photographic History* (Philadelphia: Temple University Press, 2002).

6. See Steven C. Dubin, "Symbolic Slavery: Black Representations in Popular Culture," *Social Problems* 34.2 (April 1987): 122–140.

ABOUT THE CONTRIBUTORS

There is but a handful of scholars working with African American children's literature specifically, fewer doing what I do to blur the line between the relevance of adult literature and importance of children's literature. My goal in this project is to raise awareness of the complicated and important issues in this body of work that both embraces and transcends the academy. Having only scholars respond would limit the potential of what this book might do for a more diverse audience of parents, librarians, students, educators, and the like. Including non-academics in the project demonstrates that the issues raised in my chapters and raised in the books about which I have written are relevant, especially to those who relegate children's and young adult literature to second-class status as compared with "real" adult literature. The chapters are never just about the children's books I have examined, but rather, are about issues and ideas beyond the books, which is why it was not necessary that respondents know the texts. In this same manner, I have solicited responses from non-literature specialists as well as from non-African Americanists. Whether an academic or not, each respondent has been a child, may be a parent, but is certainly an adult that interacts with youngsters on some level. The responses also connect more easily than I had imagined with real life experience — the test of any meaningful intellectual discussion.

Stacy Augustine, J.D., specializes in mediation, especially civil rights mediation, and lives in Phoenix, Arizona.

Jim Blasingame, Jr., Ph.D., is an associate professor of English Education at Arizona State University.

ben clark is a candidate for a master's degree in social work at Boston University.

Olga Idriss Davis, Ph.D., is an associate professor in the Hugh Downs School of Human Communication at Arizona State University.

Kim Curry-Evans is the director of 40 Acres Art Gallery in Sacramento, California.

Joseph L. Graves, Ph.D., is dean of University Studies and professor of Biological Sciences at North Carolina A&T State University.

C. A. Hammons is a visual artist, poet, writer, and arts educator in Phoenix, Arizona.

Jasmine Z. Lester is a senior at Desert Vista High School in Phoenix, Arizona. Jasmine's interests include photography and graphic design. She is also a member of the Phoenix Children's Chorus.

Vincenza Mangiolino, R.P.A.-C., is a physician assistant at J. R. Medical in Bayshore, New York.

Khafilah McCurdy, Ph.D., is an independent scholar and founding editor of the new *Journal of African American Children's Literature.*

Elizabeth McNeil, Ph.D., is the assistant director of Undergraduate English Studies at Arizona State University.

C. W. Sullivan III is editor of *The Children's Folklore Review* and is a professor of English at East Carolina University.

Nathan Stamey Winesett, J.D., is an attorney with Thorpe North and Western, L.L.P., in Sandy, Utah.

WORKS CITED

Adams, James T. "No Other Word Fuels Passions Like 'N-Word.'" *Birmingham News,* 3 September 1995: C1, C4.

American Academy of Child & Adolescent Psychology. "Facts for Families: Normal Adolescent Development." <http://www.aacap.org/page. ww?section= Facts+for+Families&name=Normal+Adolescent+Develop ment+Part+I> (accessed 15 February 2006).

Angelou, Maya. Foreword to *Crowns: Portraits of Black Women in Church Hats,* by Michael Cunningham and Craig Marberry, 2–3. New York: Doubleday, 2000.

———. "The Human Family." In *I Shall Not Be Moved,* 4–5. New York: Bantam, 1991.

———. *I Know Why the Caged Bird Sings.* New York: Bantam, 1971.

Ansa, Tina McElroy. *Baby of the Family.* San Diego: Harcourt Brace Jovanovich, 1989.

Applebee, Arthur N., Judith A. Langer, Martin Nystrand, and Adam Gamora. "Discussion-Based Approaches to Developing Understanding: Classroom Instruction and Student Performance in Middle and High School English." *American Education Research Journal* 40.3 (2003): 685–730.

Asante, Molefi Kete. *Afrocentricity.* Trenton, NJ: Africa World Press, 1988.

Atwell, Nancy. *In the Middle: Writing, Reading, and Learning with Adolescents.* Portsmouth, NH: Heinemann, 1987.

Bambara, Toni Cade. "The Golden Bandit." In *Jump Up and Say! A Collection of Black Storytelling,* edited by Linda Goss and Clay Goss, 207–210. New York: Simon and Schuster, 1995.

"Barbie Bride-to-Be (Danbury Mint)." Advertisement. *Parade Magazine,* 10 February 1991: 9.

Barwick, Mary. *Alabama Angels.* Montgomery, AL: Black Belt, 1989.

———. *Alabama Angels in Anywhere, L.A. (Lower Alabama).* Montgomery, AL: Black Belt, 1991.

"Beautiful Beginnings Children's No-Lye Relaxer." Advertisement. *Essence,* February 1997: 125.

"Beauty Answers." *Essence,* August 1993: 18.

Berry, Bertyce. "Fight Against Racism Begins in the Home." *Birmingham News,* 12 April 1992: E8.

Bickmore, Kathy. "Why Discuss Sexuality in Elementary School?" In *Queering Elementary Education: Advancing the Dialogue about Sexuality and Schooling,* edited by William J. Letts IV and James T. Sears, 15–25. Boulder, CO: Rowman and Littlefield, 1999.

Bland, Karina. "Hurtful Words Abuse, Too: Kids' Self-Image Easily Harmed by Careless Remarks." *Arizona Republic,* 12 April 1998: A1, A8.

Blount, Lucy. *Letters to the Precious Group.* Montgomery, AL: Light-bearers, 1990.

"The Book of Mean People," Review from the publisher, Hyperion Books for Children. http://search.barnesandnoble.com (accessed 28 July 2003).

Bonetti, Kay. "Interview with Toni Morrison." Columbia, MO: American Audio Prose Library, 1983. 172–173.

Brooks, Gwendolyn. "To Those of My Sisters Who Kept Their Naturals (Never to Look a Hot Comb in the Teeth)." In *Confirmation: An Anthology of African American Women,* edited by Amiri Baraka and Amina Baraka, 84–85. New York: William Morrow, 1983.

Bullins, Ed. "Street Sounds: Dialogues with Black Experience." In *The Theme Is Blackness,* 144–181. New York: Morrow, 1973.

Bunting, Eve. *The Wednesday Surprise.* New York: Houghton Mifflin, 1989.

Burnett, Carol. *Goldilocks and the Three Bears.* Lincoln, IL: Passport Books, 1990.

Cahill, Betsy J., and Rachel Theilheimer. "Stonewall in the Housekeeping Area: Gay and Lesbian Issues in the Early Childhood Classroom." In *Queering Elementary Education: Advancing the Dialogue about Sexualities and Schooling,* edited by William J. Letts IV and James T. Sears, 39–48. Boulder, CO: Rowman and Littlefield, 1999.

Caldwell, Paulette W. "A Hair Piece: Perspectives on the Intersection of Race and Gender." *Duke Law Journal* 1991.2 (April 1991): 365–396

Carvin, Andy. "The Mind of Robyn Hitchcock." http://edwebproject.org/hitchcock.html (accessed 7 September 2001).

Cashorali, Peter. *Fairy Tales: Traditional Stories Retold for Gay Men.* New York: HarperCollins, 1997.

Chambers, Veronica. "Dreading It…or How I Learned to Stop Fighting My Hair and Love My Nappy Roots." *Vogue,* June 1999: 171, 178.

Chappe, Kevin. "How Black Inventors Changed America." *Ebony,* February 1997: 40–50.

Chasnoff, Debra, and Helen S. Cohen. *It's Elementary: Talking about Gay Issues in School.* San Francisco: Women's Educational Media, 1999.

Chavis, Benjamin F. "The Virus of Racism Spreads to Children." *California Voice,* 7 February 1992: 3.

Chenzira, Ayoka. *Hair Piece: A Film for Nappy Headed People.* New York: Women Make Movies, 1985.

Chocolate, Deborah M. Newton. *Talk, Talk: An Ashanti Legend*. Mahwah, NJ: Troll, 1993.

Christian, Barbara. "The Race for Theory." *Cultural Critique* 6 (Spring, 1987): 51–63.

Clarke, Cheryl. "The Failure to Transform: Homophobia in the Black Community." In *Home Girls: A Black Feminist Anthology*, edited by Barbara Smith, 197–208. New York: Women of Color Press, 1983.

Cleaver, Eldridge. "As Crinkly as Yours." In *Mother Wit from the Laughing Barrel: Readings in the Interpretation of Afro-American Literature*, edited by Alan Dundes, 9–21. Jackson: University Press of Mississippi, 1990.

Coleman, Evelyn. *White Socks Only*. Morton Grove, IL: Whitman, 1996 (unpaged).

Coles, Robert. *The Story of Ruby Bridges*. New York: Scholastic, 1995 (unpaged).

Collins, Billy. "First Reader." In *Questions About Angels*. Pittsburg: University of Pittsburgh Press, 1999.

Collins, Patricia Hill. "Knowledge, Consciousness, and the Politics of Empowerment." In *Black Feminist Thought: Knowledge, Consciousness, and the Politics of Empowerment*, 221–238. New York: Routledge, 1991.

Comodromos, Eliza A. *Teacher's Guide to the Bluford Series*. West Berlin, NJ: Townsend Press, 2001.

Conquergood, Dwight. "Between Experience and Meaning: Performance as a Paradigm for Meaningful Action." In *Renewal and Revision: The Future of Interpretation*, edited by Ted D. Colson, 26–59. Salado, TX: Omega, 1986.

———. "Poetics, Play, Process and Power: The Performative Turn in Anthropology." *Text and Performance Quarterly* 9.1 (1989): 82–88.

Cooper, Wendy. *Hair: Sex, Society, Symbolism*. New York: Stein and Day, 1971.

Corcoran, John, with Carole C. Carlson. *The Teacher Who Couldn't Read*. Colorado Springs, CO: Focus on the Family, 1994.

"Court Battle Looms for Children's Books on Homosexuality." *Maranatha Christian Journal: News and Views of Today's Online Christian*. http://www.mcjonline.com/news3275.html (accessed 19 February 2002).

Crump, Fred, Jr. *Rapunzel*. Nashville: Winston-Derek, 1991.

Crutcher, Chris. "Healing through Literature." In *Author's Insights: Turning Teenagers into Readers and Writers*, edited by Don Gallo, 33–40. Portsmouth, NH: Boynton Cook, 1992.

Cullen, Countee. "Incident." In *The Black Poets*, edited by Dudley Randall, 98–99. New York: Bantam Books, 1971.

Cunningham, Michael, and Craig Marberry. *Crowns: Portraits of Black Women in Church Hats*. New York: Doubleday, 2000.

Cunningham, Michael, and George Alexander. *Queens: Portraits of Black Women and Their Fabulous Hair*. New York: Doubleday, 2005.

Currie, Tracie. "Review of *The Big Box* by Toni and Slade Morrison." *Black Issues Book Review* 2.1 (January/February 2000): 68.

Davis, Charles T., and Henry Louis Gates, Jr., eds. *The Slave's Narrative*. New York: Oxford University Press, 1985.

Davis, Gussie L. "When They Straighten All the Colored People's Hair." *Remember That Song* 3 (October 1983): 8–9.

Day, Caroline Bond. *A Study of Some Negro-White Families in the United States*. Cambridge: Peabody Museum of Harvard University, 1932.

DeLuise, Dom. *Goldilocks*. New York: Simon and Schuster, 1992 (unpaged).

dePaola, Tomie. *Oliver Button Is a Sissy*. San Diego, CA: Harcourt Brace, 1979. (unpaged).

De Veaux, Alexis. *An Enchanted Hair Tale*. New York: Harper Trophy, 1991 (unpaged).

Dorson, Richard M. "Why the Negro Has Kinky Hair." In *American Negro Folktales*, 176–177. Greenwich, CT: Fawcett, 1956.

Douglas, Kelly Brown, and Cheryl J. Sanders. "Introduction." In *Living the Intersection,* edited by Cheryl J. Sanders, 9–17. Minneapolis, MN: Fortress, 1995.

Douglass, Frederick. *Narrative of the Life of Frederick Douglass, An American Slave, Written by Himself.* 1845. In *The Norton Anthology of World Masterpieces*, edited by Maynard Mack, 646–719. New York: Norton, 1985.

DuBois, W. E. B. "The True Brownies." *Crisis* 6 (1919): 286–302.

———. *The Souls of Black Folk*. 1903. In *Three Negro Classics*, 207–389. New York: Avon Books, 1965.

Duff-Brown, Beth. "Indian Woman Garners Attention in Dowry Dispute." *Arizona Republic*, 18 May 2003: A25.

Dusek, Karen H. "Frederick Douglass, Abolitionist Writer." *Cobblestone: The History Magazine for Young People,* 10 February 1989: 21–23.

Edmonds, B. L. "Review of *Mama Eat Ant, Yuck!*" (n.d.). Review from Barbie's House Books Publishing, http://www.amazon.com/exec/obidos/ASIN/0965670023/ref=pd_sim_books/002–8032028 (accessed 19 February 2002).

Ellison, Ralph. *The Invisible Man*. New York: Vantage, 1947.

———. "Flying Home." In *Dark Symphony: Negro Literature in America*, edited by James A. Emanuel and Theodore L. Gross, 254–279. New York: Free Press, 1968.

Epstein, Aaron. "NAACP Protests Dictionary Definition of Epithet." *Arizona Republic,* 18 October 1997: A15.

Evans, Bergen. *Dictionary of Quotations*. New York: Delacorte, 1968.

Evans, Mari. "Vive Noir!" In *The Poetry of Black America: Anthology of the 20th Century*, edited by Arnold Adoff, 188–190. New York: HarperCollins, 1973.

Fader, Ellen. "Review of *The Big Box*." *School Library Journal* 45.9 (September 1999): 227.

Ford, Michael. *Happily Ever After: Erotic Fairy Tales for Men.* New York: Masquerade Books, 1996a.

———. *Once Upon a Time: Erotic Fairy Tales for Women.* New York: Masquerade Books, 1996b.

Foucault, Michel. *Discipline and Punish: The Birth of the Prison.* Translated by Alan Sheridan. New York: Vintage, 1977.

Freire, Paulo, and Donaldo Macedo. *Literacy: Reading the Word and the World.* Boston: Bergin and Garvey, 1987.

Galley, Michelle. "Mother-Daughter Work Day to Shift Focus, Include Boys." *Education Week,* 21.33 (1 May 2002): 4.

Gates, Henry Louis, Jr., ed. *"Race," Writing, and Difference.* Chicago: University of Chicago Press, 1985.

Gillespie, Marcia Ann. "Mirror Mirror." *Essence,* January 1993: 73–74, 96.

Giovanni, Nikki. "Nikki-Rosa." In *African-American Literature: An Anthology,* edited by Demetrice A. Worley and Jesse Perry, Jr., 294–295. Lincolnwood, IL: NTC Publishing Group, 1998.

Glenn, Mel. Personal interview. 9 November 2004.

Goldin, Augusta. *Straight Hair, Curly Hair.* New York: Crowell, 1966.

Goldie Locks and the 3 Bi Bears. Directed by William Hunter. Arleta, CA: Totally Tasteless Video, 1997.

Graves, Joseph L., Jr. *The Emperor's New Clothes.* New Brunswick, NJ: Rutgers University Press, 2001.

———. *The Race Myth.* New York: Dutton, 2004.

Green, Kim. "The Pain of Living the Lye." *Essence,* June 1993: 38.

Gregory, Dick. *Nigger, An Autobiography.* New York: Washington Square Press, 1986.

Grimes, Nikki. *Wild, Wild Hair.* New York: Scholastic, 1997 (unpaged).

Hair advertisement. *Jet,* 27 October 1997: 17.

Hamilton, Alison. "Nigger, Please." *Image,* October 1994: 16–19, 55–56.

Hansberry, Lorraine. "The Negro in the American Theatre." In *American Playwrights on Drama,* edited by Horst Frenz, 160–167. New York: Hill and Wang, 1965.

Harder, Arlene F. "The Developmental Stages of Erik Erikson." *The Learning Place Online* (2002). http://www.learningplaceonline.com/stages/organize/Erikson.htm (accessed February 15, 2006).

Harris, Violet J. "African-American Conceptions of Literacy: A Historical Perspective." *Theory Into Practice* 31 (Autumn 1992): 276–286.

Herron, Carolivia. *Nappy Hair.* New York: Knopf, 1997 (unpaged).

Hoffman, Mary. *An Angel Just Like Me.* New York: Dial Books for Young Readers, 1997 (unpaged).

hooks, bell. "Straightening Our Hair." In *Reading Culture: Contexts for Critical Reading and Writing,* edited by Diana George and John Trimbur, 290–299. New York: HarperCollins, 1992.

_____. *Happy to Be Nappy.* New York: Jump at the Sun/Hyperion Books for Children, 1999 (unpaged).

Hopson, Darlene Powell and Derek S. Hopson. *Juba This & Juba That: 100 African-American Games for Children.* New York: Fireside, 1996.

Hughes, Langston. *Black Misery.* New York: Oxford University Press, 1994.

_____. "Golden Gate." In *Simple's Uncle Sam*, 94–97. New York: Hill and Wang, 1965.

_____. "Mother to Son." In *Selected Poems of Langston Hughes*, 187. New York: Vintage, 1974.

Hunt, Angela Elwell. *If I Had Long, Long Hair.* Nashville, TN: Abingdon Press, 1988.

Hurston, Zora Neale. *Their Eyes Were Watching God.* Chicago: University of Illinois Press, 1978.

_____. "Characteristics of Negro Expression." In *The Sanctified Church: The Folklore Writings of Zora Neale Hurston*, 49–68. Berkeley, CA: Turtle Island, 1981.

India.Arie. "I Am Not My Hair." *Testimony: Volume 1, Life and Relationship.* New York: Motown Records, 2006. B0006141-02.

"Intra-racism." *Oprah Winfrey Show,* 12 May 1987. Transcript W172.

Jacobs, Harriet A. *Incidents in the Life of a Slave Girl, Written by Herself.* Cambridge: Harvard University Press, 1987.

Janzen, John M., and Reinhild Kauenhoven Janzen. *Do I Still Have a Life? Voices from the Aftermath of War in Rwanda and Burundi.* Lawrence, KS: Publications in Anthropology, University of Kansas, 2000.

Jeffreys, Garland. "Don't Call Me Buckwheat." *Don't Call Me Buckwheat.* New York: Black and White Alike, 1991. B000024L3S.

Jellon, Tahar Ben. *Racism Explained to My Daughter.* New York: New Press, 1999.

Jennings, Kevin. *Always My Child: A Parent's Guide to Understanding Your Gay, Lesbian, Bisexual, Transgendered or Questioning Son or Daughter.* New York: Simon and Schuster, 2003.

_____. *Becoming Visible: A Reader in Gay and Lesbian History for High School and College Students.* Los Angeles, CA: Alyson Publications, 1994.

Johnson, Angela. *Tell Me a Story, Mama.* New York: Orchard Books, 1988 (unpaged).

_____. *The First Part Last.* New York: Simon & Schuster Books for Young Readers, 2003.

Johnson, Diane, and Catherine Lewis. Introduction. *African American Review* 32 (1998): 1, 5–22.

Johnson, Dolores. *Papa's Stories.* New York: Macmillan, 1994 (unpaged).

Jones, Isis. "Nappy Hair." In *And Then We Rose from the Sun.* 1998, unpublished.

Jones, Tayari. "An Open Letter to Syria Who Recently Stopped Straightening Her Hair." 29 March 1999, unpublished.

"Judge: Light Sentence Given Because Slain Were Homosexuals." *Birmingham News*, 16 December 1988.

Kantrowitz, Barbara, and Anne Underwood. "Dyslexia and the New Science of Reading." *Newsweek*, 22 November 1999: 72–79.

Kastle, Carl F. *Literacy in the United States: Readers and Reading since 1880.* New Haven, CT: Yale University Press, 1991.

Katz, Jonathan Ned. "The Invention of Heterosexuality." In *The Social Construction of Difference and Inequality: Race, Class, Gender and Sexuality,* edited by Tracy E. Ore, 137–150. Mountain View, CA: Mayfield Publishing, 2000.

Kaufman, Joanne. "Review of *Whitewash* (video)." *Family Life,* June–July 1998: 110.

Kemp, Kathy. "Angelic Acts Are 'Gifts from God.'" *Birmingham Post-Herald,* 28 October 1991: A6.

Kenan, Randall. "Run, Mourner, Run." In *Let the Dead Bury Their Dead,* 163–191. Orlando, FL: Harcourt Brace, 1992.

Kennedy, Adrienne. "Funnyhouse of a Negro." In *Adrienne Kennedy in One Act,* 1–24. Minneapolis: University of Minnesota Press, 1988.

King, James P., and Jenifer Jasinski Schneider. "Locating a Place for Gay and Lesbian Themes in Elementary Reading, Writing, and Talking." In *Queering Elementary Education: Advancing the Dialogue about Sexualities and Schooling,* edited by William J. Letts IV and James T. Sears, 125–136. Boulder, CO: Rowman and Littlefield, 1999.

King-Smith, Dick. *The School Mouse.* New York: Hyperion, 1997.

Kozol, Jonathan. *Illiterate America.* New York: New American Library, 1985.

Krass, Peter. *Black Americans of Achievement: Sojourner Truth.* New York: Chelsea House, 1988.

Kroll, Virginia. *Jaha and Jamil Went Down the Hill: An African Mother Goose.* Watertown, MA: Charlesbridge, 1995.

LaBaw, Dominique. "Bad Hair." *Interrace Magazine,* August–September 1994: 17.

Land, Mike. "Faith Helps Woman Share Gift of Story." *Montgomery Advertiser and Alabama Journal,* 24 December 1989: 1F.

Larche, D. W. *Father Gander Nursery Rhymes.* Santa Barbara, CA: Advocacy Press, 1985.

Larkin, Alile Sharon. *Dreadlocks and the Three Bears.* Los Angeles, California: Inter Image Video, 1991.

Lee, Harper. *To Kill a Mockingbird.* New York: Warner Books, 1960.

Lee, Spike. "'Straight and Nappy': Good and Bad Hair." In *Uplift the Race: The Construction of School Daze,* 143–164. New York: Fireside, 1988.

————. with Lisa Jones. *Do the Right Thing.* New York: Fireside, 1989.

Lester, Jasmine Z. "Homophobia in Children." 11 August 2006. http://www.myspace.com/xcoldwater14x (accessed September 19, 2006).

Lester, Julius. *What a Truly Cool World.* New York: Scholastic Press, 1999.

Lester, Neal A. "Nappy Happy: A Review of bell hooks's *Happy to Be Nappy.*" *Children's Folklore Review* 22.1 (1999): 45–55.

_____. "'Life for me ain't been no crystal stair': Readin', Writin', and Parental (Il)literacy in African American Children's Books. Part I." *Arizona Reading Journal* 29 (2003a): 2, 26–37.

_____. "'Life for me ain't been no crystal stair': Readin', Writin', and Parental (Il)literacy in African American Children's Books. Part II." *Arizona Reading Journal* 30 (2003b): 1, 14–20.

"Letters: God Is Watching." *USA Today*, 30 June 2003: A11.

Letts, William J., IV, and James T. Sears. *Queering Elementary Education: Advancing the Dialogue about Sexualities and Schooling*. Boulder, CO: Rowman and Littlefield, 1999.

Lexau, Joan. *Don't Be My Valentine*. Columbus, OH: Weekly Reader Books/ Harper & Row, 1985.

Linn, Melissa. "All That Hair." In *Revolutionary Tales: African American Women's Short Stories, from the First Story to the Present*, edited by Bill Mullen, 246–250. New York: Dell, 1995.

Lipsyte, Robert. "The Forum: For Sake of Straight Kids, Quit Tyrannizing Gay Sports Stars." *USA Today*, 1 July 2003: A13.

"Literacy and Life." http://www.edentek.net/litlife.htm (accessed 26 January 2000).

Little, Benilde. *Good Hair*. New York: Simon and Schuster, 1996.

Lofting, Hugh. *The Voyages of Doctor Dolittle*. Philadelphia: Lippincott, 1951.

Lorbiecki, Marybeth. *Sister Anne's Hands*. New York: Dial Books for Young Readers, 1998 (unpaged).

Lorde, Audre. "There Is No Hierarchy of Oppression." *Interracial Books for Children Bulletin*, 14 (Special Issue: Homophobia and Education: How to Deal with Name-Calling), 1983: 9.

_____. "Is Your Hair Still Political?" *Essence*, September 1990: 40, 110.

Major, Clarence, ed. *Juba to Jive: A Dictionary of African American Slang*. New York: Penguin, 1994.

Malcolm X. *The Autobiography of Malcolm X*. New York: Ballantine, 1964.

Malveaux, Julianne. "Just a Nappy-Headed Sister with the PC Blues." *Black Issues in Higher Education*, 24 December 1998: 30.

Mandell, Phyllis Levy. "1995 Award-Winning Films and Videos: Social Studies." *School Library Journal*, April 1996: 62.

_____. "Recommended Videos." *Peace Review* 11.2 (June: 1999), 353.

Margolick, David. "For Black Prosecutor, There Is No Allure in the Simpson Case." *New York Times*, 22 January 1995: Y13.

Mastalia, Francesco, and Alfonse Pagano. *Dreads*. New York: Artisan, 1999.

Matsunaga, Fay L. "Review of *Whitewash* (video)." *School Library Journal* 41.5 (May 1995): 65.

McCall, Cecelia. "A Historical Quest for Literacy." *Interracial Books for Children Bulletin* 19 (n.d.): 3–6.

McCray, Nancy. "Review of *Whitewash* (videocassette)." *Booklist*, 1 April 1995: 1432.

McDonald, Laughlin. "Minority Vote Dilution: The Fourteenth Amendment and the Voting Rights Act." 4 January 1980. http://www.aclu-e/course3_mcdonald3.html.

McGee, Leo, and Harvey G. Neufeldt. *Education of the Black Adult in the United States: An Annotated Bibliography.* Westport, CT: Greenwood, 1985.

McGruder, Janie. "The Nurture of Boys: Moms Have to Buck He-Man Culture to Raise Emotionally Healthy Sons." *Arizona Republic,* 8 May 2003: El, E3.

McGuire, Tim. "Meanness Destroys Healthy Workplace." *Arizona Republic,* 12 July 2003: 9.

McLaren, Peter. "Decentering Culture: Postmodernism, Resistance, and Critical Pedagogy." In *Current Perspectives on Current Perspectives on the Culture of Schools,* edited by Nancy Wyner, 213–257. Massachusetts: Brookline Books, 1991.

———. "The Liminal Servant and the Ritual Roots of Critical Pedagogy." *Language Arts* 65 (1988): 2, 164–179.

———. "Schooling the Postmodern Body: Critical Pedagogy and the Politics of Enfleshment." In *Postmodernism, Feminism, and Cultural Politics: Redrawing Educational Boundaries,* edited by Henry A. Giroux, 144–173. Albany: State University of New York Press, 1991.

McWilliams, Kelly. *Doormat.* New York: Delacorte, 2004.

Medearis, Angela Shelf. *Too Much Talk: A West African Folktale.* Cambridge: Candlewick Press, 1995.

Melendez, Mel. "Girls Take Mean to a New Level: Psychological Warfare on Others Amounts to Abuse." *Arizona Republic,* 4 September 2002: 1, 5.

Mercer, Kobena. "Black Hair/Style Politics." *New Formations* 3 (1987): 33–54.

Merriam, Eve. *The Inner City Mother Goose.* New York: Simon and Schuster Books for Young Readers, 1996.

Meyers, Taro. *Rap, Rap, Rap Rapunzel and Little Red Ride 'N the Hood.* Performed by Patti Austin. Beverly Hills, CA: Dove Audio/Tarom Entertainment, 1992. 30870.

Miller, Ron. "Fairy Tales that Take on Rainbow Hues: Happily Ever After, Fairy Tales for Every Child." *San Jose Mercury News,* 23 March 1995: E1, E6.

Miller, William. *The Bus Ride.* New York: Lee and Low Books, 1997.

Mollel, Tololwa M. *The Princess Who Lost Her Hair: An Akamba Legend.* New York: Troll, 1993.

Monk, Jacklyn. "How to Get Good Hair." *Heart and Soul,* October–November 1995: 57–61.

Morrison, Toni. *The Bluest Eye.* New York: Washington Square Press, 1970.

———. *Beloved.* New York: Knopf, 1987.

———. Nobel Lecture 1993. http://www.nobel.se/cgi-bin/print.

———. (with Slade Morrison). *The Big Box,* illustrated by Giselle Potter. New York: Jump at the Sun/Hyperion Books for Children, 1999 (unpaged).

_____. (with Slade Morrison). *The Book of Mean People*, illustrated by Pascal Lemaitre. New York: Hyperion Books for Children, 2002 (unpaged).

Morrow, Willie L. *Four-Hundred Years Without a Comb: The Inferior Seed*. San Diego, CA: California Curl Limited, 1989.

Mother Goose Rhymes—Jack and Jill. (n.d.). http://www.mother.com/~prdesign/JacknJill.html (accessed 25 March 2002).

Murphy, B. O. "Greeting Cards and Gender Messages." *Women and Language* 17.1 (2004): 25–29.

Myers, Walter Dean. *The Beast*. New York: Scholastic Press, 2003.

_____. *Brown Angels: An Album of Pictures and Verse*. New York: Harper-Collins, 1996.

The N Word: Divided We Stand. DVD. Directed by Todd Larkins. 2004. Thousand Oaks, CA: UrbanWorks Entertainment, 2006.

"*Nappy Hair* Controversy." *Today,* NBC, 2 December 1998: 33–35.

Naylor, Gloria. "Mommy, What Does 'Nigger' Mean?" In *Common Ground: Reading and Writing about America's Cultures*, edited by Laurie G. Kirszner and Stephen R. Mandell, 379–383. New York: St. Martin's Press, 1994.

New Titles for 1992–1993: Fiction, Biography, Regional History, Poetry, Children's Literature. Montgomery, AL: Black Belt, 1992.

Noble, Kenneth B. "The Simpson Defense: One Hateful Word." *New York Times* (19 March 1995): 1, 4.

"Notable Films/Videos, Recordings and Computer Software, 1995." *School Library Journal* (April 1995): 35–36.

Nursery Rhymes for Grown Ups. (n.d.). http://www.office-humour.co.uk/item.cfm?itm=296 (accessed 17 October 2004).

Odanaka, Barbara. "Children's Books in Light of a Very Dark Day." *Skateboardmom.com*. http://skateboardmom.homestead.com/sept11.html (accessed 5 December 2005).

Oliver, Elizabeth Murphy. *Black Mother Goose Book*. Brooklyn: Dare Books, 1981.

Oliver, Stephanie Stokes. "Word from the Editor." *Heart and Soul,* October–November 1995: 55.

_____. "A Hair-Raising Story." Essence, February 1997: 18, 148, 150.

Olney, James. "'I Was Born': Slave Narratives, Their Status as Autobiography and as Literature." In *The Slave's Narrative*, edited by Charles T. Davis and Henry Louis Gates, Jr., 148–175. New York: Oxford University Press, 1985.

O'Meally, Robert G. "Frederick Douglass' 1845 *Narrative*: The Text Was Meant to Be Preached." In *Afro-American Literature: The Reconstruction of Instruction*, edited by Dexter Fisher and Robert B. Stepto, 192–211. New York: MLA, 1978.

Papp, Joseph. "A Colored Girl: Ntozake Shange." Television interview recorded in New York. WGBH Boston: 11 November 1979.

Parker, KRS-1. "Ya Strugglin'." *Edutainment*. New York: Boogie Down Productions, 1990. B0000004WO.

Peterson, V. R. "Talking with Toni Morrison." *People* 52, 1 November 1999, 65.

Pineau, Elyse Lamm. "Teaching Is Performance: Reconceptualizing a Problematic Metaphor." In *Performance Theories in Education: Power, Pedagogy, and the Politics of Identity*, edited by Bryant K. Alexander, Gary L. Anderson, and Bernardo P. Gallegos, 15–39. Mahwah, NJ: Erlbaum, 2005.

Platzner, Rebecca. "Learning to Listen." 20 February 1999. http://email.rutgers.edu/pipermail/child_lit/1999-February/006507.html.

Probst, Robert E. "Dialogue with a Text." *English Journal* 77.1 (1988): 32–38.

"Quotations about Literacy." http://www.literacytrust.org.uk/database/quote.html (accessed 3 September 1999).

Rado, James, and Gerome Ragni. *Hair: The American Tribal Love-Rock Musical*. New York: Tams-Witmark Music Library, 1968.

Rahaman, Vashanti. *Read for Me, Mama*. Honesdale, PA: Boyds Mills, 1997 (unpaged).

Randall, Dudley. "On Getting a Natural, for Gwendolyn Brooks." In *The Poetry of Black America*, edited by Arnold Adoff, 141. New York: Harper & Row, 1973.

"Quotation by Kwame Kilpatrick." Rants & Raves. *The Advocate*, 12.

Raspberry, William. "We Give This Slur Its Power." *Tuscaloosa News,* 11 April 1995: n.p.

————. "Review of *Whitewash* (book)." *Notable Children's Trade Books in the Field of Social Studies* (April–May 1998): 6.

Reeves, Garland. "*Alabama Angels* Enters Fourth Printing." *Birmingham News,* 12 December 1990: 1F.

"Review of *The Big Box*." *Publishers Weekly,* 12 July 1999: 95.

Richardson, Lynda. "61 Acts of Bias: One Fuse Lights Many Different Explosions." *New York Times,* 28 January 1992: B1, B6.

Riggs, Marlon. *Ethnic Notions: Black Images in White Minds*. San Francisco: California Newsreel, 1987.

————. "Tongues Untied." In *Brother to Brother: New Writings by Black Gay Men*, edited by Essex Hemphill, 200–205. Boston: Alyson, 1991.

"Roark Bradford (1896-1948)." www.kirjasto.sci.fi/rbradf.htm (accessed 24 September 2006).

Robotham, Rosemarie. "Still Friends." *Essence,* August 1997, 95–96, 136–138.

Rollins, Charlemae, ed. "Introduction." In *We Build Together. A Reader's Guide to Negro Life and Literature for Elementary and High School Use*, xiii–xvi. Champaign, IL: National Council of Teachers of English, 1967.

Rooks, Noliwee M. *Hair Raising: Beauty, Culture, and African American Women*. New Brunswick, NJ: Rutgers University Press, 1996.

Rosenblatt, Louise. *Literature as Exploration*. New York: D-Appleton Century, 1938.

Rosenthal, Elisabeth. "China Area Is Rife with the Sale of Girl Babies." *Arizona Republic*, 20 July 2003, A21.

Ross, Raymond S. "Racially Potent Words." In *We Build Together: A Reader's Guide to Negro Life and Literature for Elementary and High School Use*, edited by Charlemae Rollins, xiii–xvi. Champaign, IL: National Council of Teachers of English, 1967.

Rue, Nancy N. *Coping with an Illiterate Parent.* New York: Rosen, 1990.

Russell, Kathy, Midge Wilson, and Ronald Hall. *The Color Complex: The Politics of Skin Color among African Americans.* New York: Anchor Books, 1993.

"Sadness and Shame in the Bronx." *New York Times,* 10 January 1992: A26.

Sanders, Dori. *Clover.* Chapel Hill, NC: Alonquin Books, 1990.

Sapphire. *Push.* New York: Vintage Books, 1996.

Schenden, Laurie. "School's 'Out' for Summer: Documentary on Homosexual Tolerance Raises Ire of Christian Right." *The Advocate,* 8 June 1999: 2. http://www.findarticlaes.com/cf_dls/m1589/199_June_8/54796510/p1/article.html.

Schraff, Anne. *A Matter of Trust.* Bluford Series no. 2. West Berlin, NJ: Townsend Press, 2001.

———. *Lost and Found.* Bluford Series no. 1. West Berlin, NJ: Townsend Press, 2001.

———. *Until We Meet Again.* Bluford Series no. 7. West Berlin, NJ: Townsend Press, 2001.

Scott, Jerry and Jim Borgman. "Zits." *Arizona Republic,* 10 January 2003: E4.

Sears, James T. "Teaching Queerly: Some Elementary Propositions." In *Queering Elementary Education: Advancing the Dialogue about Sexualities and Schooling,* edited by William J. Letts and James T. Sears, 3–14. Boulder, CO: Rowman and Littlefield, 1999.

Shange, Ntozake. *Betsey Brown.* New York: St. Martin's Press, 1985.

———. *Nappy Edges.* London: Methuen, 1978 (unpaged).

———. "Ntozake Shange Interviews Herself." *Ms.,* December 1977: 35, 70, 72.

———. *spell #7.* In *Three Pieces,* 1–52. New York: Penguin Books, 1979.

———. *Whitewash.* New York: Walker, 1997. (unpaged).

Shenitz, B. "Fighting Back." *Out,* March 2002: 99–103, 118, 120.

Sims, Naomi. *All About Hair Care for the Black Woman.* New York: Doubleday, 1982.

Singer, Bennet, ed. *Growing Up Gay/Growing Up Lesbian: A Literary Anthology.* New York: The New Press, 1994.

Smith, Aaron "Skip." "A History Lesson." *Parade Magazine,* 8 September 1996: 17.

Smitherman, Geneva. *Black Talk: Words and Phrases from the Hood to the Amen Corner.* Boston: Houghton Mifflin, 1994.

Sporn, Michael. *Whitewash* (videocassette). Eugene, OR: Churchill Media, 1994.

Stortz, Diane. *The Always-Late Angel.* Ashland, OH: Landoll, 1993.

Sutton, Roger. "Review of *The Big Box.*" *Horn Book Magazine,* September/October 1999: 598.

Tarpley, Natasha. "Haircut." *Obsidian II: Black Literature in Review* 6 (Winter 1991): 83.

———. *I Love My Hair!* New York: Little, Brown, 1998 (unpaged).

Tatar, Maria. "Introduction." In *The Classic Fairy Tales*, ix–xviii. New York: Norton, 1999.

Thomas, Joyce Carol. *Crowning Glory.* New York: Joanna Cotler Books/HarperCollins, 2002.

"Toni Morrison Talks about *The Big Box*." 2003. Interviews and Essays. Barnes and Noble.Com-The Big Box. http://search.barnesandnoble.com.

"The Typical Adult Non-Reader." http://indianriver.fl.us/living/services/als/typical.html (accessed 26 January 2000).

Udis-Kessler, A., and C. Thompson. "Beyond Gay or Straight: Increasing Our Choices about Sexual Identity." The Campaign to End Homophobia. 1995. http://www.endhomophobia.org/BeyondGay.html.

Villarosa, Linda, ed. "Straight Women, Gay Men: A Talk between Friends." *Essence* 62–64 (August 1993): 111–112.

Walker, Alice. *In Search of Our Mother's Gardens.* New York: Harcourt Brace Jovanovich, 1983.

———. "Oppressed Hair Puts a Ceiling on the Brain." *Ms.,* June 1988: 52–53.

———. "Olive Oil." In *Erotique Noire/Black Erotica*, edited by Miriam de Costa-Willis, Reginald Martin, and Roseann P. Bell, 362–366. New York: Doubleday, 1992.

Wallace, Michele. "Anger in Isolation: A Black Feminist's Search for Sisterhood." In *Invisibility Blues*, 18–25. New York: Verso, 1990.

Ward, Sara (n.d.). *Grim Fairy Tales: The Role of Rhetoric in Gender Roles and Sexuality.* http://www.cbu.edu/Academics'honors/hj2k3_grim.html (accessed 1 October 2004).

Weir, Albert E. *Songs of the Sunny South.* New York: Appleton, 1929.

West, Diana. "Review of *Whitewash* (videocassette)." *American Spectator,* July 1995: 64–65.

"Whoopi Goldberg: Direct from Broadway." Home Box Office, 1985.

"Why CIBC Is Dealing with Homophobia." *Interracial Books for Children Bulletin* 14 (Special Issue: Homophobia and Education: How to Deal with Name-Calling), 1983: 3, 9.

Wilde, Susan. "Celebrity Coaching: Eight Tips for Stars Writing Children's Books." *Independent Weekly Online*, 26 April 2000. http://www.indvweek.com/durham/200-0426/ae.html.

Wolfe, George C. "The Hairpiece." *The Colored Museum.* New York: Broadway Play, 1987.

Wood, Tom, and Jenny Wood. *Goldilocks and the Three Bears.* Somerset, UK: Oyster Books, 1991.

Woodson, Stephani Etheridge. "Popular Cultural and the Performance of Childhood: Our Dirty Little Secret (An Occasional Paper)," 1–21. Tempe: Arizona State University, Joan and David Lincoln Center of Applied Ethics, Fall 2002.

Wright, Blanche Fisher. *The Real Mother Goose*. Chicago: Rand McNally, 1944.

Wright, Marie. "Review of *Whitewash* (book) by Ntozake Shange." *School Library Journal* 44 (May 1998): 125–126.

Wright, Richard. "The Ethics of Living Jim Crow." *Uncle Tom's Children*, 3–15. New York: Harper & Row, 1965.

Yara, G. "'Q' and 'U' Say 'I Do' in Kindergarten." *Ahwatukee Foothills News*, 12 April 2002: A1, A5.

Yarbrough, Camille. *Cornrows*. New York: Coward-McCann, 1979.

Zemach, Margot. *Jake and the Honeybunch go to Heaven*. New York: Farrar Straus and Giroux, 1982.

CHILDREN'S LITERATURE AND CULTURE
JACK ZIPES, SERIES EDITOR

INDEX